Constructive Dissonance

Constructive Dissonance

Arnold Schoenberg
and the Transformations of
Twentieth-Century Culture

EDITED BY

Juliane Brand and Christopher Hailey

UNIVERSITY OF CALIFORNIA PRESS
Berkeley   Los Angeles   London

University of California Press
Berkeley and Los Angeles, California

University of California Press, Ltd.
London, England

© 1997 by
The Regents of the University of California

Library of Congress Cataloging-in-Publication Data

Constructuve dissonance : Arnold Schoenberg and the transformations of
    twentieth-century culture / edited by Juliane Brand and Christopher
    Hailey.
        p.   cm.
    Papers delivered at a conference held at the Arnold Schoenberg
Institute, University of Southern California, Nov. 15–17, 1991.
    Includes bibliographical references and index.
    ISBN 0-520-20314-3 (cloth)
    1. Schoenberg, Arnold, 1874–1951—Congresses.   I. Brand, Juliane.
II. Hailey, Christopher.
ML410.S283C66   1997
780′.92—dc20   96-24712
                                                                      CIP
                                                                      MN
Printed in the United States of America
9   8   7   6   5   4   3   2   1

This book is dedicated to Leonard Stein

CONTENTS

CONNECTIONS

ILLUSTRATIONS

FIGURES

MUSICAL EXAMPLES

TABLES

INTRODUCTION

The second half of this century will spoil by overestimation
whatever the first half's underestimation left unspoilt.
ARNOLD SCHOENBERG, 1949

In many ways the second half of the twentieth century has been preoccupied with sorting out the shock waves of the first, which included two world wars, countless struggles for national and ethnic independence and autonomy, political and economic upheaval, and genocide, population dislocation, and emigration on an unprecedented scale. Since 1950, however, the political and economic structures that emerged following the Second World War have been undergoing not violent shifts but rather a process of expansion, decay, and transformation. Inherited ideologies, critically evaluated, have gradually been modified or abandoned, barriers have disintegrated, and certain issues once thought parochial have assumed global import. This phenomenon is no less evident in the arts, where the first half of the century brought revolutions of material and language, of media and means of dissemination, and of the interrelationship between artists, their audience, and their craft. By midcentury an array of "isms" had crystallized around a few fixed reference points.

One of those fixed points was Arnold Schoenberg. By the time he died in 1951 Schoenberg had come to be regarded as one of the pivotal figures of twentieth-century musical culture. An entire generation of younger composers was bred upon the dogma of a musical progress in which Schoenberg's innovations were a necessary and inevitable consummation, and even that other central figure, the archneoclassicist Igor Stravinsky, adopted Schoenbergian twelve-tone and serialist techniques in his last years. Now, nearly half a century later, Schoenberg and his music have become the object of reappraisal. Although a number of major figures still build upon the foundations of Schoenberg's method, others have abandoned serialism or ignore it altogether. Moreover, many of Schoenberg's principal twelve-tone works have yet to find a place in our concert repertory comparable to that enjoyed by the mature works of other twentieth-century masters such as Berg and Bartók. How then are we to evaluate Schoenberg's contribution to twentieth-century culture?

The partisan battles of the inter- and postwar years created an image of Schoenberg as a lonely, isolated figure—a latter-day prophet preaching in the wilderness of contemporary culture. Such an image obscured the ways in which the composer's life was an integrated part of some of the central experiences of twentieth-century history. The very stations of his professional biography—from the hothouse ambience of turn-of-the-century Vienna to the frenetic environment of the Berlin of the Weimar Republic, and on to exile in Los Angeles—reflect the representative quality of his life. Of course, mere chronological and geographic coincidence would be of little significance if the scope of Schoenberg's intellect and curiosity had not penetrated so many facets of contemporary life. Schoenberg was an articulate observer with strongly held and often idiosyncratic opinions on virtually any subject. His energy and vitality, his forceful presence, are documented in his music, letters, essays, and books. What is more, his passion for preservation insured the survival of the artifacts of his life, from a richly annotated library to a massive body of correspondence spanning sixty years. It is the controversial and often problematic position that Schoenberg has occupied in twentieth-century music history that compels historians to examine and reexamine his legacy. Beyond that, the wealth and quality of the source material provide the scholar with unmatched resources for taking the measure not only of the man but also of his time. Together these strands of inquiry make possible a critical evaluation of Schoenberg and his relationship to twentieth-century culture as well as of our relationship to the inherited structures that *we* are now in the process of transforming.

• • • • •

Schoenberg is often referred to as a *conservative* revolutionary, and as a product of Hapsburg Vienna he could hardly have been otherwise. The retrospective cast of Viennese intellectual thought is balanced, however, by a critical spirit that could be at once ironic and pedantic. Schoenberg was inspired by such Viennese contemporaries as Karl Kraus and Gustav Mahler to draw radical consequences from his profound identification with his musical heritage. Much has been written about the prophetic qualities of prewar Vienna—a testing ground, as Kraus wrote, for the "end of the world." But did a world come to an end, or was it taking shape from the energies of a newly self-confident middle class? The energies of that class were nourished not only by a critical assessment of the past but also by a head-on confrontation with the present. For Schoenberg that confrontation with the present was most intense during his years in Berlin.

Schoenberg lived in the German capital during three periods of his life: as an untried novice (1901–1903), as a radical revolutionary (1911–1915), and, finally, during the last years of the Weimar Republic (1926–1933), as an established master, increasingly out of touch with the younger generation. On each occasion he was attracted by prospects of financial security and wider resonance for his works. It was here that he was most directly confronted with the bracing and not always salutary winds of the present— new literary impulses and technological wonders on the one hand, economic chaos and political madness on the other. The works Schoenberg wrote in Berlin and those that were influenced by his sojourns there—from his cabaret songs of 1901 to the *Pierrot* settings of 1912 and his film music of 1929—reflect this encounter with the "present." It is also in Berlin that Schoenberg was increasingly compelled to take a stand on the social, moral, and ethical issues confronting modern society.

Schoenberg was among the first to recognize the futility of remaining in Nazi Germany, and in 1933, at the age of fifty-nine, he became an exile in America. Welcomed, like many of his fellow émigrés, as a master from the Old World, he soon learned that he had to adjust to a new set of cultural assumptions. His American experiences enriched his creative thought (although performances of his music remained in inverse proportion to his growing reputation as a "modern enigma") and gave him new outlets for his teaching (it was in America that he wrote his principal practical textbooks and exerted the widest influence as a pedagogue). And yet, during the very decade in which Schoenberg and others arrived from Europe, indigenous American artistic culture was taking wing. Did the wave of European émigrés enrich or retard that process of finding an "American" voice? The concrete and continuing influence of Schoenberg's teaching, and the teaching of other émigrés, poses questions about the tension between inherited and grafted culture, about the nature and relevance of the émigré experience, and about our present assessment of Schoenberg's relationship and pertinence to twentieth-century culture as a whole.

•   •   •   •   •

It is on the basis of these reflections, developed together with Leonard Stein, the founding director of the Arnold Schoenberg Institute, that the conference "Constructive Dissonance: Arnold Schoenberg and Transformations of Twentieth-Century Culture," on which this volume is based, was organized. The conference was to be Leonard Stein's farewell to the Institute, the final event of an eventful seventeen-year stewardship of Schoenberg's legacy.[1] It was Leonard's vision to offer a forum for synthesis and interdisciplinary discussion, in which the geographic sites of Schoenberg's professional career—Vienna, Berlin, and Los Angeles—were to serve as a framework for exploring his relationship to crucial themes of twentieth-century culture. Analysis of individual works or compositional method was to take second place to an examination of the historical, aesthetic, and intellectual issues that shaped Schoenberg's artistic philosophy as well as an assessment of our contemporary response to the modernist legacy of the first half of this century. It is a mark of the success of the conference, which took place at the Arnold Schoenberg Institute on the campus of the University of Southern California 15–17 November 1991, that much of the most stimulating interchange took place in the freewheeling discussions between papers and sessions, often late into the night. The present volume includes thirteen of the twenty-three papers delivered at the conference (in addition to one submitted subsequently) in a selection that the editors hope is representative of the goals and achievements of that event as well as a fitting tribute to Leonard Stein, whose imagination and enterprise made it possible. Given the time that has elapsed since the conference, most of the papers have been significantly revised to take account of recent scholarship as well as of the impulses generated by the conference itself.

The essays of the first section illuminate the trajectory of Schoenberg's creative and intellectual development through an investigation of cultural and biographical contexts. Leon Botstein explores the cultural fissures in turn-of-the-century Vienna as well as the overarching retrospective cast of the city's ideology of modernism. Alexander L. Ringer argues that Schoenberg's confronting and accepting the historical dissonance of his Jewish identity was a mainspring of his creative life and that it is an essential perspective for understanding the aesthetic consistency of his works. Questions of identity also underlie Peg Weiss's discussion of the ethnographic dimensions of Vasili Kandinsky's relationship with Schoenberg and the surprising degree to which that relationship resonated in Kandinsky's paintings. The late Alan Lessem paints a dark picture of Schoenberg's American years, emphasizing the dislocation of exile and Schoenberg's gradual withdrawal into a lonely isolation with his God.

In the second section the focus shifts to specific works and to the interplay between creative impulse and aesthetic articulation. The most tumultuous years in Schoenberg's creative life were those between 1908 and 1911, during which the composer not only broke with tonality but experimented with the radical rejection of inherited forms and structures. Ethan Haimo's close reading of the *Harmonielehre* of 1911 suggests ways in which the roots of Schoenberg's atonal thinking are embedded in his concept of tonal practice. Walter Frisch examines how Schoenberg's Chamber Symphony, op. 9, served as a vehicle for confronting and transcending the dialectical tensions between the symphonic and chamber traditions of Viennese classicism. Questions of gender politics, psychological theory, and aesthetic philosophy intertwine in the essays by Bryan R. Simms and Joseph Auner on the operas *Erwartung* (1909) and *Die glückliche Hand* (1910–1913), respectively—works of pivotal importance in Schoenberg's short-lived attempt to create an expressive language directly responsive to emotional impulse and unmediated by formal constraints. Jan Maegaard's reflections on his catalog of Schoenberg's incomplete works, fragments, and sketches remind us of that vast shadow land of discarded projects from the composer's fertile imagination. Patricia Carpenter and Severine Neff offer an overview of one of Schoenberg's most ambitious unfinished projects, a comprehensive theory and philosophy of composition, which occupied him in one way or another for most of his creative life.

The essays of the final section address Schoenberg's relationship to contemporary thought. My own essay on Schoenberg and the Canon argues that Schoenberg's lasting legacy may rest less on his having expounded timeless truths than on his having provided timely responses to issues of his age. Hermann Danuser demonstrates how Schoenberg's *Kunstbegriff,* or concept of art, with its dialectical opposition of tradition and innovation, heart and brain, is at once historically dated and surprisingly relevant to the creative dilemmas of our own time. Jonathan Dunsby's praise for Schoenberg as "the central architect of present-day theory and practice" likewise emphasizes his role as an "irritant to the orthodoxies" that are everywhere challenged by postmodernist perspectives. Reinhold Brinkmann suggests differing ways of approaching Schoenberg's career as a narrative telos that transformed language from an artifact of aesthetic self-reflection to an agent of moral engagement. What Brinkmann calls Schoenberg's *Durchbruch,* or breakthrough, in the works of his last years is in no small part a triumph of self-definition, a theme that resonates with several other essays in this collection.

In 1911 Kandinsky wrote of a fast-approaching time "of reasoned and conscious composition, when the painter will be proud to declare his work constructive."[2] It is from this perspective of conscious creation that the conference and the resulting collection of essays draw their title. Schoenberg's emancipation of dissonance served not only to colonize new terrain within our universe of artistic expression but also to acknowledge that that universe might include irreconcilable difference as a constructive principle. If Schoenberg no longer occupies a central position in our musical discourse—a discourse that may no longer even have a center—his voice can still be heard among the plurality of voices, not least because he was among the first to anticipate their dissonance.

The editors wish to express their gratitude to all the participants who helped make the original conference such a stimulating and productive experience. The National Endowment for the Humanities provided vital financial assistance, as did the Getty Center for the History of Art and the Humanities, whose capable staff, including Associate Director Tom

Reese and Assistant Director for Visiting Scholars and Conferences Herbert Hymans, provided additional logistical support and advice. The smooth operation of the conference itself was made possible by the dedicated staff of the Arnold Schoenberg Institute, among them Andrea Castillo-Herreshoff, Christian Kiefer, JoAnn Roe, and especially Assistant Director Heidi Lesemann.

Special thanks are due Wayne Shoaf, the archivist of the Arnold Schoenberg Institute, for assistance in tracking down nagging source and reference questions during the preparation of this volume. We are particularly grateful to Nuria, Ronald, and Lawrence Schoenberg for their support and kind permission to reproduce pictures and musical examples from the Schoenberg legacy. A similar debt of gratitude is due to the Artists Rights Society for permission to reproduce the Kandinsky plates. Finally, our hearty thanks to Doris Kretschmer, Rose Anne White, and the University of California Press for their constructive criticism and encouragement.

Christopher Hailey
Los Angeles, 1996

NOTES

1. See the *Journal of the Arnold Schoenberg Institute* 14/1 (June 1991) for tributes to Leonard Stein and a chronology of the events at the Institute from 1974 through 1992.

2. Wassily Kandinsky, *Concerning the Spiritual in Art,* trans. M. T. H. Sadler (reprint, New York: Dover Publications, 1977), 57.

SOURCE NOTE

Source references cite published English translations where available; the text of the German original is provided only for material that is unpublished or not readily accessible. Most German-language sources are listed among the following frequently cited sources (which appear by short title in the annotations):

Adorno, Theodor W. "Arnold Schoenberg," in *Prisms,* trans. Samuel Weber and Shierry Weber. Cambridge: MIT Press, 1981. For the original text, see *Prismen* (Frankfurt am Main: Suhrkamp, 1955).

Berg, Alban, and Arnold Schoenberg. *The Berg-Schoenberg Correspondence: Selected Letters.* Ed. and trans. Juliane Brand and Christopher Hailey, ed. Donald Harris. New York: W. W. Norton & Company, 1987.

Busoni, Ferruccio. *Ferruccio Busoni: Selected Letters.* Ed. and trans. Antony Beaumont. New York: Columbia University Press, 1987. For the original German letters between Schoenberg and Busoni, see Jutta Theurich, "Briefwechsel zwischen Arnold Schönberg und Ferruccio Busoni 1903–1919 (1927)," *Beiträge zur Musikwissenschaft* 19/3 (1977).

Kandinsky, Wassily, and Franz Marc, eds. *The Blaue Reiter Almanac.* Documentary edition, ed. Klaus Lankheit, trans. Henning Falkenstein. New York: Viking Press, 1974. For the German original, see *Der Blaue Reiter,* ed. Wassily Kandinsky and Franz Marc (Munich: R. Piper & Co. Verlag, 1912; reprint, 1967).

Maegaard, Jan. *Studien zur Entwicklung des dodekaphonen Satzes bei Arnold Schönberg.* 2 vols. Copenhagen: Wilhelm Hansen, 1972.

Reich, Willi. *Schoenberg: A Critical Biography.* Trans. Leo Black. New York and Washington: Praeger Publishers, 1971; New York: Da Capo Press, 1981. For the German original, see *Schönberg oder Der konservative Revolutionär* (Vienna: Verlag Fritz Molden, 1968).

———. ed. *Arnold Schönberg: Schöpferische Konfessionen.* Zurich: Verlag der Arche, 1964.

Rosen, Charles. *Arnold Schoenberg.* Princeton, N.J.: Princeton University Press, 1981.

Rufer, Josef. *The Works of Arnold Schoenberg.* Trans. Dika Newlin. London: Faber and Faber, 1962. For the German original, see *Das Werk Arnold Schönbergs* (1959; 2d ed., Kassel: Bärenreiter, 1972).

Schoenberg, Arnold. *Arnold Schoenberg Letters.* Ed. Leonard Stein, trans. Eithne Wilkins and Ernst Kaiser. London: Faber and Faber, 1964. Unless otherwise noted, the original German letters are found in *Arnold Schoenberg: Ausgewählte Briefe,* ed. Erwin Stein (Mainz: B. Schott's Söhne, 1958).

―――. *Style and Idea: Selected Writings of Arnold Schoenberg.* Ed. Leonard Stein, trans. Leo Black. 1975. Rev. ed., Berkeley and Los Angeles: University of California Press, 1984. Unless otherwise noted, the German original is found in Arnold Schönberg, *Stil und Gedanke: Aufsätze zur Musik,* in *Gesammelte Schriften,* vol. 1, ed. Ivan Vojtêch (Nördlingen and Reutlingen: S. Fischer Verlag, 1976).

―――. *Theory of Harmony.* Trans. Roy Carter. Berkeley and Los Angeles: University of California Press, 1978. For the German original, see *Harmonielehre* (1911; 3d rev. ed., Vienna: Universal Edition, 1922).

Schoenberg, Arnold, and Wassily Kandinsky. *Arnold Schoenberg, Wassily Kandinsky: Letters, Pictures and Documents.* Ed. Jelena Hahl-Koch, trans. John C. Crawford. London and Boston: Faber and Faber, 1984. For the original German letters, see *Arnold Schönberg, Wassily Kandinsky: Briefe, Bilder und Dokumente einer aussergewöhnlichen Begegnung,* ed. Jelena Hahl-Koch (Salzburg and Vienna: Residenz Verlag, 1980).

SOURCE ABBREVIATIONS

ASI   Arnold Schoenberg Institute, Los Angeles

ASC/LC   Arnold Schoenberg Collection, Library of Congress, Washington, D.C.

Contexts

ONE

Music and the Critique of Culture

Arnold Schoenberg, Heinrich Schenker, and the Emergence of Modernism in Fin de Siècle Vienna

Leon Botstein

> *But I wept as I listened to the Fourth Quartet. Now I know for certain that you are the last Classical composer: your cradle was Beethoven's Grosse Fuge, where there is none of that Russian, French, or English folklore, and the barbarism of presenting a symbol instead of a direct experience. . . . Bach, Beethoven, and Schoenberg are the last composers capable of erecting a musical structure that can—must—be regarded as an organic world. . . . All music but theirs is either galvanized, artificially stimulated folkweave . . . or purely abstract geometry with queer sounds and odd effects touting for the listener's custom.*
> OSKAR KOKOSCHKA TO ARNOLD SCHOENBERG 19 AUGUST 1949

I

Arnold Schoenberg's contemporary, the painter Oskar Kokoschka, grasped the historical paradox represented by Schoenberg's career precisely in 1949. Like Schoenberg, Kokoschka at the start of his career in pre–World War I Vienna was regarded as an outsider and as the quintessential modernist enfant terrible.[1] Although Schoenberg's work was heralded and reviled during the first quarter of this century as the embodiment of radical modernism, from the vantage point of the last quarter of this century he may turn out to have been, as Kokoschka observed, the last great exponent of a late-eighteenth- and early-nineteenth-century tradition of music and music making. As Kokoschka shrewdly observed, in the name of Schoenberg's innovations a modernism entirely foreign to Schoenberg's own work had come into being during the 1940s.

Hegel's notion about the "cunning of reason" in history comes to mind when one considers that a crucial factor behind Schoenberg's notoriety as a standard-bearer of modernism was the debt his work demonstrated to a nostalgic, idealized conception of classicism. Before 1914 his music was regarded as offensive by audiences and critics because it challenged a conceit of musical connoisseurship in Vienna, a place that Schoenberg in 1909 sarcastically called "the city of song." Schoenberg's first Viennese opponents saw themselves as the standard-bearers of a unique local musical sensibility

3

derived from Viennese classicism. The demands made by Schoenberg's pre–World War I compositions on listeners revealed, however, that the Viennese rhetoric of defense on behalf of hallowed cultural values masked a deterioration of the very values conservatives claimed needed protection from an arrogant new generation of artists.

The circumstances of late-nineteenth-century Vienna and Schoenberg's relationship to them suggest that Schoenberg's modernism was shaped by the politics of culture. His music triggered audience insecurity and doubt. Evident beneath the expressions of distaste were fears about appearing inept, superficial, and self-deluded. Like the child in the fairy tale about the emperor's new clothes, Schoenberg pointed out to the powerful—affluent Viennese middle-class music lovers and amateurs—that they were naked, as it were, when they paraded around defending classical notions of beauty and refinement. Schoenberg's music explicitly asserted a traditional ideal of musical discourse that exceeded the capacities of the audience. The radically modern was the premodern past reborn.

The role Arnold Schoenberg played in defining the future course of twentieth-century music history has one clear historical precedent from the nineteenth century: the pervasive influence exercised by Richard Wagner. Schoenberg's importance, like Wagner's, did not derive solely from his compositions and the originality of his musical imagination. No doubt the first performances of the two quartets, opp. 7 and 10, and the Chamber Symphony, op. 9, between early 1907 and late 1908 in Vienna and the premiere of *Pierrot lunaire* in Berlin in 1912 were watersheds in the history of twentieth-century concert life.[2] The sharp and divided responses by audiences, critics, and musicians were turning points in twentieth-century modern art and culture.

As in the case of Wagner, the extramusical resonance emanating from Schoenberg's work and its reception was striking. While this might be said as well of Gustav Mahler and Richard Strauss, in the context of Vienna during the nearly twenty years between 1892, when *Don Juan* was first performed at the Vienna Philharmonic, and the Viennese premiere of *Der Rosenkavalier* in 1911, a qualitative difference can be discerned.[3] Shouting and scuffling accompanied the 1908 premiere of Schoenberg's Second Quartet in the Bösendorfersaal. A near-riot erupted on March 31, 1913, at an orchestral concert in Vienna in which works by Mahler, Berg, Webern, Zemlinsky, and Schoenberg were played. By then Schoenberg's name and public reputation were as responsible for the disruptions as the sounds of music that emerged. Why did Schoenberg's music and name—years before the development of his mature style—become a cause célèbre in the reaction against early-twentieth-century modernism?

As Walter Frisch's excellent recent monograph on the early Schoenberg shows, the composer's early music is remarkable in its synthesis of simplicity and clarity.[4] However, the more admiring we become of Schoenberg's compositional mastery and profound understanding of traditional practices revealed in the years between 1893 and 1908 (as he moved from his first neo-Brahmsian works to a period marked by closer affinities to Wagner and then to his own "direction"), the more baffling the pattern of reception he encountered early in his career becomes. These works lost their appearance of radicalism long ago.

Schoenberg's efforts to deflect research into his early career by his cursory but authoritative accounts of his own development are evidence of the importance of the Vienna years.[5] In retrospect, Schoenberg knew that the pre–World War I reaction to him set the pattern of response to his later music and to musical modernism for most of the rest of the century. The particular cast he gave to musical modernism in response to the cultural politics of Vienna at the turn of the century had far-reaching biographical, aesthetic, and rhetorical consequences.

Mahler's music was dismissed as crude, bloated, and pretentious. Strauss, accused of theatrical vulgarity, was facile and perhaps too gifted, eager to shock the public with lavish surface effects. Mahler and Strauss seemed partly decadent and ultimately banal.[6] Their faults derived from their striking surface accessibility; there seemed little new that could not be connected back to Wagner. Likewise, the criticism of new works by Pfitzner, Zemlinsky, and Bartók in 1904 and 1905 seemed not to inspire the outrage expressed at Schoenberg.[7]

How and why did Schoenberg succeed in communicating an "arrogant" (as the Viennese critic Robert Hirschfeld described him in his 1905 review of *Pelleas*) critique of contemporary musical values and cultural life? His staunchest defenders in pre–World War I Vienna, including Gustav Mahler, Karl Kraus, and David Josef Bach, recognized that Schoenberg stood for something that transcended the aesthetic debate about music in the 1890s surrounding Mahler and Strauss.[8] If one can rely on Alma Mahler (who was a devoted lifelong friend of Schoenberg's), Mahler's public defense of Schoenberg was based more on his conviction that it was imperative to uphold the principle of a young generation's right to chart new paths than on any sympathy toward the music itself. Schoenberg's work was a welcome ally in a struggle against philistine audiences and critics who, in the name of cultured taste, resisted and denigrated the new. His appearance reconfigured the radicalism of the the music of Mahler and Strauss, which appeared, by contrast, benign.[9]

Schoenberg's revolution seemed to exceed the proper boundaries of any composer's search for musical originality. In 1909 Hans Liebstöckl, the critic of the *Illustrirtes Wiener Extrablatt*, accused Schoenberg of requiring one to "deposit one's whole personality in the cloakroom." Schoenberg sought Karl Kraus's aid in 1908 in taking up cudgels against Ludwig Karpath, a Viennese critic for whom Kraus (for other reasons) had nothing but contempt. Kraus freely admitted that he had limited interest and expertise in matters musical (with the exception of a passion for Offenbach). He sensed that in Schoenberg's aesthetic ambitions lay an assault similar to his own on an underlying nexus of corrupt social and cultural habits and alliances in Vienna.[10]

Schoenberg challenged Karpath to a public duel in the form of a contest about who was more competent in harmony and counterpoint. Karpath had written a scathing dismissal of the Second Quartet, to which Schoenberg sought to respond. Karpath alleged that "for the first time in [his] twenty years as a critic" he felt compelled to shout "Stop" at a concert. The critic became the public defender for the majority of the audience. The fact was, according to Karpath, that what Schoenberg had written was not a work of musical art. To prove it Karpath argued from authority—his knowledge of the standard "musical disciplines" of harmony, formal analysis, and the like.

Wagner helped invent the rhetoric of how the truly revolutionary artist would find himself at odds with an ignorant and corrupt press and its adherents—the audience of regular *haute bourgeois* urban concertgoers and newspaper readers. These critical fulminations, tinged with an anti-Semitism that cast the assimilated Jew as the archetype of the philistine journalist and culture monger, were disingenuous, however. As Schoenberg observed, Wagner knew just how, through his music, to win over the audience of his own time.[11] Wagner succeeded in his explicit ambition to become the most lionized and popular composer of his age, particularly within social strata he relished castigating. He exploited the limited powers of musical discernment characteristic of late-nineteenth-century audiences. At first hearing, rapid accessibility to the expressiveness, defined in extramusical terms, in Wagner's works generated a welcome audience recognition of novelty, danger, decadence, and modernity.

Although Wagner's most ardent admirers came from generations younger than his own, and Wagnerism in France and in German-speaking Europe became a battle cry against reigning conservative tastes, by the mid-1870s the struggle had been largely won. Wagner returned to Vienna to conduct in triumph in 1875, one year after Schoenberg's birth. His supporters then included key members of an older, established Viennese social, cultural, and political elite—Johann Herbeck and Josef Standhartner, for example—as well as such enthusiastic younger adherents as Hugo Wolf, Guido Adler, and Gustav Mahler. In the Vienna of Schoenberg's youth, Wagner had become in rhetoric and music an inspiration to the young as well as an object of enthusiasm among the affluent and well-established citizenry that patronized music. After 1875 his disciple Hans Richter dominated Vienna's concert life. Despite a lingering anti-Wagnerian conservatism in the faculty and curriculum of the Vienna Conservatory, all the students of the late

1870s and the 1880s knew of Anton Bruckner's devotion to the Bayreuth master.

In contrast to Wagner, Schoenberg's music and the rhetorical strategy employed in its defense (designed largely by Schoenberg himself) never achieved wide acceptance. Most apparent in this failure to replicate the Wagnerian pattern was the inability to win the audience over by offering the middle-class concertgoer and amateur musician that alluring Wagnerian combination of becoming emotionally mesmerized by a work of art and at the same time feeling flattered that one was flirting safely with radicalism and novelty. At first only *Verklärte Nacht* became part of the repertoire (a fact that annoyed the sixty-year-old Schoenberg during his first years in America). Franz Schreker's success with the 1913 premiere of *Gurrelieder* in Vienna came too late to change the dynamics between Schoenberg and the public. Wagner's conquest of the musical world can be compared with Franz Joseph Haydn's triumph with the public in London in the 1790s.[12] Despite Wagner's self-serving rhetoric about being a revolutionary, he, like Haydn, was in the business of winning the public over.[13]

Although Schoenberg rather liked being seen as challenging norms and practices, he was ambivalent about how defensive and stubborn the audience had become. He blamed performers rather than listeners and toward the end of his life hoped to achieve widespread recognition. But from the beginning, in the face of controversy, his assertion of artistic integrity assumed a nearly puritanical facade of ethical superiority. Schoenberg's envy of Stravinsky, Ravel, Respighi, and Bartók took the form of high-minded moralizing about aesthetic concessions and superficialities.[14]

The critics who ridiculed and dismissed the young Schoenberg, unlike their historical counterparts who attacked Wagner when he first came on the scene, were never betrayed by their readers' changing tastes. In terms of Karl Mannheim's sociology of culture, musical modernism in the tradition of Schoenberg failed to enter and become part of the "objective culture." In the twentieth century the hostile critic has remained the spokesperson of the audience. Listeners continue to hear, particularly in the mature Schoenberg, an attack directed at themselves that offers little possibility of an honorable capitulation. As Schoenberg's response to Karpath revealed, in the music itself lay the allegation that "those savage potentates who wear only a cravat and a top hat" were unequal to the task of understanding the very tradition of music from Bach, Wagner, and Brahms that they so cherished. In 1925 Schoenberg wrote, "[L]isteners must have ears, and ears to detect the difference between music and shibboleths."[15]

Among Schoenberg's early Viennese advocates, particularly those with socialist leanings, the implicitly contemptuous attitude toward the audience was troublesome. David Josef Bach warned the small cadre of Schoenberg enthusiasts that their hostility betrayed an unattractive sense of superiority at odds with the hope that radical change through art might advance the larger struggle for a more just and egalitarian world.[16] Bach was perhaps the first to notice—as Hanns Eisler and Kurt Weill later did—an inherent contradiction between the claims of twentieth-century musical modernism and the possible role of musical art in societal reform directed at bettering the lot of the working classes through political and economic emancipation.

Schoenberg the polemicist learned from Wagner. Like Wagner, he wrote about music extensively in a manner that underscored new music's aura of cultural critique.[17] Like Wagner, he cultivated disciples and adherents. Despite the admirably eclectic programming of contemporary music sponsored by the Verein für musikalische Privataufführungen in Vienna and Prague after World War I, Schoenberg the teacher and mentor helped create a geography of the good and the bad in which the boundaries remained unmistakable. The Verein was not Bayreuth, but both initiatives share the conviction that an alternative to the everyday commerce of culture was essential for the proper presentation of one's own work.

From the generation of Egon Wellesz, Willi Reich, and Theodor W. Adorno to that of René Leibowitz, Pierre Boulez, Glenn Gould, and Milton Babbitt a nearly canonic literature of justification has come into being. Schoenberg's followers, like Wagner's, did little to hide their contempt for those who did not share their enthusiasms. Just as Wagner helped alter the way future generations would understand the place in music history occupied by past masters such as Beethoven and Mendelssohn, Schoenberg defined the terms by which the past should be interpreted. Although Schoenberg the writer shaped the way the narrative of the history of music in the twentieth century has come to be understood, the plausibility of his explanatory paradigm of progressive and regressive modernism in music has been placed into doubt among scholars and musicians, in part by the failure of modernist music inspired by him to succeed with audiences.

The pre–World War I controversy surrounding Schoenberg was rooted in the fear that he would become the future. By the end of the twentieth century he seems more like Kokoschka's conception of him as the last but unacknowledged exponent of a dying tradition. Postmodernism has helped to devastate the already thin popularity Schoenberg's music had achieved by midcentury. Only the more accessible early works still come around. And the limited success of later works (for example, the String Trio) derives from their being heard as creations of late-Romantic musical rhetoric.

Dedicated advocacy by the American and Western European academic world has sustained Schoenberg's succès d'estime.[18] Wagner fanatics still exist in significant numbers. Wagner societies sell Valkyrie helmets, T-shirts, and mementos at meetings attended by ordinary concertgoers and record collectors. Wagner's capacity to enthrall new audiences who have no idea of the historical Wagner continues unabated. The cultural and political reform project whose mantle of leadership Schoenberg assumed in the fin de siècle remains unrealized. At the end of his life, Schoenberg dreamed that perhaps in the new state of Israel the chances might be better than in Europe or America for a modernism based on the restoration of a genuine musical culture derived from a preindustrial cultural heritage.[19]

II

Three factors specific to Vienna in the years 1874–1901 (after which Schoenberg moved briefly to Berlin) decisively influenced Schoenberg's evolution. First, by comparison to contemporary Viennese musicians, Schoenberg's status was that of an outsider. He was an autodidact, and he was exceptional in that he was not extremely proficient at any instrument. He was also an assimilated Jew from the lower middle classes, without a university education. Second, there was a rift within the Viennese community of avowedly antiestablishment writers, painters, architects, and composers. By 1901 two loosely defined camps were visible, each with a different conception of the modern. Despite individual friendships between both camps, Schoenberg entered the rift clearly on one side. Third, there was a widespread public debate in fin de siècle Vienna regarding the quality of musical life, culture, and education in a city that had come to regard its status as the world capital of music as axiomatic and indisputable.[20] The popular musical and theatrical culture in fin de siècle Vienna was under attack as cheap and debased. Schoenberg's reaction against the influences of late Romanticism was deepened by his exposure to Vienna's popular commercial musical culture. The Viennese ideology of modernism with which he associated himself possessed a nostalgia for the role of culture and art in the pre-1848 world, including its popular art forms.

Schoenberg's autodidactic process of learning music can be compared usefully to the early career of Robert Schumann. Schoenberg's oft-repeated tribute to the influence of Richard Dehmel on his music is reminiscent of Schumann's remark that he learned more about counterpoint from Jean Paul than from anyone else.[21] The significance of this mediation of the musical through the literary in Schoenberg's case is twofold. First, Schoenberg developed his compositional craft primarily through the writing of songs. In contrast to the later ideology expressed in the preface to *Pierrot* and the 1912 essay for *Der Blaue Reiter,* at the start of his compositional career words as carriers of meaning were keys to the use of time through music and therefore musical form. Ordinary language as the medium for the narration of emotional states remained significant for Schoenberg as late as 1904–1905. Although according to Frisch "the real importance" of the String Quartet, op. 7, lies in Schoenberg's innovative adaptation of the "absolute instrumental tradition" of composition, the "secret" extramusical program may be as important in understanding the structure of the work.

Frisch observes that in the Second Quartet, with its inclusion of voice and text, "thematic transformation"—that is, a technique of "absolute" instrumental composition—is now "put into the service of a programmatic statement."[22] Even according to this view, the early Schoenberg emanates from an engagement with the relationship between language and music in which the impetus, in part because of Schoenberg's training, came first from language. The extent to which music, biographically speaking, was a secondary medium whose command came later to Schoenberg (in terms of comparative biography) than to other composers may explain his later obsession with the autonomy of musical elements. Yet Schoenberg's lifelong adherence to structural and aesthetic criteria—as in his use of the dicotomy implied by the terms *style* and *idea*—derived from the intense Viennese modernist engagement with the nature of language and its relationship to thought. In Schoenberg's case, as in that of the early Schumann, the role of thinking about language generated musical innovation.[23] The initial subordination of the musical to the linguistic stands in contrast to the ideology characteristic of Brahms's early development or the training of a conservatory student like Zemlinsky.

Dehmel exercised an influence on Schoenberg's German-speaking generation not unlike that of Oscar Wilde in the English-speaking world. A key difference was that the medium of Dehmel's influence in the 1890s was lyric poetry. He believed that his philosophical views—on sexuality, the power of nature, and the primacy of individuality and freedom as means to social justice—and his mystical belief in a metaphysical dialectic that reconciled apparent contradictions (for example, male-female, subjectivity-objectivity) were reflected formally in the poetic work. As Dehmel wrote to Gustav Kühl in 1897, art functions indirectly as a moral instrument through its form. Aesthetic form realizes the essential underlying unity of experience that human beings are otherwise blocked from encountering.

According to Dehmel, the overarching structure of his poem *Verklärte Nacht* interconnects each unit so that "under the influence of a mood of nature, a momentary spiritual expression of both male and female" can be felt as one reads and contemplates the impression of the whole. The constituent elements and the larger shape are integrated not by the argument but by the structural transformation of ordinary word meaning and grammar that poetry generates. The "psychology of poetic creativity" leads to the use of the aesthetic, in formal terms, to achieve a sense of higher human truth and unity than ordinary speech allows. A reconciliation between individuality and the universal is thus realized.

Dehmel's significance to Schoenberg bridged the first two phases of the composer's early development—the neo-Brahmsian period and the more Wagnerian phase. If Dehmel's ambitions regarding the use of art to change the self-image of the individual vis-à-vis life were reminiscent of those of the Nietzsche of *Zarathustra*, the intensity of Dehmel's engagement with love, sexuality, and gender was Wagnerian. But his notions of an organic unity of form derived from the unique powers of the poetic were similar to Brahms's view on the autonomy and structural integrity of aesthetic forms in music.[24]

Dehmel believed that, much like the great composers of the past, he had to challenge the reigning standards of what constituted acceptable poetic language and subject matter. Modernity and innovation were essential. His influence on the young Schoenberg, therefore, can be construed as setting an example for the necessity of communicating meaning, as in op. 7, "secretly" through novel musical procedures, just as he had sought to do in his own poetry. The impulse was Wagnerian, but the strategy Brahmsian. Dehmel's achievement justified the link between the obligation to extend the boundaries of what was regarded as acceptably musical (for example, norms of formal continuity and harmonic practice) and the task of transcending through art the limitations of received ethical norms and a rigid epistemology.[25] In Schoenberg's view Dehmel seemed ideally suited to writing *Die Jakobsleiter.* He wrote, "[T]he mode of speech, the mode of thought, the mode of expression should be that of modern man; the problems treated should be those that harass us."[26]

At the same time Schoenberg's particular path to composition made him defensive and skeptical. Deprived of the institutional validation expected of an aspiring Viennese professional musician, Schoenberg, unlike Dehmel, sought to reconcile the modern with counterintuitive virtuosity in terms of rigor and technique. The assertion that higher standards in the realm of harmony, counterpoint, and compositional practice in the conventional sense were audible in the modern was also a strategy by which to deflect criticism. Schoenberg was vulnerable where Mahler and Zemlinsky were not. Both were prize-winning graduates of the Vienna Conservatory and therefore unlikely candidates for the charge of fakery or ineptitude.

Schoenberg's status as a Jew in Vienna vis-à-vis the career of musician and composer was unexceptional and did not distinguish him from other Jews such as Karl Kraus, Otto Weininger, and Mahler in terms of the complex mix of marginality, envy, and discrimination that affected Jews in fin de siècle Vienna.[27] Nevertheless, being Jewish was a factor for those with artistic ambitions. As Dehmel's own fleeting anti-Semitism demonstrated, Wagner had succeeded in popularizing the idea that Jews were incapable of true creativity.[28] Weininger's views on the creative impotence of the Jew were well known to Schoenberg, as was Kraus's special form of contempt for the Jewish elites of Vienna.

In the Viennese worlds of music and painting with which Schoenberg was most closely allied, the two most admirable individuals of Jewish origin were Mahler and Zemlinsky. Nearly half of the audience and the majority of the critics in Vienna were Jews.[29] And yet at the fin de siècle Schoenberg, the Jewish modernist, came under attack not primarily from ultraconservative Gentile camps but from within the ranks of educated, acculturated Viennese Jews for whom participation in the city's musical culture was a crucial dimension of their self-image as assimilated, legitimate Viennese. Schoenberg's pre–World War I affinity to Karl Kraus's vicious denunciation of artists of Jewish origin and the Jewish public for music and theater in Vienna shows the disfigurement created by Viennese anti-Semitism; it was deflected onto the Jews themselves. By 1933 Schoenberg had freed himself of this intraethnic dynamic.[30] Kraus never did.

•   •   •   •   •

By 1901 the remarkable, complex, and intertwined amalgam of artists and writers that dominated cultural life in Vienna had developed into two distinct focal points. One was oriented around Gustav Klimt and Arthur Schnitzler. The second was grouped around Karl Kraus and Adolf Loos. Clearly many key figures in Vienna (such as Otto Wagner, Sigmund Freud, Viktor Adler, Theodor Herzl, and members of the university faculties in philosophy and economics) were independent of these two groups or maintained peripheral and sometimes overlapping ties. But the distinctions between the two main groupings defined the debate about modernism and the role of art.

Klimt and Schnitzler, despite controversies surrounding their work, were visible successes and the objects of widespread adulation and patronage. The 1897 Secession building, designed by Joseph Maria Olbrich, was dedicated by Emperor Franz Joseph II. Its honorary head was the grand old man of Austrian scene painting, Rudolf von Alt. Schnitzler was triumphant in the arena of Vienna's main stage, the Burgtheater. Klimt and Schnitzler's nearest counterpart in music was Gustav Mahler, whose accession in 1897 to the leadership of the Imperial Opera immediately made him a lionized personality. Despite all the intrigues and criticisms leveled at him during his ten-year reign at the opera, his achievements and talents never lacked for recognition in the city. For Klimt, Schnitzler, and Mahler controversy and spectacular success went hand in hand.

This achievement helped arouse the suspicions of initially sympathetic contemporaries. Kraus and Loos posed the question: For all the claims made on behalf of the heralded new painters, composers, and writers that they represented a new modern sensibility and a new age—particularly in the critical praise lavished by Ludwig Hevesi and Hermann Bahr—was there anything fundamentally new or worthwhile in the Secession and the Young Vienna writers movement? Were these new artists and writers (Hofmannsthal, for example) more than mere aesthetes who reveled in the shock value of candor on matters psychological and sexual? Did they just exploit the sensual and decorative surface of art without getting at the ethical and epistemological essence of an older generation's corrupt taste?

If the enemies of the modern were historicism and late-Romantic sentimental realism, the new in Klimt's and Mahler's hands seemed at best a superficial, if not decadent, response. Kraus, and later Schoenberg, developed a nearly paranoid suspicion of a conspiracy linking the commerce of art (including patronage and the politics of arts institutions), the philistine audience, the press, and the self-styled modern artist. Kraus was perpetually alert to such alliances in Vienna, especially within its self-appointed avant-garde.

The group around Kraus—the second axis in Viennese fin de siècle culture—included Peter Altenberg and eventually the expressionist painters. At stake for this group was a belief in art as a profound instrument of ethical and moral transformation. Kraus admired Frank Wedekind rather than Schnitzler, Else Lasker-Schüler rather than Hofmannsthal. Wedekind challenged the sensibilities of conventional morality in the service of ethical truth, not mere psychological perception, entertainment, or titillation. This second group sought to revive pre-1848 Viennese satirical traditions, particularly the work of Johann Nestroy and Friedrich Kürnberger. The advocates of the Klimt-Schnitzler axis wrote criticism for the daily newspapers of Vienna. The voice of the second group was Karl Kraus's magazine, *Die Fackel,* and, briefly, Loos's publication *Das Andere.* Ludwig Wittgenstein and Elias Canetti would be influenced by Kraus and Loos, as were Schoenberg and Berg.

Schoenberg's attraction to this group stemmed not only from a sense of his own exclusion from the mainstream of Viennese cultural institutions and his marginal position vis-à-vis the city's dominant social circles. Kraus's acerbic moralism and sarcasm fit his personality. Even more to the point was his intense and puritanical attitude toward the use of language. It was from Kraus that Schoenberg developed the fundamental distinction between idea and style, or, in Loos's vocabulary, between structure and ornament.

Modernism, as argued by the circle around Kraus, needed to be a critique of journalism, modern popular culture, and fashion. Most fin de siècle modernism appeared to pander to a debased sense of art and reveled in a facile bohemianism designed to enhance the journalistic fame associated with the making of new art. In contrast, Kraus and his followers argued that the exemplary vehicle for art—language—was also the instrument of truth telling. Inherent in language—and therefore in music and the elements of visual art—were sacred normative verities that went beyond the use of language evident in ordinary realist and naturalist strategies.[31] Schoenberg's conception of the essential character of the materials of music—as autonomous elements with immanent structural possibilities but also with an inherent ethical resistance to abuse and misuse—and his own views on the history of music owe much to the example of Kraus. Adherence to limited notions of syntax, grammar, and narration in music suppressed the intrinsic possibilities of musical art.

Conventional boundaries between the new and the old were therefore redrawn. In Kraus's canon, Offenbach and Wagner were praised but Heine disparaged. Nestroy and Wilde were idealized but not Hofmannsthal and Stefan George. The emergence of these two groups at the fin de siècle made for strange alliances. Some conservative critics such as Robert Hirschfeld were praised by Kraus and his group, even at the expense of Mahler.

$$\bullet \quad \bullet \quad \bullet \quad \bullet \quad \bullet$$

Kraus's view of the task of modern art led him and his group to reassert classicism as a possible model. The achievements of the pre-1848 world in theater, literature, architecture, design, and music seemed immune from the corruptions of commerce and mass society. They exceeded the boundaries of bourgeois realism and representation. Kraus went beyond the motto of the Secession ("To each age its art, to art its freedom"). He sought to merge a normative aesthetic philosophy with a teleology. No doubt the present day demanded something more than a rehash of the past. For Loos and Schoenberg, technological progress and economic and social change rendered aesthetic nostalgia or the use of art to camouflage historical change repugnant. However, in the assertion of the modern, ethical and aesthetic truth took precedence over convention and contemporaneity.

Not only did the classical masters appear exemplary, but so too did Brahms. Despite Schoenberg's appropriation of Wagnerian musical innovations and his acceptance of a Wagnerian historical narrative in which Wagnerian practice played a decisive role toward the emancipation of the dissonance and the normalization of remote harmonic relationships, it was the classical notion of motivic variations and transformations in musical form that held the most promise. Schoenberg's sharp reaction against the neoclassicism of the 1920s stemmed not so much from the impulse to look at the eighteenth century for models as from the neoclassicists' superficial conception of what could be learned from the eighteenth century. In his view, Stravinsky and his emulators merely exploited the evident decorative symmetries of the past.[32]

What made the application of Karl Kraus's strategy within the arena of music particularly apt was the fact that a public debate regarding the dete-riorating state of musical culture in Vienna was already under way by the early 1890s. The rhetoric of cultural decline had become quite famil-iar. The extension of general literacy and the concomitant spread of music education, propelled in part by the wide distribution of pianos and piano instruction in Vienna after 1848, carried with them the doubt that this democratization of culture was compatible with the sustaining of late-eigh-teenth-century standards.

Part of the special allure of concert music for the late-nineteenth-century Viennese population was its historical association with eighteenth-century aristocratic habits. By the late nineteenth century the population of Vienna was composed mostly of individuals not born in the city. Given Vienna's sense of itself as a city of music, the acquisition of musical culture was par-ticularly useful to newcomers in the psychological process of feeling at home and part of the city. The intense social pressure for music education fueled the suspicion that true connoisseurship was not compatible with ef-forts to make music education more accessible. By the mid-1880s the sim-plification of piano instruction, the proliferation of explanatory literature about music, and a popular music journalism available to the growing ranks of eager consumers of culture appeared to many observers as dangerous developments.[33]

Heinrich Schenker, who was six years older than Schoenberg but who arrived in Vienna from Galicia only in the mid 1880s, began to write criti-cism in Vienna in the early 1890s.[34] There was an uncanny correspondence between his diagnosis of the Viennese musical scene and the views of the young Schoenberg. Schenker's basic argument was that music presented a particular challenge to the audience consistent with its character. Unlike the other arts, music—as represented by the folk song, the simplest and most "natural" of creations and the "easiest" (in terms of the instrumental technique required to play it)—was ultimately the most difficult to grasp. The "artistry" of a great tune, for example, represented an almost meta-physical mystery. It was not comparable to the simple sentence or the clear image. Although poetry shared with music a nonconventional logic, as in other visual and linguistic arts there was a basic level of comprehension that almost everyone could attain. The dimension that artistic creation added to language was essentially transformative and supplemental—from the simple to the complex.

This was not the case in music. In fact, the influence of Wagner had seriously undermined the recognition of the essence of music. The chal-lenge of modernism was to reverse the efforts of the late Romantics in music, who subordinated musical sound to the expectations it raised de-rivative of the other arts. The unique essence of music, embedded in the simple, was obliterated.[35]

As in mathematics, the magic of music stemmed from the unique flexibility of its elements. The independent meaning of variables was fundamentally nonreferential. Musical significance derived from combinations of these elements with one another. Furthermore, as elements worked together in individual circumstances, they became adapted, in an unstable, highly individualized manner, to being "filled up with emotions." Upon each hearing, with each individual, there was the potential for the attachment of changing emotional and extramusical meaning.[36] Such extramusical meanings were crucial to music, but they were not fixed or illustrative. If they emanated from formal musical strategies, they could be protean and expansive beyond the range of words and images.

For this reason the conventions of late-nineteenth-century program music were fundamentally in error. Like Schoenberg, Schenker came to regard the creation of musical form through the imitation of poetic meaning, visual imagery, and linguistic narrative as an inappropriate procedure for modern music. As a model for the sequence, character, and duration of events, the extramusical defined in terms of language and the pictorial was fundamentally at odds with the nature of music. Schenker argued that in contrast to Wagner, the great classical masters—from Haydn, Mozart, and Beethoven to Brahms—created musically coherent works that possessed an infinitely differentiated and individual opportunity for the ascription of emotional meaning. Therefore a certain kind of active and not passive listening was required so that the power of music could be unlocked in a personally meaningful manner by the lay individual.

Schenker recognized that historically there had been a constant struggle between the word and musical sound. Because all laypersons had access to meaning through images and words in painting, poetry, and prose, it was only natural that with the expansion of the audience in the late nineteenth century, words and images became the accepted route to musical appreciation. Not only did composers begin to subordinate sound to word, but the audience sought to understand all music as if it were little more than translations into sound. Even performers shaped renditions of historical repertoire as if the music had been organized around an extramusical narrative—a secret linguistic and visual program.

This procedure actually blocked the audience's ability to listen actively, since if true musical appreciation were cultivated each individual would not be reduced to passively recognizing a program associated with a piece of music but would be enabled to listen so that the temporal experience of music could be profoundly personalized to fit the moment and the hearer's imagination. Any translation of sound into word would bear the stamp of the individual. What, then, was required for the possession of skills adequate to an "active appreciation"? A lay appreciation of music analogous to the understanding of the principles of mathematics was viewed as a possible and desirable starting point.[37]

Schenker realized that the contemporary public applied skills of ordinary literacy and culture, mediated through words and pictures, onto music. Since the contemporary audience consisted of passive spectators, its judgment was flawed. Schenker wrote scathingly of music teachers and the time wasted teaching myriads of middle-class people instrumental techniques—the mechanical ability to reproduce music themselves—without ever increasing their understanding of the logic of music. What was required in contemporary musical culture was the training of lay, "self-activated listeners" who no longer would be dependent on getting only the "spirit"—extramusically understood—of the musical experience.[38]

The crucial point of comparison between Schenker and the young Schoenberg was their shared conviction that music, although independent of words, operated by laws that were analogous to those of linguistic grammar. Structural elements such as the refrain, for example, had both linguistic and musical functions that were not identical, although overlapping. The divergence between the two men rested on their assumptions about the possible future range of evolution for musical grammar, and not on the principle that music required the use of formal structures adequate to its autonomous character. For Schoenberg, musical grammar had both a teleology and an evolutionary history. For Schenker its nature was fixed. But for both men the pinnacle of recognition of the unique character of music and the high point in its realization as art had been the classical era.[39]

Regardless of their fundamental differences with respect to the possibilities presented to the composer in modern times, their views on the inadequacies of the Viennese listening public were nearly identical. Since fin de siècle Viennese concertgoers were dependent on routinized extramusical associations, as Schenker observed in 1894, an "unmusical criticism" reigned. An "immorality" dominated musical life. Commercial social utility and advancement had become the dominant factors motivating musical life, not a love or appreciation of musical art. Both men shared a particular contempt for performance practices that obscured musical structure, even though Schoenberg and Webern, unlike Schenker, retained an affection for a rhythmically flexible, Romantic performance approach to the classical repertoire.[40]

In a trenchant 1894 essay entitled "Hearing in Music" Schenker sought to find in the modern world a way to encourage the transformation of the spontaneous, naive response to music into a "conscious, active" experience for the layperson in which the totality of a work, as well as its constituent material elements, could be enjoyed. A new kind of comparative science of music was required. The elements that needed transmittal were the principles of polyphony, harmony, and "organic" structure. Once a musical apperception was cultivated, ordinary language could help active appreciation, but music appreciation would no longer be tied to some language-based, cliché-ridden scheme of musical meaning.

Schenker identified the need for a new kind of musical upbringing (*Erziehung*). Weaning listeners from descriptive and programmatic narratives could reveal to them "an entire metaphysical" realm hidden in music. The simple formulas of music teachers were at fault. The desire on the part of amateurs to use music to express individuality was thwarted by a mechanical definition of technique that fostered a mindless dexterity.

In order to match the soul of the listener with the secrets of the work of art, a cleansing of the historical surface of the classical tradition had to be achieved. Teaching manuals and printed editions of the classical repertoire that used an overlay of interpretive and expressive commentary masking the essence of even the simplest lullaby, robbing it of its vitality and many-sided adaptability to each individual, had to be abandoned.[41] Likewise, Schenker was critical of local performance practice. In contrast to the established critics of Vienna, he was not an unqualified admirer of Hans Richter.[42] He found Wagner's influence on the performance of the classical repertoire to be deleterious, for it fostered the imposition of extramusical programs. In orchestral concerts there was a new emphasis on sound effects and instrumental color as opposed to musical structure.

Hans von Bülow was more to Schenker's liking. However, Schenker realized that the public of the future, particularly in orchestral concerts, would become even more dependent on the virtuoso conductor, whose qualities would be judged not by musical results perceptible aurally but by visual impressions. Although a well-rehearsed orchestra needed a minimum of gestures from the conductor, the audience was increasingly tied to the conductor's physical realization of the line of the music and its salient events. The conductor's virtuosity constituted a visual compensation for the inadequacies of listening. The music associated with the Wagnerian and post-Wagnerian trends exemplified by Richard Strauss and Gustav Mahler fit the need to reduce the musical to effect an illustration. As Schenker wrote in 1897, the death of Brahms represented a staggering loss. Brahms was the last master of the truly musical.[43]

Bruckner, in contrast, was the symphonist of effects, despite a false reputation as a master of counterpoint. His popularity was based on his sonorities. Only Bruckner scherzos were musically original. Despite the extensive Mozart celebrations of 1891 and the perception during the 1890s of an overt "Mozart renaissance," a return to the real essence of Mozart had yet to materialize. Too much of the Mozart revival of the 1890s was cast in the spirit of Wagner and designed to demonstrate that Mozart prefigured Wagnerian aesthetics, when in fact Mozart represented its antithesis.

Schenker, like Schoenberg, sought to fashion a post-Romantic credo. Both men, coming of age in the late nineteenth century in Vienna, confronted what they regarded as the corruption of musical culture in their own time. The objective of a new aesthetic, therefore—of a break with the past—was to find a way out of the legacy of Wagnerism, not only in compositional practice but also in music education and the dynamics of public musical life. Although the conclusions they drew were different, Brahms emerged as the pivotal figure for them both.

From the perspective of the late twentieth century, the critique on the part of a younger generation of the musical culture of fin de siècle Vienna set the stage for a modern movement in both composition and music scholarship that explicitly sought to delegitimate the social and cultural consequences of the popularization of concert music during the late nineteenth century. The contempt for the audience and critics mirrored, for Schoenberg and Schenker, a post-Nietzschean reformist radicalism exhibited by Karl Kraus and Adolf Loos. Not only art but culture at large, including the institutions, political arrangements, laws, and mores of the late nineteenth century, were at stake. In the 1920s and 1930s this fin de siècle merger of musical modernism and an agenda of societal reform assumed a compelling plausibility in the struggle against Fascism.

Schenker died in Europe in 1935. Schoenberg immigrated to America. Both men exerted a dramatic and transformative influence on musical composition and scholarship in America. The allure of their approaches to several generations of American musicians and scholars may be explained, in part, by the resonance felt vis-à-vis America to the critique of late-nineteenth-century culture and society implicit in their work.

Our distance from the horrors of the European midcentury and more than a decade of neoconservatism in American politics may have weakened our appreciation of the cultural critique located in Schoenberg's aesthetic evolution at the turn of the century. At the same time it is unlikely that the insights about musical culture, listening, and the audience that Schoenberg and Schenker developed along parallel lines before World War I have become entirely irrelevant. We might be well advised to locate this critique of modernity in Schoenberg's music itself in new ways—much as Schenker argued ought to be done when listening to any great music. After all, at stake in the music of Arnold Schoenberg, from the start of his career, was more than just music.

NOTES

This is a revised version of the opening address given at the Schoenberg conference in November 1991 at the Arnold Schoenberg Institute in Los Angeles. I have sought to retain the character of an opening speech in which the frame of a general argument is retained. The critical apparatus is designed to refer readers to the sources.

1. The parallel is not precise, but it is appropriate. See Werner J. Schweiger, "Zwischen Anerkennung und Verteuflung: Zur Rezeptionsgeschichte von Kokoschkas Frühwerk, " in *Oskar Kokoschka: Symposion,* ed. Erika Patka (Salzburg: Residenz Verlag, 1986), 114–126.

2. This selection of premieres is based on the level of the public controversy they raised. The January 1910 concert at the Ehrbar Saal in which the op. 15 Stefan George cycle and op. 11 were premiered was less dramatic. The premiere of *Pelleas* in the winter of 1905 can be considered in the light of the subsequent discussion, however.

3. See Franz Grasberger, *Richard Strauss und die Wiener Oper* (Tutzing: Hans Schneider, 1969), 7–24.

4. Walter Frisch, *The Early Works of Arnold Schoenberg 1893–1908* (Berkeley and Los Angeles: University of California Press, 1993).

5. See Schoenberg's "A Self-Analysis" (1948), "My Evolution" (1949), and "How One Becomes Lonely" (1937), in *Style and Idea.*

6. The best source for Viennese criticism of Mahler's music is Henry-Louis de La Grange, *Gustav Mahler: Vienna: The Years of Challenge (1897–1904)* (Oxford: Oxford University Press, 1995); for Strauss, see Leon Botstein, "Richard Strauss and the Viennese Critics (1896–1924)," in *Richard Strauss and His World,* ed. Bryan Gilliam (Princeton, N.J.: Princeton University Press, 1993).

7. See Leon Botstein, "Music and Its Public" (Ph.D. diss., Harvard University, 1985), 1,184–1,199.

8. See Ulrich Thieme, *Studien zum Jugendwerk Arnold Schoenberg: Einflüsse und Wandlungen* (Regensburg: Bosse Verlag, 1979), 40–53.

9. Alma Mahler, *Gustav Mahler: Memories and Letters,* ed. Donald Mitchell (New York: Viking Press, 1969), 77, 111–112.

10. See the text of Schoenberg's response to Karpath, and Kraus's supportive contextualization, in *Die Fackel* 272–273 (15 February 1909), 34–35.

11. Josef Rufer, *The Works of Arnold Schoenberg,* 147–148.

12. See Simon McVeigh, *Concert Life in London from Mozart to Haydn* (Cambridge: Cambridge University Press, 1993).

13. It is significant that in those mature works with a tie to the political realities of European anti-Semitism—*Moses und Aron, Kol Nidre, Ode to Napoleon Buonaparte,* and *A Survivor from Warsaw*—Schoenberg succeeded, without apology, in using music to reach an audience at first hearing, even in the case of the posthumous first performance of *Moses und Aron.* The Wagnerian impulse is discernible. A contrast becomes most apparent when one compares each of these works with other Schoenberg compositions written at the same time that lack this particular extramusical meaning.

14. See "Circular to My Friends on My Sixtieth Birthday" (1934), in Schoenberg, *Style and Idea,* 27; and *Schoenberg Letters,* 270. On Stravinsky, see the short comments by Schoenberg from 1926 and 1928 in *Style and Idea,* 481–483.

15. Schoenberg, "Tonality and Form," *Style and Idea,* 257; see also the scathing comment on page 97 about "the Viennese conductor" who rejected the op. 9.

16. David Josef Bach, "Feuilleton: Der neuste Fall Schoenberg," *Arbeiterzeitung* (Vienna), 2 January 1909, 1–2.

17. The 1911 *Harmonielehre* is perhaps the most significant example. One also thinks of the essays on Brahms and Mahler. Schoenberg's polemical writings are found in Schoenberg, *Style and Idea*; of particular interest are the pre–World War I essays "About Music Criticism," and "Problems in Teaching Art," "A Legal Question," and "The Music Critic." See also "Ein Interview" in *Stil und Gedanke*.

18. See the excellent opening statement in Ethan Haimo, *Schoenberg's Serial Odyssey: The Evolution of His Twelve-Tone Method, 1914–1928* (Oxford: Oxford University Press, 1990), 2–6.

19. See *Schoenberg Letters*, 287.

20. The argument in this essay is abbreviated, of necessity, in terms of its detail. The reader may wish to consult any number of well-known books on turn-of-the-century Vienna, including the classic work by Carl Schorske, *Fin-de-Siècle Vienna: Politics and Culture* (New York: Alfred A. Knopf, 1980). For those interested in Schoenberg vis-à-vis Vienna, see Edward Timms, *Karl Kraus: Apocalyptic Satirist* (New Haven, Conn.: Yale University Press, 1986), 3–29.

21. *Schoenberg Letters*, 35. One might also compare Schoenberg's attitude toward Dehmel to that of Charles Ives toward Emerson.

22. Frisch, *Early Works of Arnold Schoenberg*, 266.

23. See John Daverio, *Nineteenth Century Music and the German Romantic Ideology* (New York: Schirmer Books, 1993).

24. See Reinhold Brinkmann, *Late Idyll: The Second Symphony of Johannes Brahms* (Cambridge: Harvard University Press, 1995), 84.

25. See letters of Richard Dehmel to Georg Ebers, 29 September 1891; to Wolfgang Kirchbach, 3 October 1891; and to Gustav Kühl, 21 September 1896 and 11 February 1897, in Richard Dehmel, *Ausgewählte Briefe aus den Jahren 1883 bis 1902* (Berlin: S. Fischer Verlag, 1922), 58–69, 252–256, and 260–262.

26. Schoenberg to Dehmel, 13 December 1912, *Schoenberg Letters*, 35.

27. See Alexander L. Ringer, *Arnold Schoenberg: The Composer as Jew* (Oxford: Oxford University Press, 1990). Schoenberg's self-image as Jew and his reactions to anti-Semitism have a social-class dimension. In contrast to his critics of Jewish origin and other younger talents identified as Jews (including whose who had converted or who were born converted)—such as Kraus and Hofmannsthal—Schoenberg was relatively poor and represented the first generation of his family in Vienna to assimilate fully.

28. See Dehmel, *Ausgewählte Briefe*, 196–199.

29. See Leon Botstein, *Judentum und Modernität* (Vienna: Böhlau Verlag, 1991), 126–148.

30. See Michael Mäckelmann, *Arnold Schoenberg und das Judentum: Der Komponist und sein religiöses, nationales und politisches Selbstverständnis nach 1921* (Hamburg: Verlag der Musikalienhandlung Karl Dieter Wagner, 1984).

31. See, for example, the impression made by Kraus on Berg in early 1915 during Kraus's tireless effort to expose the role of the press in glorifying the war effort; *Berg-Schoenberg Correspondence*, 229–230. See also Alexander Goehr, "Schoen-

berg and Karl Kraus: The Idea behind the Music," *Music Analysis* 4/1–2 (1985), 59–71.

32. Schoenberg, *Style and Idea*, 481.

33. A example of the type of Viennese publication directed at middle-class consumers of culture, particularly music, was the journal *An der schönen blauen Donau: Belletristisch-musikalische Zeitschrift*, which began in 1885 and appeared twice a month. It was a family magazine (*"Unterhaltungsblatt für die Familie"*) with a sheet-music insert in each issue, in addition to articles, poems, essays, and short stories.

34. See Helmut Federhofer, *Heinrich Schenker: Nach Tagebüchern und Briefen in der Oswald Jonas Memorial Collection* (Hildesheim: Georg Olms Verlag, 1985), and Nicolas Meeus, *Heinrich Schenker: Une introduction* (Liege: Mardaga, 1993). See also Allan Keiler's parallel discussion in his "The Origins of Schenker's Thought: How Man Is Musical," *Journal of Music Theory* 33/2 (fall 1989), 273–298. The argument that follows takes issue with some of Keiler's claims, but remains essentially consistent with his basic thesis.

35. Helmut Federhofer, ed., *Heinrich Schenker als Essayist und Kritiker: Gesammelte Aufsätze, Rezensionen und kleinere Berichte aus den Jahren 1891–1901* (Hildesheim: Georg Olms Verlag, 1990), 249–250.

36. Ibid., 100.

37. Ibid., 138–140. It is possible to speculate that the mature Schoenberg's concentration on a row of twelve pitches and its permutations as a basic underlying unit of composition mirrors the very same understanding of music's essence as is exhibited in Schenker's discussion of intervallic relationships within the thematic unit as containing the structural cell in complex—as regards surface and duration—works of musical art.

38. Ibid., 62.

39. See Heinrich Schenker, *Harmonielehre* (1906; Vienna: Universal Edition, 1978).

40. Consider, for example, Webern's 1932 performance of his arrangements of the Schubert German Dances. Included in the Boulez Webern set SONY SM3K 45845.

41. Federhofer, *Schenker als Essayist*, 154–166, 216–221, 248–252.

42. Compare Schenker's 1894 description of Richter with Ludwig Karpath's 1898 essay. See Federhofer, *Schenker als Essayist*, 79; and Ludwig Karpath, "Hans Richter," in *50 Jahre Hoftheater: Geschichte der beiden Wiener Hoftheater unter der Regierungszeit des Kaisers Franz Josef I*, ed. Rudolph Lothar and Julius Stern (Vienna: Steyermühl, 1898), 81–83. Schenker also wrote an essay in 1901 critical of Mahler's performance (with reorchestrations) of Beethoven's Ninth Symphony; see *Schenker als Essayist*, 259–268.

43. Federhofer, *Schenker: Nach Tagebüchern*, 238–239, 257–259; Federhofer, *Schenker als Essayist*, 230–235.

TWO

Assimilation and the Emancipation of Historical Dissonance

Alexander L. Ringer

Few twentieth-century composers, if any, have been as closely examined by musical theorists in recent decades as Arnold Schoenberg, whose very name invariably evokes the "method of composing with twelve tones related only to one another" that in the wake of the World War II exerted such startling fascination on countless musical minds desperate for relief from their nagging creative malaise. Why, however, of all the great talents of his generation this largely self-taught descendant of a modest Austro-Hungarian Jewish family should have been the one to alter the course of twentieth-century music in such decisive ways remains a rather obvious, though admittedly complex, question that has hardly been seriously asked, let alone meaningfully answered. Indeed, were it not for some strikingly self-revelatory statements in Schoenberg's own published writings, what enabled him to pursue his lonely path so doggedly against all historical and purely aesthetic odds might yet be shrouded in even greater mystery than it undoubtedly is.

Talk of spiritual development seems rather beside the issue where an unreconstructed purist is concerned whose philosophical outlook barely changed in the course of a long creative life. The implication of some kind of steady evolution in Schoenberg's dauntless quest for truth simply does not square with his oft-expressed, unshakable, and infallibly proven faith in the essential immutability of all fundamental precepts. Organic change was a central aspect of his creative approach, sustained as much by the precipitous events of the disturbing times in which he lived as by that intangible inner necessity he felt compelled to obey. By the same token, however, that very quality served to reinforce the overarching sense of lawful unity at the heart of all of his varied artistic responses to a world in turmoil.

A relentless drive for unity and a well-nigh ascetic passion for self-imposed restraint emerged early on as hallmarks of Schoenberg's artistic personality. "At the very start I knew that restriction could be achieved by two methods, condensation and juxtaposition," he recalled in 1948.[1] Seven years earlier he had conluded his University of California lecture titled "Composition with Twelve Tones" with the suggestion that "when Richard Wagner introduced his *Leitmotiv*—for the same purpose as that for which I introduced my Basic Set—he may have said: 'Let there be unity.' "[2] So consistently did this deeply embedded creed determine his work and thought that already in 1937 he felt compelled to tell an American audience: "I have not discontinued composing in the same style and in the same way as at the very beginning. The difference is only that I do it better now than before; it is more concentrated, more mature."[3] But then, he had long since reached the conclusion that truly creative visions will always be conceived "in harmony with the Divine Model."[4]

Schoenberg's absolute commitment to rigorous discipline and structural unification became in a sense a condition of inner survival, given the disquieting climate of psychological and social dissonance in which he grew up and spent the first quarter century of his productive life. What distinguished him more than anything else from other intellectually and artistically gifted contemporaries of similarly assimilated Jewish background was his remarkable ability to turn such shared sociocultural liabilities into decisive creative assets. Thus it was that his uncanny "emancipation" of the insidious "historical dissonance" affecting all but the most insensitive of "modern" Jews brought to full fruition what the much heralded emancipation of musical dissonance had merely promised: a seemingly inescapable element of perpetual unresolved tensions, unconditionally accepted as such, now furnished the liberating ethical wherewithal for aesthetic exploits of an entirely new order.

That this crucial feature has been so sorely neglected is no doubt due at least in part to the decidedly Gentile nature of historical musicology, a scholarly daughter of Romanticism raised on philological models at the behest of a thousand years of Christian musical civilization. Assimilated Jewish music historians, beginning with Gustav Mahler's close friend Guido Adler, readily fell into line, if only because the study of a Christian art did seem to call for Christian expertise and perspectives. Christianity had, after all, seen to it that Jews remained excluded from European musical life well into the nineteenth century. A musical past that was for all practical purposes *judenrein* hardly cried out for any intrinsically Jewish input. Then, too, historians almost by definition rely extensively on documentary evidence. Although Schoenberg's published essays do offer occasional hints regarding his general state of mind in certain contexts, they reveal little about his day-to-day preoccupations, let alone his more intimate musings. He did, of course, write copious notes to himself and from time to time made a personal matter the subject of a letter to a trusted friend. His dramatic exchange of letters with Vasili Kandinsky in April 1923, on the other hand, forms an exception in almost every way. For one, it reveals his profound consciousness of the assimilated Jew's historical dilemma in unusually forceful terms. Above all, however, the fearful predictions of the fate awaiting those unable or unwilling to draw the inescapable conclusions from their ominously dissonant existence turned out to be terrifyingly prophetic.

"What made young Arnold run" in this direction in the first place can only be inferred from what is generally known about turn-of-the-century Jewish Vienna in conjunction with the more specific conditions of his maturation into a feeling, thinking human being who was resolutely oriented toward·action. Attempts to dig below the obvious surface are beset with interpretive pitfalls. Apart from the need for a host of "objective" data, any such attempt calls for a measure of empathy with Jewish culture, religious as well as secular, that is apt to elude even otherwise highly qualified scholars, for most of them are accustomed to dealing with musical works of art primarily in splendid isolation, as structural entities answering only to their own intrinsic laws. Musical anthropologists recognized long ago that as a form of symbolic behavior music is always inextricably bound up with the sociocultural factors that engender and nurture it; traditional musicology by contrast still prefers to leave "extraneous" considerations of this kind to general historians with a taste for the arts, whose comments may or may not be incorporated into the requisite erudite footnotes. Nor should it be forgotten that academic musicology treated the twentieth century until quite recently as a wayward stepchild preferably left to the care of professional theorists, not a few of whom turned out to be "note counters" of the sort that incurred Schoenberg's repeated wrath. Last but by no means least, anything smacking even remotely of *Geistesgeschichte* is bound to get short shrift this side of the Atlantic, where the historical falsifications and vilifications of National Socialist and Stalinist ideologists are still keenly remembered. As a historical phenomenon, however, Arnold Schoenberg, a victim as well as vocal opponent of these aberrations, can hardly be understood without proper reference to the humanistic premises and contributions of Geistesgeschichte. Surely, as long as familiarity with New England transcendentalism or American individualism is considered indispensable for a meaningful appraisal of Charles Ives and his particular mission, Arnold Schoenberg, his exact contemporary and eventual fellow American, deserves equally serious attention in equivalent Jewish terms.

The Schoenberg household differed very little from many others established in Vienna during the second half of the nineteenth century by Jews from the far-flung reaches of the empire seeking a better future in the big city. Though for the most part traditionally religious—Arnold Schoenberg's ancestry included rabbis as well as cantors—Vienna's Jews nevertheless succumbed quite readily to the lures of assimilation and, in more extreme cases, equated the desired opening to Austrian society at large with whole-sale renunciations—indeed, denunciations—of Jewish religious practices or customs. What religious observances Samuel Schönberg had endeavored to maintain apparently fell into disuse soon after his untimely death. His son's later helplessness in dealing with Hebrew texts would suggest that he lacked even that minimum of Jewish education generally accorded twelve-year-old boys in preparation of their first public reading from the Torah—the central part of the bar mitzvah ceremony, whereby they become full-fledged members of their religious community. Whether Arnold Schoenberg ever assumed his religious duties in this time-honored manner is still an open question. For all we know, his "confirmation" involved something like the family party described by Arthur Schnitzler, whose "modern" parents went out of their way to behave "like everybody else."[5] Unfortunately, "everybody else" did not necessarily respond positively to those earnest strivings of a minority but recently emerged from centuries of involuntary separateness. Rising fears of "unfair competition" and, far worse, rumors about an alleged Jewish plot to bastardize the Aryan race (that mythical brainchild of post-Romantic apostles of purity touting misbegotten evolutionistic theories), not to speak of the still festering blood libel, continued to preclude broadly based social acceptance. The very improvements in the legal and material position of Central European Jewry, tokens of outward progress, also contained the seeds of ultimate destruction.

Arnold Schoenberg was barely seven years old when the German Reichstag seriously debated a proposal to rescind substantial portions of Jewish civil rights that had been granted less than two decades earlier. In imperial Russia the assassination of Czar Alexander II unleashed a chain of murderous pogroms. For who but those unholy servants of the Antichrist could have committed this heinous deed? Vienna witnessed the realization of one of Richard Wagner's fondest wishes when hundreds of Jews were among the many victims of the fire that engulfed the Ringtheater during the sold-out second performance of Offenbach's *Tales of Hoffmann*. Wagner, of course, had imagined a Jewish holocaust at a performance of Lessing's *Nathan, the Wise*.[6] Still, he might have been cheered a few months after the Vienna disaster by the news that Dresden, the city where he had nurtured his incipient hatred of everything Jewish, was hosting the founding congress of organized political anti-Semitism. Actually, at that point Wagner himself began to have second thoughts, albeit too late. The aging sorcerer had clearly lost control, and his eager apprentices, boosted by the "scientific" claims of the new racism, lost no time setting in motion the notorious *Antisemitenstreit* of Berlin's leading historians. Eventually, not to be left behind, ranking French army officers staged the bogus treason trial of Captain Henri Dreyfus that turned the Viennese journalist and playwright Theodor Herzl, once like Gustav Mahler a proud member of Vienna's pan-German Wagner-

Association, into the progenitor of modern Zionism. Other Jewish activists meanwhile carried their fight against domestic anti-Semitism straight into the Austrian political arena. One of their most prominent leaders, Josef Bloch, even won a libel suit against a dangerous agitator fittingly answering to the name Rohling, who had publicly asserted that Jews killed Christians as a sacred duty mandated by the Talmud.

The novel phenomenon of Jews fighting back was hardly lost on Arnold Schoenberg, who heard the pros and cons passionately debated in his favorite coffeehouses no less than at home in Leopoldstadt. Here the events of this seemingly endless drama created far greater concern than, say, the unexpected failure of a Schnitzler play. Those hardworking Jewish residents were anything but strangers to anti-Semitic harassment, in particular from that traditionally bigoted section of the petite bourgeoisie that Adolf Hitler later gratefully remembered for its contribution to his early awareness of the pernicious Jewish influence on Austrian society. Hitler shrewdly linked that crucial awakening with his consuming hatred for the Hapsburg monarchy, which, unlike its Russian counterpart, was happy to take advantage of the Jewish population's talents and far-flung connections, the very qualities that had induced Joseph II in Mozart's day to issue his famous *Toleranzpatent* for the benefit of a limited number of economically "useful" Jews. Seen in this light, Arnold Schoenberg's occasional nostalgia for the Austrian imperial house betrayed a healthy dose of political realism rather than the simple reactionary tendencies often ascribed to him by left-leaning critics who view the world pointedly through non-Jewish glasses.

Socially suspended, as it were, between the interests of the state and the animosity of many of its citizens, not to mention that of the extremely powerful Roman Catholic clergy, Austria's Jews, while still barred from state employment by imperial decree, contributed far more than their proportional share to the free professions, whether medical, legal, literary, or artistic. But their very successes in these and a number of other walks of life encouraged a false sense of security that proved their undoing in the long run. In the meantime, though, growing numbers of conservative businessmen as well as radical intellectuals celebrated the consummation of their assimilation by deserting the Jewish community altogether. Some, like the famous Adler brothers, embraced socialism as a new religion that promised the elimination of all social distinctions, including those between Christians and Jews. Others, with more serious spiritual concerns but woefully ignorant of their own religious heritage, persuaded themselves that Judaism was too old-fashioned for the modern world and accepted Protestantism as a viable alternative to the official state church. Still, as Heinrich Heine put it when Jews were first led to believe that their future depended on rapid assimilation, if not outright conversion: Jewishness is not easily "washed off." This well-documented truth caused a few to carry the gospel of progress so far as to agree in essence with Richard Wagner's conclusion, first stated in the final sentence of his "Judaism in Music," that it would be in the best interests of all concerned if the Jewish people once and for all vanished from the earth.

Arnold Schoenberg became a Protestant in 1898, presumably under the influence of his Lutheran friend Walter Pieau. However, this official act changed his overt religious behavior as little as did his solemn declaration of returning to the Jewish fold as a refugee in Paris thirty-five years later. Important Christian holidays had long since become festive occasions of a general nature, and nonbelievers, too, hoped for universal peace on earth. Thus nearly ten years after his baptism Schoenberg still bypassed the Gospels in favor of a nineteenth-century poem in his musical appeal for *Friede auf Erden*. Clearly none of the religious institutions of his time, let alone their often rather self-glorious representatives, proved a match for the spiritual challenges this genuine believer derived from his close reading of the Hebrew Bible, albeit in Martin Luther's German translation. Thrice alienated, much like his mentor Gustav Mahler—as a Jew among Austrians, a Christian among Jews, and a musical secessionist among his peers—he actually never ceased to identify with the manifest destiny of those ancient wanderers in the desert to whom, as he explained to his cousin Malvina at the mature age of sixteen, all civilization owed its moral and social foundations.[7]

Earlier in the century, during those heady post-Napoleonic days when Central Europe's Jews expected confidently to join the majority culture, Heinrich Heine was only one brilliant representative of his generation to elect conversion as a token of sociopolitical progress. Some, among them Felix Mendelssohn, were taken to the baptismal font by anxious parents hoping to protect their youngsters from continuing anti-Jewish abuse. Others, like Adolf Bernhard Marx, turned Lutheran only after years of earnest soul searching. Typically, though, both Marx and Mendelssohn, who later became close friends, always regarded their Jewish roots with pride, drawing heavily upon the Old Testament, the Hebrew Bible, for lifelong inspiration. With his best-known work, *Moses*, Marx in fact anticipated Schoenberg not merely in writing his own oratorio text but, interestingly enough, also in allowing its composition a prolonged incubation period. Like Schoenberg, too, Marx was a prolific theorist and teacher whose devotion to the cause of Bach and Beethoven shaped the musical outlook of many a German composer. It was in fact the discovery of Mozart's Requiem and Handel's *Messiah* that induced him to study the Bible seriously for the first time, which ultimately led to his baptism—against the wish of a loving father who, despite his own distinctly rationalist leanings, remained loyal to his Jewish heritage. It is no wonder that under these by no means rare circumstances the younger Marx continued to be guided as much by "the genuine message of Judaism" as by the spirit of the Gospels,[8] the twin foundations of Schoenberg's early thought as well. And Schoenberg surely knew Marx's pioneering Beethoven studies, the first to stress the "*Zug nach dem Ganzen*" (drive toward the whole) as a central trait of all large-scale musical structures.[9]

By the end of the nineteenth century, at any rate, it may well have looked as if

> cultural commonality and occasional contact had shaped a common basis for the Jewish minority and the non-Jewish majority. Under these conditions the change of religion was no leap over an abyss. To many Jews, especially in the higher social, intellectual, and artistic circles, the conversion to Christianity marked the completion of their incorporation into the dominant culture, in the shaping of which they took part.[10]

The majority population did not always see it that way, however, treating in particular Jews who had undergone baptism "without any religious experience" with a good deal of suspicion, if not outright cynicism. And lingering conflicts of this sort, personal as well as collective, inevitably reinforced the Jewish sense of existential dissonance, with often devastating consequences. Budding intellectuals unequipped to cope in more traditional terms often retreated into seemingly unassailable radical positions, while others, the precocious genius Otto Weininger among them, were driven to suicide once their irrational public expressions of self-hatred failed to provide tangible relief. Max Brod's protégé, the talented young composer Alfred Schreiber, did remain faithful to his Jewish background. But the dissonant clash of his hopes with the reality of the Jewish situation proved too much, and he, too, put an abrupt end to his budding creative life.

With growing interest Arnold Schoenberg, ever constructive in thought and deed, watched the rash of Jewish political activity—Josef Bloch's fight for official recognition of Austria's Jews as one of the empire's many minorities no less than Theodor Herzl's relentless efforts on behalf of an independent Jewish state in the biblical land of old. Ultimately he made his choices unswayed by any of the principals in the great debate surrounding the "Jewish question." Given the Viennese cultural scene of the early twentieth century, his personal and professional contacts naturally involved many individuals of Jewish descent whose thinking, speech, and general attitudes inevitably reflected the early impact of Jewish lore and customs, if only in their propensity for self-deprecating Jewish jokes. In short, one way or another Schoenberg confronted his Jewish origins every day. Had he wished to look the other way, the outside world would have interfered, though perhaps not always as brutally as in the summer of 1921 at Mattsee, the Austrian resort town that barred Jews under the new political order as it had under the old. Characteristically, Schoenberg refused the requested proof that he and his family were proper Christians. Instead he accepted a Jewish friend's offer of sanctuary in Traunkirchen, where a surprised Josef Rufer first learned of the new method of composing with twelve tones. One wonders therefore whether the composer's rejoinder that this ensured Germany's musical supremacy for another hundred years did not in those circumstances contain a strong admixture of irony. At any rate, given the specific nature of the twelve-tone technique, it could hardly have referred to Wagner or even Brahms, whose "progressiveness" Schoenberg was yet to discover. More likely he had the melodic-rhythmic outlook of the same Johann Sebastian Bach in mind whom Joachim Quantz once cited in support of his prediction that German music would always be based on a mixed, as opposed to a uniquely national, style. Beethoven, the true executor of Bach's musical bequest as well as of that of the French Revolution, certainly proved the point. Schoenberg, pursuing that grand tradition further and further, for his part finally reached that step on his personal *Jakobsleiter* where air of another planet rendered conventional forces of musical gravity as inoperative as those historical dissonances in the despairing hearts and minds of so many of his contemporaries.

The chain of traumatic experiences from the Dreyfus trials through the humiliating *Judenzählung* of 1916 (the official census of Jewish soldiers in response to charges that Jews had managed to avoid their military duty; the census proved the opposite) on to Mattsee and beyond reflected a kind of perverse logic to which Schoenberg reacted, logically as always, with a thorough reevaluation of his own dissonant socioreligious past in light of the mandates of his artistic mission. As he told Kandinsky the year after Mattsee, the strength that permitted him to persevere on his chosen path came entirely from religion, "though without any organisational fetters."[11] As evidence he referred to his *Jakobsleiter* text. Yet by 1923 it was no longer a generalized matter of faith:

> For I have at last learnt the lesson that has been forced upon me during this year, and I shall not forget it. It is that I am not a German, not a European, indeed perhaps scarcely even a human being (at least, the Europeans prefer the worst of their race to me), but I am a Jew."[12]

In 1921 the London *Times* had managed to unmask the virulently anti-Semitic "Protocols of the Elders of Zion" as nothing but a series of "clumsy plagiarisms," a thinly disguised parody of the 1865 French political pamphlet "Dialogues in Hell between Machiavelli and Montesquieu." But this hardly diminished the flow of anti-Semitic propaganda through a Gentile world looking for convenient scapegoats in the aftermath of a disastrous war.[13] And Schoenberg's explicit statement that he was thenceforth perfectly content to be a Jew and no longer wished to be treated as an exception actually reflected a growing general tendency among artists and intellectuals of Jewish descent. The year 1921 saw no less than three major literary figures of decidedly different backgrounds and orientations reasserting their Jewish pride in print. Jakob Wassermann in a short but unsparing autobiographical essay entitled *Mein Weg als Deutscher und Jude,* which he dedicated to his close friend Ferruccio Busoni, came to the firm conclusion that as long as the rest of the world was determined to find fault with them, regardless of what they did or did not do, the Jews would simply have to go it alone.[14] Franz Kafka's friend Max Brod in his magisterial *Heidentum, Christentum, Judentum* drew attention to the disastrous consequences of the historical alliance of Christian otherworldliness and pagan materialism in comparison with the traditionally Jewish concerns for a dignified life in the present for all created in God's image.[15] Finally, Jacob Klatzkin, taking issue with the emphasis of his own teacher, Hermann Cohen, on Judaism's worldwide messianic mission, in his *Krisis und Entscheidung im Judentum* insisted rather on land and language as indispensable prerequisites of any meaningful Jewish future.[16] Not surprisingly, it was Klatzkin with whom Schoenberg corresponded while working on *Der biblische Weg,* the spoken drama spawned by the tragic events of an era that witnessed the brazen assassination of, among others, Walter Rathenau, the Jewish foreign minister on whose prestige and skill the fledgling Weimar Republic had placed so much hope for its future.

Unlike Hans Stuckenschmidt and, for that matter, Willi Reich, the late Michael Mäckelmann accepted the thesis of the paradigmatic significance of Schoenberg's Mattsee experience sufficiently to make it the starting point of his on the whole impressive doctoral dissertation. Inexplicably, though, he referred to that brief, if decisive, episode as a pogrom. In so doing he conveyed an erroneous impression not only of what actually happened but also of the nature and appropriateness of the composer's reaction.[17] For, despite the fact that White Russian as well as Polish soldiers and peasants had turned on Jewish communities within their reach as soon as the Czarist and Hapsburg regimes collapsed, it was an act of mental rather than physical violence that sensitized Schoenberg to the fragility of the *conditio judaica* in post–World War I Europe.[18] By then, to be sure, the name of the Cossack leader Petlura had become a symbol of rape, burning, looting, and the collective death of those who found themselves in the path of the undisciplined hordes roaming the Eastern European countryside in search of Jewish victims. On 16 June 1921, about the time Schoenberg and his family vainly sought peace and quiet in Mattsee, Koitschitz, a town near Minsk, suffered a grievous extension of the pogroms already visited upon Homel, Vitebsk, and Minsk itself. "The cruelty and barbarism can be gauged from the fact that while only fifty people were wounded, eighty-seven Jews were killed, among them an infant and his mother . . . [and] a few women were violated," reported the American Jewish Committee. Nine days later an armed band

> attacked the railroad station at Staravee, district of Bobrouisk, disarmed one of the two policemen, and robbed and pillaged the Jewish houses. They killed twelve Jews, including a boy of nine and a man of sixty, violated and killed a girl of nineteen, and wounded eleven Jews, among them two little girls.[19]

In Poland roving bands of soldiers made a special practice of attacking Jews on trains and in railroad stations. It took a stern American protest for the army's commanders to issue an explicit countermanding order.

Like most of his friends and colleagues, Schoenberg had taken little notice of the misfortunes of those strange-looking *Ostjuden* from beyond the new Austrian Republic's eastern border. Thousands of impoverished refugees were passing through or had settled in Vienna, glad to have escaped with their lives. No doubt Schoenberg, too, had heard and perhaps even repeated derogatory stories about those wretched souls whose unfamiliar garb and behavior lent themselves to jokes in poor taste. He soon recognized, however, that these for the most part strictly Orthodox creatures were the ones who perpetuated what Adolf Bernhard Marx had called "the genuine message of Judaism," a message so firmly imprinted on his mind that nothing could erase it. Emanuel Swedenborg's Christian gnosticism, as the composer understood it from his reading of Balzac's *Séraphita*, may actually have reinforced long-standing cabalistic tendencies—for example, in its rejection of clear distinctions between the realms of nature and the spirit. If proof were needed for Schoenberg's intrinsically Talmudic modes of reasoning and acting, the very first sentence of his *Harmonielehre* of 1911 should do nicely. "*Dieses Buch habe ich von meinen Schülern gelernt*" (This book I learned from my students)[20] amounts to a concise paraphrase of that well-known saying attributed to Rabbi Chanina: "I learned much from my teachers, from my colleagues even more than from my teachers, but from my pupils more than from all of them together."[21] Schoenberg's manner of teaching likewise recalls those rabbis of old, intensely engaged with their disciples in a never-ending search for new meanings and a better understanding of the Law's intricate meanings. As Schoenberg himself declared: "The teacher who does not exert himself because he tells only 'what he knows,' does not exert his pupils either. Action must start with the teacher himself; his unrest must infect the pupils. Then they will search as he does."[22]

If there was a trenchant difference between the author of the first edition of the *Harmonielehre* and that of the third, published in 1922, it reflected in no small measure the eternal lesson of the Jewish experience that words alone won't do—that, with survival at issue, thought must be matched by action. As he pointedly asked Kandinsky, now clearly no longer oblivious to the plight of Eastern European Jews, "What is anti-Semitism to lead to if not to acts of violence? Is it so difficult to imagine that?"[23] In August 1921 Adolf Hitler spoke before a gathering of the radical right on the subject "Why we are anti-Semites." Soon thereafter the *Völkischer Beobachter*, the official newspaper of the National-Socialist Workers Party, gleefully reported his solemn pledge not to rest until all Jews were safely locked up in concentration camps. And when the first storm-troop battalions took to the streets, the die was cast. Yet very few among Germany's intelligentsia appreciated the horrendous truth in Arnold Schoenberg's well-nigh clairvoyant apprehensions.

Irrevocably convinced that the historical experiment of assimilation was doomed to failure and that the sociocultural dissonance it had generated was likely to remain forever unresolved, Schoenberg unconditionally accepted the inner as well as outer contradictions of Jewish existence as fundamental aspects of the fate and mission of a unique people chosen, as he saw it, for the sake of a single abstract proposition: the divinely ordained idea of unity. In this, its emancipated form, historical dissonance became as effective a source of creative energy as it had been in the days of old, when the children of Israel chose to abandon Egypt's fleshpots for that "biblical road" which, though obviously fraught with dangers, also promised beyond sheer physical escape from the perennial pharaohs of this world a future truly consonant with the spiritual aspirations of those who, "having left behind everything material," wish only to be permitted to dream their ancient "dream of God."[24]

NOTES

1. Schoenberg, "A Self-Analysis" (1948), in *Style and Idea*, 78.
2. Schoenberg, "Composition with Twelve Tones (1)" (1941), in *Style and Idea*, 244.
3. Schoenberg, "How One Becomes Lonely" (1937), in *Style and Idea*, 30.
4. Schoenberg, "Composition with Twelve Tones (1)" (1941), 215.
5. Arthur Schnitzler, *Jugend in Wien* (Frankfurt am Main: Fischer Taschenbuch Verlag, 1981), 60.
6. See *Cosima Wagner's Diaries*, ed. Martin Gregor-Dellin and Dietrich Mack, trans. Geoffrey Skelton, vol. 2, *1878–1883* (New York and London: Harcourt, Brace, Jovanovich, 1980), 773.
7. See H. H. Stuckenschmidt, *Schönberg* (Zürich and Freiburg: Atlantis Verlag, 1974), 25.
8. See Herzl Shmueli, "Adolf-Bernhard Marx (1795–1866): Deutscher Musiker jüdischer Herkunft (Eine Dokumentation)," *Orbis Musica* 10 (1990/91), 219.
9. See Adolf Bernhard Marx, *Die Musik des neunzehnten Jahrhunderts und ihre Pflege* (Leipzig: Breitkopf & Härtel, 1873), 35.

10. Jacob Katz, *From Prejudice to Destruction: Antisemitism 1700–1933* (Cambridge: Harvard University Press, 1980), 81.

11. Schoenberg to Kandinsky, 20 July 1922, *Schoenberg Letters*, no. 42, 70–71, esp. 71.

12. Schoenberg to Kandinsky, 20 April 1923, *Schoenberg Letters*, no. 63, 88.

13. Still today Louis Farrakhan draws upon the alleged authority of the "Protocols" for his absurd charges of a worldwide Jewish conspiracy. At the time Henry Ford's *Dearborn Independent* took care of that sort of thing. When the evidence of forgery turned out to be incontrovertible, Ford simply stopped printing new accusations and reprinted the old ones.

14. Jacob Wassermann, *Mein Weg als Deutscher und Jude* (Berlin: S. Fischer Verlag, 1921).

15. Max Brod, *Heidentum, Christentum, Judentum*, 2 vols. (Munich: Kurt Wolff Verlag, 1921).

16. Jacob Klatzkin, *Krisis und Entscheidung im Judentum: Probleme des modernen Judentums*, 2d ed. (Berlin: Jüdischer Verlag, 1921).

17. Michael Mäckelmann, *Arnold Schönberg und das Judentum: Der Komponist und sein religiöses, nationales und politisches Selbstverständnis nach 1921* (Hamburg: Verlag der Musikalienhandlung Karl Dieter Wagner, 1984), 13–14. But see Alexander L. Ringer, *Arnold Schoenberg: The Composer as Jew* (Oxford: Clarendon Press, 1990), 4 and passim.

18. For a discussion of the *conditio judaica* in connection with Gustav Mahler in particular, see Nikolaus Vielmetti, "Das Judentum im zeitgenössischen Musikleben," in *Bruckner Symposion 1986*, ed. Othmar Wessely (Linz: Anton Bruckner Institut, Linzer Verlagsgesellschaft, 1989), 49–57.

19. American Jewish Committee, *American Jewish Yearbook 5683* (Philadelphia: Jewish Publication Society of America, 1922), 24:61.

20. Schoenberg, *Harmonielehre* (Leipzig and Vienna: Universal Edition, 1911), v.

21. See Nikolaus Vielmetti, "Lorenzo Da Ponte—Emanuele Conegliano," *Orbis Musica* 10 (1991/1992), 201.

22. Schoenberg, *Harmonielehre*, vii; Schoenberg, *Theory of Harmony*, 2.

23. Schoenberg to Kandinsky, 4 May 1923, *Schoenberg Letters*, no. 64, 92–93.

24. These are the concluding words of Schoenberg's *Der biblische Weg*.

THREE

Evolving Perceptions of Kandinsky and Schoenberg

Toward the Ethnic Roots of the "Outsider"

Peg Weiss

In a letter written two weeks after witnessing what his new friend the Russian-born artist Vasili Kandinsky might have called a "thundering collision of worlds," Franz Marc linked the names of Kandinsky and Schoenberg with observations on primitive art and "Oriental" music, which, he said, had retained its intrinsic "primitive" characteristics.[1] As is well known, that metaphorical thundering collision had taken place at the beginning of January 1911, when Kandinsky and his friends had celebrated the New Year by attending a concert of Schoenberg's music.[2] They heard the First String Quartet in D Minor, op. 7, the Second String Quartet in F-sharp Minor, op. 10, and the Three Piano Pieces, op. 11. Kandinsky's response had been immediate: within two days he had moved from the first sketches to the completed painting *Impression III (Concert)*, a work that with its aggressive yellow visual blast (like the fanfare of trumpets, in Kandinsky's color language), anchored by the ironic black form of the instrument, so brilliantly echoes the concert's aural impact on an artist for whom synesthetic perceptions could be shattering (see figure 1). Black, he wrote in his manifesto *Über das Geistige in der Kunst*, is "musically represented by a completely closing pause after which a continuation follows as if at the beginning of another world, because what is closed by *this* pause is ended for all time: the circle is closed."[3] In that passage he went on to compare black with the silence imposed by death but concluded that, although "externally the most soundless color," black was the one color "against which every other color, even the weakest sounding, sounds stronger and more precise." Thus, in choosing to pit strong yellow against black, the artist had unleashed the loudest coloristic sound he could imagine—like the lash of a whip—while heralding the "beginning of another world."[4]

In his letter of 14 January 1911 to August Macke, Marc had exclaimed:

Fig. 1. Kandinsky, untitled study for *Impression III (Concert)*, January 1911. Charcoal on paper, 10 × 14.7 cm. Musée National d'Art Moderne, Centre Georges Pompidou, Paris. From *Kandinsky*, ed. Christian Derouet and Jessica Boissel (Paris: Musée National d'Art Moderne, 1984). Copyright © 1996 Artists Rights Society (ARS), New York/ADAGP, Paris.

> Can you imagine a music in which the tonality (that is, the holding to some kind of tonal system) is completely lifted? When listening to this music, which lets every tone struck stand for itself (a kind of *white canvas* between the color spots!), I had to think continually of Kandinsky's great Composition, which also allows no trace of tonal system . . . and also of Kandinsky's "leaping spots."

At that point Marc knew the great *Composition II* that had first attracted his attention to Kandinsky when it caused an uproar at the second exhibition of the Neue Künstler-Vereinigung the preceding autumn. Although local critics castigated the artist not only as "Eastern" but also as "insane," and the work as a failed craftsman's "design for a carpet," Marc had written an open letter to the director of the gallery declaring Kandinsky's "Compositions"—regarded strictly as "pictures"—more than a challenge to the great Persian tapestries then on view in the famous Mohammedan exhibition, exclaiming: "What artistic insight does this unique artist harbor!"[5]

Marc's January letter to Macke continued: "Schoenberg starts from the principle that the conceptions of consonance and dissonance do not exist at all. A so-called dissonance is only a consonance that lies further apart."

Fig. 2. Kandinsky, *Romantic Landscape*, 3 January 1911. Oil on canvas, 94.3 × 129 cm. Städtische Galerie im Lenbachhaus, Munich. Copyright © 1996 Artists Rights Society (ARS), New York/ADAGP, Paris.

And Marc outlined how in his painting he, too, wanted to operate with independent primary colors free of bondage to the paradigm of the prism. Primary colors may be spread out across the canvas, he wrote, in a sense creating "partial dissonances" that in the overall effect of the entire painting would actually create a new consonance, or, as he adds parenthetically, "harmony." Marc had at this time very likely begun work on his *Blue Horse I*.[6]

Little notice has been taken of the fact that on that same postconcert day Kandinsky's hypercreativity had resulted in yet a second painting, *Romantic Landscape*, with its trio of horsemen careening across a barren landscape ambiguous in time and space (see figure 2). Whereas the downward plunge of the horsemen is abruptly halted by the upward thrusting form at left, any sense of three-dimensional space suggested by the difference between the scale of this form and the great black form at the right on the one hand and the riders on the other is abolished by the swath of white that brings its brilliant vermilion sun smashing forward again to the plane of the canvas. It is a dizzying space, at once dense and immense, a space in which asteroids, too—Kandinsky's "leaping spots"—seem to inhabit the air. One feels indeed the "air of another planet."

In fact, it would seem that the poetry of Stefan George had served as a kind of springboard both for Kandinsky, whose own early work often echoed the poet's words and concepts, and for Schoenberg, whose Second String Quartet, played that day in Munich, closed with two movements that were essentially settings of two poems from George's *The Seventh Ring* cycle: "Litany" and "Ecstasy." It was the latter that seems most to have captured Kandinsky's imagination and to have inspired *Romantic Landscape,* which also contains echoes of poems from George's earlier *Algabal* series.[7] Is it any wonder, then, that Schoenberg—who had set fifteen other poems of George's—was, on seeing this painting for the first time the following December at the Neue Secession in Berlin, immediately attracted to it and wrote to Kandinsky: "The one that pleased me most was *Romantic Landscape.*"[8]

The Schoenberg quartet and the George poem underlying its last movement have other dimensions—other subtexts, as it were—that parallel dimensions in Kandinsky's experience. These are expressed in the painting *Lyrical,* and in the series of folkish *All Saints Day* paintings, all from the same year, 1911.[9] A key to these connections is hinted at in Marc's perceptive January letter to Macke, in which he combines observations on the theoretical relationships between Kandinsky and Schoenberg with ruminations on another and parallel experience that he described as "shattering":

> I have been thoroughly through the Völkermuseum in order to study the artistic means of "primitive peoples" (as . . . most contemporary critics put it when they characterize our efforts). Finally I found myself caught up, stunned and shattered, before the carvings of the Cameroons. . . . In this short winter I have become quite another person.

Indeed, the *Cameroons House Post* from Munich's great anthropological museum—an institution with which Kandinsky had been familiar since long before his arrival in Munich—was subsequently reproduced in *Der Blaue Reiter* almanac.[10] Marc described the "jolt" given him by the Schoenberg concert and its inspirational effect upon his artistic thinking but concluded that the real goal would be to bring forth a new art not out of theory but instinctively, in the manner of "the primitive peoples." Schoenberg, he surmised, seemed to be "convinced of the relentless dissolution of European laws of art and harmony, and grasps after the musical means of the Orient, which have (to date) remained primitive."

Here two chords are struck: the notion of primitive art as "shattering," even transformative, because it was somehow "instinctual"; and the equation of this "primitive" with the concept "Oriental." For it is clear that both Kandinsky, the Russian in whose veins flowed Mongolian blood, and Schoenberg, the Jew, were perceived as "Oriental," as we see by the words of critics and friends alike. Alexander Ringer has demonstrated the "Oriental" ramifications of Schoenberg's Judaic grounding and pointed out that in musical criticism since the nineteenth century the epithet *Oriental* often served as a synonym for *Jewish.*[11] Kandinsky, too, whose father had been born in far eastern Asia among the Mongols and Buriats of Kyakhta, was labeled Oriental and thus situated by the critics in that metaphorical Eastern diaspora—equated even, as one Munich critic would have it, with the "*kannibalischstische Naturvölker*" (cannibalistic nature-peoples).[12] As my research demonstrates, Kandinsky's own ethnographic expedition into the far reaches of Vologda Province in 1889 had been motivated at least in part by a desire to trace his own roots among the Finno-Ugric Zyrian (Komi) peoples. It was also an attempt to get in touch with the roots of those ancient members of his father's clan who had emigrated from the Ural mountain area of the Ob River, from the place known as Kondinsk, to far eastern Siberia—first to Yakutia and then to the even more eastern areas of Kyakhta on the Mongolian border, and Nerchinsk, areas inhabited by the Buriat and Tungus peoples. Ethnic mixing was not uncommon in the vast Russian empire, and there is genealogical evidence of a Buriat intermarriage in the Kandinsky family. Many nineteenth-century ethnographers and linguists thought there were ancient links between the Finno-Ugric and Mongolian peoples, a theory that drove expeditions such as those of Andreas Sjögren and Alexander Castrén, whose reports Kandinsky cited in his own ethnographic writings. Kandinsky himself believed in his Oriental origins and often boasted that he had Mongolian blood in his veins; indeed, the faintly Oriental features of Kandinsky's visage were frequently mentioned by his friends and acquaintances.[13]

The fact is that both Kandinsky and Schoenberg were "outsiders" struggling to find their individual voices in a hostile environment. No wonder they were drawn to one another. No wonder they sought to transcend their environments by similar means, relying on that inner springboard of the human spirit that Kandinsky called "inner necessity." And no wonder Kandinsky found Schoenberg's outward-turning *Visions* discomfiting and openly admitted to the composer that he much preferred the landscapes and the *Self-Portrait from the Back* (also known as *Self-Portrait from Behind;* see figures 3 and 4), in which he found "things as they are and living 'as such' innerly," or, as he also phrased it: "pure 'fantasy' in hardest material."[14] He recognized in these paintings a primal force that made "things as they are" *live,* and he equated them with his own in terms of inner power. Indeed, on the very page in the *Blaue Reiter* almanac on which the *Self-Portrait* was reproduced appeared Kandinsky's famous equation: "Realism = Abstraction, Abstraction = Realism. *The greatest difference in the external becomes the greatest likeness in the inner.*"[15] It is a witty visual and verbal pun, for the portrait encountered here—the "greatest difference" from what we expect—does not gaze out at us but rather walks away and, in turning its back to our gaze, jolts us into recognition of that inner "abstract" essence. In fact,

Fig. 3. Schoenberg, *Vision*, as reproduced in *Der Blaue Reiter* (Munich: R. Piper & Co. Verlag, 1912). Oil on canvas, 32 × 20 cm. From *Der Blaue Reiter*, facsimile reprint (Munich: R. Piper & Co. Verlag, 1979). Reproduced courtesy of Lawrence Schoenberg.

ARNOLD SCHÖNBERG

hältnis umgekehrt zu sein scheint, so sind im letzten Grunde (= Ziele) diese zwei Pole einander gleich. Zwischen diesen zwei Antipoden kann das Zeichen des Gleichnisses gestellt werden:

Realistik = Abstraktion,

Abstraktion = Realistik.

Die grösste Verschiedenheit im Aeusseren wird zur grössten Gleichheit im Inneren.

* * *

Einige Beispiele werden uns aus dem Gebiete der Reflexion in das Gebiet des Greif- baren versetzen. Wenn der Leser irgendeinen Buchstaben dieser Zeilen mit ungewohnten Augen anschaut, d. h. nicht als ein gewohntes Zeichen eines Teiles eines Wortes, sondern erst als Ding, so sieht er in diesem Buchstaben ausser der praktisch-zweckmässig vom Menschen geschaffenen abstrakten Form, die eine ständige Bezeichnung eines bestimmten

Fig. 4. Schoenberg, *Self-Portrait from the Back,* as it was illustrated in the almanac *Der Blaue Reiter.* From *Der Blaue Reiter,* facsimile reprint (Munich: R. Piper & Co. Verlag, 1979). Reproduced courtesy of Lawrence Schoenberg.

examples of both types of Schoenberg's paintings were reproduced within Kandinsky's essay "Über die Formfrage" ("On the Question of Form"), along with other examples of "naive" realism such as works by Henri Rousseau, Bavarian *Hinterglasmalereien* and "miracle pictures," children's paintings, and, tellingly enough, one of Matisse's *Music* paintings.[16] Not surprisingly, of course, Kandinsky concluded that there was no question of form; any form might be appropriate so long as it arose out of inner necessity.

No wonder both Kandinsky and Schoenberg were drawn, though at different times, to seek their voices in their own roots. Indeed, Kandinsky could laugh up his sleeve at his uneducated critics, being himself a trained ethnologist well read in the universal lore of folk mythology as well as in such specialized areas as Finno-Ugric and Siberian shamanism. Schoenberg's reference in the second movement of the Second String Quartet to the old Viennese folk tune "Ach du lieber Augustin" would instantly have caught his attention, for he knew that the text was an ethnographic relic that, slight as it was, with its seemingly innocent, fragile, poignant tune, referred to earth-shattering occurrences: the Great Plague and the recurrent "end time" prophecies of apocalyptic tradition. He himself had played on simple Bavarian folk-art tradition to express millennial concerns, as in his *Hinterglasmalereien;* this method at the same time allowed him to re-affirm his own grounding in old Russian mythology and folklore and to explore his fascination with *dvoeverie,* that characteristic synthesis of pagan and Christian belief systems that he had made the core of his own ethnographic studies.[17]

This is perhaps most easily demonstrated in a watercolor study for his 1911 glass painting *All Saints Day II* (see figure 5). In this benignly duplicitous depiction of "saints" we can easily detect at the upper right Saint Elias, or Elijah, and his chariot—a saint who, among the Finno-Ugric peoples, with whose beliefs Kandinsky was familiar, was identified with the pagan god of thunder Perun, or Thor. Pointedly, Elias/Thor drives a Russian troika. At the lower left is Saint Simeon Stylites, a double reference to Simon or Semyon of the Russian folk tale "The Seven Semyons": it was Semyon who forged the iron pillar (a shamanic device) from which to survey the world and foretell the future; and the saint of the same name was noted for his conversions of the pagans. Note that he stands here in close alliance with a horseman hitherto identified only as Saint George but who actually lived a double life as another horseman of Finno-Ugric lore, known as the World-Watching-Man—always depicted, as we shall see, with outstretched arms on horseback. And, lastly, at the lower right, there is the figure of the Zyrian shaman Pam, whose confrontation on the banks of the Vychegda River with Saint Stephen, the bishop of Perm—the cleric responsible for converting the Zyrians—was part of a legend Kandinsky knew from his own visit to the Vychegda River area of Vologda Province, the center of his re-

Fig. 5. Kandinsky, sketch for the glass painting *All Saints Day II* (also known as *Composition with Saints*), 1911. Watercolor, ink, and pencil. Städtische Galerie im Lenbachhaus, Munich. Copyright © 1996 Artists Rights Society (ARS), New York/ADAGP, Paris.

search as a student of ethnography in the summer of 1889. Here Pam, in his distinctive sorcerer's hat, rows off in a boat, pursued by *rusalki*, Zyrian water sprites, one of whom tries to climb into his boat. Sorcerers in pointed caps or in magic flight, often with arms outflung, appear elsewhere in Kandinsky's work, as in more than one vignette in *Klänge* (Resonances), his 1913 book of prose poems and woodcuts (see figure 7).

This expressed interest in folklore can be compared both to Schoenberg's exploration of mythic lore in *Gurrelieder* and to Kandinsky's devotion to the legendary saga of the Finns known as the *Kalevala,* a copy of which had accompanied him on his expedition into the farthest reaches of Vologda Province to study the beliefs of the Zyrian (or Komi) peoples in that fateful summer of 1889, at the height of his ethnographic career. Indeed, it was his devotion to the *Kalevala* that later inspired him to invite the Finnish symbolist painter and illustrator of the *Kalevala,* Axel Gallen-Kallela, to exhibit with his Phalanx society in Munich in 1904.[18] A particularly interesting demonstration of Kandinsky's vast knowledge of northern folklore can be found in the Russian version of his essay on stage composition, published in 1919, where he compared Wagner's use of the leitmotif to the Lapps' distinctive "musical motif," the *vuolle,* that each family was said to possess and by which each was identified.[19]

But there is yet another ramification of the Second Quartet's last movement that we have not explored. It is the fact that the George poem that begins "I feel the air of another planet" was entitled "Entrückung," which has been translated as "Transport" but which also bears the translation "Ecstasy." The ancient and almost universal myth of ecstatic flight was immediate in Kandinsky's imagination, for he was intimately familiar with a wide range of ethnographic literature on Finno-Ugric and Siberian shamanism. That consciously or subconsciously he should have related Schoenberg's music to ecstatic shamanic experience is hardly surprising in view of his ethnographic interest in the phenomenon of shamanism.[20] Evidence for this can be found in an observation Kandinsky made a decade later in a proposal submitted to the Institute of Artistic Culture in Moscow. There, in outlining what he termed the "parallelism" of sound and color, he recalled:

> I once happened to see how Arabs used the continuous parallelism of sound (a monotone drum) and primitive movement (a pronounced, rhythmic kind of dancing) to achieve a state of ecstasy. Even a simple, schematic [arrangement of lines] could never produce such a result. I also happened to observe the audience during one of Schoenberg's quartets, in which the manipulation of the line of the instruments, and, in particular, the incorporation of the voice, produced the impression of the lash of a whip. It is interesting to note that Arnold Schoenberg introduced the flow of parallel lines into some of his compositions with (at least for musicians) virtually the same revolutionary effect.[21]

Earlier in the proposal he urged the investigation of movements employed in ancient cultures for the purpose of "expressing primitive feelings" before they are forgotten, including those used in "rituals" and "religious rites," noting that even some of those gestures that are distinguished by "extreme sketchiness" may possess "superhuman power of expression."

What has not been noted before and seems particularly convincing in this context is that Kandinsky painted what is perhaps his most compelling homage to the shamanic legend of magical flight on 11 January 1911, just nine days after the Schoenberg concert and seven days before his first letter to the composer. In the painting *Lyrical* the shaman, as described in the ethnographic literature, flies above treetops and mountaintops on his journey to other worlds.[22] He has already "freed himself in tones—circling—weaving" ("*Ich löse mich in tönen, kreisend, webend*"). As the canvas itself becomes the singing skin of the monotonal drum, the rider becomes, as the closing line of the poem suggests, "a droning of the sacred voice" ("*Ich bin ein dröhnen nur der heiligen stimme*"). The painting is aptly named to denote the unity of the magical flight and the *Klang* or resonance of the drum.

The folklore of the northern Finno-Ugric, Lapp, and Siberian peoples, including the iconography of the shamanic drum and the legend of magical

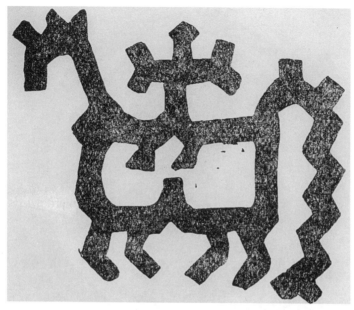

Fig. 6. Design for a sacrificial blanket depicting *Mir Susne Khum* (World-Watching-Man). Mansi (Vogul), 19th century. Watercolor on paper. From S. V. Ivanov, *Materialy po Izobrazitel'nomu Iskusstva Narodov Sibiri XIX–nachala XX v.* (Moscow: Akademi Nauk, 1954).

flight, was to remain a driving force in Kandinsky's work to the end of his life. In these motifs, so often linked to the quest for regeneration, he expressed his own search for roots, as Schoenberg in his later devotion to Judaism would express his search for rootedness and affirmation of his Jewish heritage.

Among the most ubiquitous of these ethnic motifs for Kandinsky was that of Saint George, whose image was synthesized with that of the northern mythic god known as World-Watching-Man. In the ancient folklore of the Voguls and Ostiaks, among others, this god, son of the great sky god Numi Torem, served as an intercessor between the gods and humankind, flying across the sky at night on his magical horse to keep an eye on the world. He was always depicted on horseback, with arms outflung—as in the characteristically stylized Vogul (Mansi) design for a sacrificial blanket (see figure 6). But the shaman preferred for his flight a piebald, or spotted, horse, so Kandinsky's magic horsemen rode piebald horses. This can be seen in the vignette for *Klänge*, and in an early drawing for his first *Composition*, where he had already adapted the arms-outflung figure of World-Watching-Man to the piebald horse (see figures 7 and 8).

Fig. 7. Kandinsky, vignette to the poem "Blätter" in *Klänge* (Munich: R. Piper & Co. Verlag, 1913). Städtische Galerie im Lenbachhaus, Munich. Copyright © 1996 Artists Rights Society (ARS), New York/ADAGP, Paris.

In the transformational language of Kandinsky's Bauhaus period, a time when he stripped his arsenal of forms to the bare bones of geometry—in parallel, one might say, to Schoenberg's development of the twelve-tone method—the multisignificant figure of Saint George/World-Watching-Man/shaman also underwent a transformation. This can be observed in an untitled drawing of 1924 (see figure 9), where the horse is reduced to a thrusting hooked stick representing the leaping animal's back and bent foreleg. The figure on his back has been reduced to the circular drum form, but with the same arms-outflung posture, triangular head, and an eye on his chest to remind us of his identity as World-*Watching*-Man. The serpent conquered by the hero in his Saint George alter ego writhes about the horse's body.

Lest the reader remain skeptical of this apparently drastic transformational language, we can see the same terms employed in major paintings of this era, including *In the Black Square* of 1923 and *Black Accompaniment* of 1924, which represent Saint George on his horse confronting the cosmic

Fig. 8. Kandinsky, drawing for *Composition I*. Pencil on paper, 11.3 × 18 cm. Musée National d'Art Moderne, Centre Georges Pompidou, Fonds Kandinsky, Paris. Copyright © 1996 Artists Rights Society (ARS), New York/ADAGP, Paris.

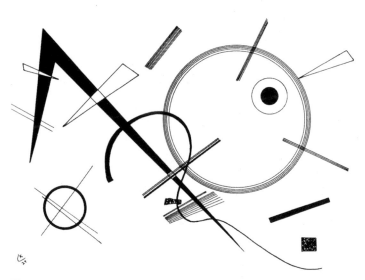

Fig. 9. Kandinsky, untitled drawing, 1924. Ink on paper, 23.5 × 32 cm. From Pierre Volboudt, *Die Zeichnungen Wassily Kandinskys* (Cologne: Verlag M. DuMont Schauberg, 1974), no. 49. Copyright © 1996 Artists Rights Society (ARS), New York/ADAGP, Paris.

dragon.[23] In *Black Accompaniment* there is nearly the same disposition of forms as in the earlier painting, but with a self-parodying humor: the horse reduced to a rearing lancelike back and bent foreleg (similar to that in the untitled drawing, which may, in fact, have been a study); the chin-strapped saint looking rather surprised, as the goggle-eyed dragon at the lower left lolls on its back below the horse's feet just as it had done in the version of saint and dragon more than a decade earlier, the 1911 *St. George III*. This hieroglyphic shorthand had in fact been suggested to Kandinsky in large part by the schematic representations of gods and animals on Lapp and Siberian shaman drums.

This brief demonstration shows not only the development of a brilliant new visual vocabulary but also the persistence of a richly symbolic imagery representing the artist's continuing quest for and affirmation of the roots of his personal heritage. Also evident is the continuity of an idealistic, Utopian vision that had from the beginning promised him the salvation of a decadent and evil world through art.

By 1923 Kandinsky had lived through the horrors of World War I, the Russian Revolution, and the ensuing plague of famine and disease; he had survived alienation, two emigrations, and a great personal loss in the death of his son Volodia, born in the midst of world catastrophe and dead at the age of three. Now back in Germany and firmly ensconced at the Bauhaus, once again surrounded by admiring students and colleagues, he sought to reestablish the vanguard of the old days by contacting his old friend Arnold Schoenberg. Their first exchange in July 1922 was as warm and cordial as ever, and both expressed the wish to meet again.

But when Kandinsky a year later invited Schoenberg to join him in Weimar, the latter's attitude had changed, and a bitterly poignant exchange ensued. Given our knowledge of how everyday life affected Kandinsky's painting and the extent to which his work expressed symbolic meaning, it will be informative to examine the paintings that bracket the 1923 exchange between Kandinsky and Schoenberg.

Just a few weeks before writing to Schoenberg with his proposal that the composer consider taking on the directorship of the Weimar Musikhochschule, Kandinsky had finished a new Saint George painting called *Through-Going Line*, of March 1923, anticipating the Russian celebration of Saint George's Day on April 24.[24] It is a confident, life-affirming picture in which the schematized but clearly recognizable figure of Saint George, riding a stick horse, unites the heavenly regions of the left-hand side of the canvas, in true shamanic style, with the worldly side on the right. According to Kandinsky's aesthetic vocabulary, the direction of his leap, from left to right, is "toward home." The symbolic serpent writhes well below, effectively trampled by the horse's legs.[25]

On 15 April 1923, a few weeks after completing this painting, Kandinsky wrote to Schoenberg with his proposal regarding the Weimar Musik-hochschule.[26] Thereafter followed, in quick succession, Schoenberg's pointed letter, dated 19 April, accusing Kandinsky of anti-Semitism and re-jecting the invitation on the grounds that, as a Jew, he understood (on the basis of rumors apparently spread by Alma Mahler) that he would be out of place at the Bauhaus; Kandinsky's stricken and poignant reply of 24 April; and finally, on 4 May, Schoenberg's long and tortured analy-sis of his condition as a Jew and human being, condemned by a society determined to recognize either the Jew or the human being but not both as once.

Kandinsky's house catalog lists the painting *Schwarz und Violett* as having been painted in April 1923. Thus it is safe to postulate that this painting was created between the time the artist received the first and second Schoen-berg letters (in his response of 24 April, the Russian Saint George's Day, Kandinsky mentions that he had received Schoenberg's first response the previous day). *Schwarz und Violett* presents on the left the head of Saint George as a black mask, with its characteristic curved and "feathered" hel-met, a motif Kandinsky used frequently. However, here one white eye is pierced by a triangular "arrow," while another triangular form, similar to the sails of the "boats" at right, pierces the cheek of the mask, lending the eerie face a tearful aspect. The other eye, half closed, is set askew. To the right—the "earthly" side of the painting, according to Kandinsky's own theories—two boatlike images seem storm-tossed on a tilting, purple plane. In *Über das Geistige in der Kunst* Kandinsky had described the color purple (*Violett*) as "a cooled-off red in the physical and the psychic sense. It has thus something sickly, quenched (like coal slag!), something sad about it. . . . The Chinese use it specifically as the color of mourning."[27] Here, then, the boatlike forms representing the two artists are tossed on a sad and slag-col-ored sea of rumor, misunderstanding, and deceit. The arrow piercing the eye is a reference to the Lapp myth, which Kandinsky knew well, of the *Ganfliege,* or arrowlike missile, sent magically by one shaman to harm an-other.[28]

When Schoenberg hurled his personal frustration and anger at his old friend Kandinsky, it is certain that he could not have guessed the artist's own tortured experiences of war and revolution, famine and disease; nor could he have known of the Kandinskys' lost child, for they kept that a secret all their lives. Schoenberg, desperately wounded, had written from the heart. Difficult as it may have been for him, Kandinsky, though stricken himself, had the wisdom to remain silent. He was forced to recognize that the halcyon Munich days were lost forever; the world was blacker than he had ever wanted to know. For succor he turned once again to the beloved image so intrinsic to his heritage and so powerful in its promise of regeneration and hope, to his own leitmotif, Saint George. The painting that immediately followed the exchange with Schoenberg was *In the Black Square,* of June 1923.

According to Kandinsky's theory, black was that "nothing without possibility," that "nothing after the quenching of the sun, an eternal silence without future and hope."[29] But Kandinsky did leave a slight opening for hope in pronouncing black also the color against which all others resonate most strongly. His resonant, regenerational Saint George in his watchful and healing roles as World-Watching-Man and shaman soars on a white trapezoidal plane that is bound to rise beyond the black silence. And indeed, as we know, a reconciliation of sorts did eventually take place between Kandinsky and Schoenberg in the summer of 1927.

Kandinsky too was soon to suffer the fate of artists driven from Germany by the Nazis. His paintings were stripped from the museums and shown in Hitler's exhibition *Decadent Art,* and he was forced into yet another exile, to end his life in Paris.[30] Perhaps it was merciful that he did not live to know that he had also been expunged from the memory of his own people and was not to be recognized by them again until 1989, one hundred twenty-three years after his birth.[31]

Both Schoenberg and Kandinsky have been seen as pioneers of the modern, inventors of new languages—in the one case of music's twelve-tone system, in the other of "abstraction" in art. Yet in both cases it has been difficult to interpret their later works within the context of twentieth-century critical insistence on "pure" formalism. Critics failed utterly either to see or to comprehend the shamanic imagery and symbolism of Kandinsky's later works such as *Open Green,* also of 1923, with its soaring Saint George shaman, or the great shaman-drum series that includes *Oval no. 2* of 1925, which is based directly on the paradigm of the Lapp shaman drum. Nor have they noticed that the deceptively geometric *Peevish,* of 1930, actually holds a richly ethnographic subtext dealing directly with shamanism.[32]

It remains to analyze one last interaction between Kandinsky and Schoenberg, which is documented by the last letter Kandinsky addressed to the composer, a response, dated 1 July 1936, thanking Schoenberg for a note that had been delivered by a mutual acquaintance, Louis Danz.[33] Kandinsky's next painting once again seems to carry a subtextual reference to his old friend. In this painting, *Triangles,* there are two personages constructed of triangles, facing each other. According to the iconographic clues I have developed, both the circle signifying the shamanic drum and the waving ribbonlike form at the far left, which is a reference to the shaman in magical flight, point to an identification of this figure as the artist himself, who appears to offer a palette of colored objects to his visitor.

Perhaps what is suggested here is an exchange of gifts. A closer look at the figure at the right reveals that it is made up of two triangles superimposed, as in the star of David. In this case the triangles are neither equilateral nor symmetrical, but slightly askew; nevertheless, I think there can be no mistaking the implication that the artist's visitor is his Jewish friend Schoenberg, who carries what might be described as a shaman's staff and whose internal world is equally colorful. Indeed, the two "shamans" appear to stand on equal footing. Poignantly, they are separated by a thin (perhaps now insignificant?) snakelike form evoking the dragons of evil in the world.[34]

A drawing that may date from the same period, one that has a motif of a shaman and ladder, may carry a hooded reference to Schoenberg's *Jakobsleiter,* which the composer had mentioned years earlier, in a letter to Kandinsky of 20 July 1922. Particularly compelling is a "lyrelike" form dangling from the figure of the shaman.[35]

The best the critics could do, even until very recently, with such late works of the Paris period as *Around the Circle* and *The Green Bond* was to use the terms *Oriental, Byzantine,* and *Scythian.* This is to ignore the fierce, almost fanatical, resolve of the artist to embrace the heritage of Siberian shamanism with near-textbook imagery based on ethnographic sources. In his preparatory drawing for the right side of the painting *The Green Bond* there is the figure of the artist as shaman, the agent of healing and intercessor between mankind and the heavens, climbing the sacred tree that grows from the summit of the cosmic mountain toward the heavens, symbolized by a cloud. He wears a feathered headdress characteristic of the Siberian shaman but also of that old *Blue Rider* Saint George of yore, and is accompanied by his magic drum and ladle-shaped beater, which float just to the left of his head and shoulder. He wears his ribbed breastplate—a symbol of his immortality—on his back. He looks back over his shoulder to observe a pointed-head idol, characteristic of the Ostiaks, a northern Russian Finno-Ugric tribe, floating in its shroud and bound with thread, in accord with the beliefs of the Zyrian peoples Kandinsky had studied, who believed that the dead shaman had to be tied up to prevent his soul form known as the *Ort* from wandering.[36]

Thus did the artist, in the last year of his life, confirm in one of his most "Oriental" paintings the multicultural inheritance of his personal genealogy. *The Green Bond* represents a grand synthesis of Russian Orthodox, Finno-Ugric, and far eastern Asiatic shamanic belief systems. And we have recently come to appreciate the full extent of Schoenberg's Judaic grounding and his final embrace of his own Oriental heritage, expressed especially in the the last years of his life in works like *Kol Nidre* and *A Survivor from Warsaw.*

Only now that we can begin to understand the strength and creative energy that each of them, both artist and composer, was able to distill from his status as outsider and from his individual Oriental heritage can we perhaps consider the breach between them healed at last.

NOTES

1. Marc to August Macke, 14 January 1911, *August Macke Franz Marc Briefwechsel*, ed. Ernst Brücher and Karl Gutbred (Cologne: Verlag M. DuMont Schauberg, 1964), 39–42, esp. 41. Unless otherwise noted, all translations are by the author.

2. The printed program makes clear that the concert took place on 2 January (not 1 January, as has previously been reported); see also Franz Marc's letter to his wife, quoted in the exhibition catalog *Franz Marc 1880–1916* (Munich: Städtische Galerie im Lenbachhaus, 1980), 29–30.

3. Kandinsky, *Über das Geistige in der Kunst* (1912; reprint, Bern-Bumplitz: Benteli, 1965), 98; translations by the author.

4. It is interesting that the most "realistic" of the sketches for *Impression III (Concert)* includes not only the accompanying musicians but also the figure of the singer who participated in the third and fourth movements of the Second String Quartet. She stands to the right of the piano. Kandinsky devoted the major portion of his treatise *Über das Geistige in der Kunst* to a discussion of color, its psychology and symbolism. Although the treatise was not to become available to the public until December 1911 (with a postpublication date of 1912), the manuscript had been essentially completed by 1910. The coincidence of this particular painting with the Schoenberg concert has been noted previously by Jelena Hahl-Koch; see *Schoenberg/Kandinsky Letters*, 207.

5. The letter was subsequently published by the Neue Künstler-Vereinigung as an offprint and of course immediately came to the attention of Kandinsky and his friends; see *Franz Marc Schriften*, ed. Klaus Lankheit (Cologne: DuMont Buchverlag, 1978), 127. The painting was destroyed in World War II, but an oil sketch remains (collection of the Solomon R. Guggenheim Museum), which is reproduced in Hans K. Roethel and Jean K. Benjamin, *Kandinsky Catalogue Raisonné of the Oil-Paintings* (Ithaca, N.Y.: Cornell University Press, 1982), 305.

6. Even before the concert Marc had linked the theoretical Kandinsky and the theoretical Schoenberg. After spending New Year's Eve in the company of Neue Künstler-Vereinigung artists, including Kandinsky, Münter, and Jawlensky, he had written to his wife the following day:

> Tomorrow awaits (perhaps) an event: I am going to the concert of Arnold Schoenberg; you know, that most modern Viennese composer, whose artistic program . . . could have been printed in the catalog of the New Society. The strangest thing about him seems to be the complete abandonment of tonality—he no longer makes a horizontal cut through the tone rows, rather vertical cuts, which, in my opinion, must have a relationship to the ideas of Kandinsky.
>
> *Franz Marc 1880–1916*, 29.

7. *Romantic Landscape* also evokes motifs from two other George poems, "I must saddle ashen horses" and the "great black somber flower" of *Algabal.* I have discussed in detail the stylistic relationship between George's poetry and Kandinsky's early works in my *Kandinsky in Munich—The Formative Jugendstil Years* (Princeton, N.J.: Princeton University Press, 1979), especially in chapter 8, pages 81–90. It is interesting in this context to recall that during a 1980 visit by the author to Judith Köllhofer-Wolfskehl, the daughter of George's and Kandinsky's Munich friend, the poet Karl Wolfskehl, the clear relationship between George's poems and Kandinsky's graphics received a startling confirmation. Then in her eighties, she paused at the illustration in my book of Kandinsky's woodcut *The Birds,* originally prepared for the portfolio *Xylographies* in 1907, and began spontaneously to recite:

> Schwalben seh ich wieder fliegen
> schnee- und silberweisse schar
> wie sie sich im winde wiegen
> in dem winde kalt und klar
> . . . .

This was the very poem to which I had compared the same Kandinsky print in the text. Although its birds are clearly not swallows, the image as a whole brilliantly expresses the contrast between the black, ravenous jungle of desire and the clear, cold light of equilibrium sought by the poem's exotic protagonist. In fact, the second verse of the poem actually speaks of the "ravens" and "*Papageien*" in the dark wood, contrasting them to the swallows of the first and last verses. Kandinsky's print contrasts the dark wood, with its ravens and silent sentinel, against the winter-barren, wind-blown tree and wind-blown maiden at the right, and a transparent bird of more exotic origin than the swallow.

For discussions of the relationship between *Jugendstil,* George's poetry, and Schoenberg's music, see also Reinhold Brinkmann, "Schönberg und George: Interpretation eines Liedes," *Archiv für Musikwissenschaft* 26 (1969), 1–28; and Klaus Kropfinger, "The Shape of Line," *Miscellanea Musicologica,* Adelaide Studies in Musicology, vol. 13 (1984), 131–167.

8. Schoenberg to Kandinsky, 14 December 1911, *Schoenberg/Kandinsky Letters,* 38–40, esp. 38. Yet despite the pleasure he obviously took in it, Schoenberg could not resist exercising his critical faculty as well: his only objection, he said, was to the large scale of the work (it is nearly a meter high and more than a meter wide—94.3 by 129 cm, to be exact). But Schoenberg gave the proportions in the form of a mathematical equation using not centimeters of canvas but colors—the white proportionately the greatest—that, he complained, seemed to escape from his vision. He had discovered that only by standing farther away from the picture did these proportions diminish, and he could then grasp the whole. Not surprisingly, Kandinsky shot back: "Are you against doubling the strength of the orchestra?" He denounced mathematical equations as just that—"artistically speaking, one minus one may equal two"—and defended his proportions by claiming them as just another artistic means to be manipulated purposefully in order, as he said, to prevent a fleeting view of his pictures, and to transform the ordinary object into "quite

another being." Kandinsky to Schoenberg, 13 January 1912, *Schoenberg/Kandinsky Letters*, 41–43, esp. 42 and 43.

9. *Lyrical* and two versions of *All Saints Day* are reproduced in Peg Weiss, *Kandinsky and Old Russia: The Artist as Ethnographer and Shaman* (New Haven, Conn.: Yale University Press, 1995), 88 and 58, 59.

10. As I first demonstrated in "Kandinsky in Munich: Encounters and Transformations," in the exhibition catalog *Kandinsky in Munich 1896–1914* (New York: Solomon R. Guggenheim Foundation, 1981), 28–82, *Der Blaue Reiter* almanac was conceived by its editors, Kandinsky and Marc, as a therapeutic metaphor for cultural salvation. Most of the ethnographic artifacts, including folk-art objects, reproduced in the almanac had originally performed a ritual function as symbols of regeneration and resurrection. Indeed, one of the essays on music was even written by a physician (Kul'bin). I have made a thorough study of the ethnographic ramifications of Kandinsky's work in *Kandinsky and Old Russia* (1995); see also Peg Weiss, "Kandinsky and 'Old Russia'—An Ethnographic Exploration," in *The Documented Image Visions in Art History*, ed. Gabriel Weisberg and Laurinda Dixon, with Antje B. Lemke (Syracuse, N.Y.: Syracuse University Press, 1987), 187–222. A more detailed analysis of Kandinsky's relationship with Munich's Staatliches Museum für Völkerkunde is to be found in Peg Weiss, "Kandinsky: The Artist as Ethnographer," *Münchner Beiträge zur Völkerkunde* 3 (1990), 285–329.

11. Alexander L. Ringer, *Arnold Schoenberg: The Composer as Jew* (Oxford: Clarendon Press, 1990), esp. 6–9 and passim.

12. M. K. Rohe, "Zweite Ausstellung der neuen Künstlervereinigung München. . . . ," *Münchner Neueste Nachrichten* 63/424 (10 September 1910), as quoted in *Franz Marc Schriften*, 216–218. Another Munich critic, Georg Wolf, not only emphasized the Oriental elements in the exhibition but castigated the artists as "*Morphium- oder Haschischtrunkene*" (morphine or hashish drunks) in *Die Kunst für Alle* (1 November 1910); cited in Weiss, *Kandinsky in Munich* (1979), 187 n. 143.

13. For more on Kandinsky's genealogical origins, see Weiss, *Kandinsky and Old Russia* (1995), 1–10, 213–215; and Weiss, "Kandinsky and 'Old Russia' " (1987). See also Vladimir V. Baraev, *Drevo Dekabristy i semeistvo Kandinskikh* (Moscow: Izdatel'stvo Politicheskoi Literatury, 1991).

Although the serious question as to whether or not Kandinsky held anti-Semitic views has not yet been confronted in the scholarship, it should be noted that Kandinsky's Weltanschauung was clearly the result of a liberal upbringing and education. He vigorously decried the pogroms that followed the 1905 revolution, which he happened to experience at first hand in Odessa. He described those excesses to Gabriele Münter in anguished words, adding that this was the reason he never wished to be called an "Odessan." Kandinsky to Münter, 3 November 1905, Gabriele Münter- und Johannes Eichner-Stiftung, Städtische Galerie, Munich.

14. Kandinsky to Schoenberg, 16 November 1911, *Schoenberg/Kandinsky Letters*, 35–36, esp. 36 (author's translation).

15. *Der Blaue Reiter*, ed. Vasili Kandinsky and Franz Marc (Munich: R. Piper & Co. Verlag, 1912), 85. See also *Der Blaue Reiter*, ed. Klaus Lankheit (new documentary ed., Munich: R. Piper & Co. Verlag, 1965), 156, 158; and *The Blaue Reiter Almanac* (New York: Viking Press, 1974), 164, 166.

16. Regarding the purposive arrangement of the illustrations in the text of the *Blaue Reiter* almanac, see Weiss, "Kandinsky in Munich" (1981), 28–82. See also— with respect to the text and illustrations for Kandinsky's stage composition, *Der gelbe Klang*, which were included in the almanac—Susan Stein, "The Ultimate Synthesis: An Interpretation of the Meaning and Significance of Wassily Kandinsky's *The Yellow Sound*" (master's thesis, SUNY/Binghamton, 1980).

17. See Weiss, "Kandinsky and 'Old Russia' " (1987); and Weiss, *Kandinsky and Old Russia* (1995), 56–63, 99, 143, and passim. Both Kandinsky and Schoenberg were, of course, well aware of the long nineteenth-century tradition of musical exploration of folk music, which had its parallel in the imitation of folkish themes and imagery in the arts and architecture. Kandinsky had frequently exploited folkloristic motifs in his early paintings and woodcuts and, indeed, would continue to do so throughout his life; as late as 1919 he also exploited the "folkish" arts of furniture decoration and glass painting, for instance, in a series of watercolors he called *Bagatelles*. Schoenberg for his part had worked with folk material in *Gurrelieder* and in a number of songs and the early opera libretto called *Aberglaube*. Both would break away from the more or less imitative tradition to conceive their work directly out of personal ethnic traditions. In his 1947 essay "Folkloristic Symphonies" (*Style and Idea*, 161–166, esp. 166, 196–203), Schoenberg pointed to the emptiness of that older tradition that could not stand before "real" folk music produced, as is all real music, "spontaneously, as an inspired improvisation."

18. See Weiss, *Kandinsky and Old Russia* (1995), 45–46; Weiss, *Kandinsky in Munich* (1979), 65–67; and Weiss "Kandinsky in Munich" (1981), 47–48.

19. See Kandinsky, "O stsenicheskoi kompozitsii," *Izobrazitel'noe iskusstvo* 1 (1919), 44. Serge Eisenstein cited this passage from Kandinsky in his notes on Wagner's use of the leitmotif for his unpublished book *Grundproblem*, which was to deal with the relationships between primitive symbol (as described in the ethnographic literature) and artistic symbol; I am grateful to the Soviet scholar Vjacheslav V. Ivanov for bringing this to my attention (see his excellent study "Eisenstein und die Semiotik der Kunst," pt. 2, in *Einführung in allgemeine Probleme des Semiotik*, ed. Wolfgang Eismann [Tübingen: Gunter Narr Verlag, 1985], 205–206). In this context it is interesting that in the 1940s the Lapp scholar Björn Collinder actually referred to the *vuolle* as a leitmotif; see Collinder, *The Lapps* (Princeton, N.J.: Princeton University Press, 1949), 189–90. See also Weiss, *Kandinsky and Old Russia* (1995), 130.

The concept of an individual identifying song that might even figure in the exchange of souls was prevalent among several cultures and was well known among ethnographers at the turn of the century. Indeed, the frequently cited ability of the shaman (especially among the Finno-Ugric peoples) to return the recovered "soul" of a patient through his ear provided further demonstration of the supreme importance of the faculty of hearing and the restorative power of sound. It is likely that Kandinsky had gotten his information from his good friend the noted ethnographer Nikolai Kharuzin, who had published extensively on the Russian Lapps and on Lapp shamanism. Kandinsky was also well informed about the folk theater of the Voguls, a northern tribe whose elaborate improvisatory "bear festival" dramas may have inspired some of his own stage compositions.

20. I discussed Kandinsky's knowledge of the musical aspects of the shamanic experience in a lecture titled "Kandinsky's Ethnographic 'Klänge,' " delivered at the Arnold Schoenberg Institute, Los Angeles, in March 1990.

21. Kandinsky, "Institut Khudozhestvennoi Kul'tury v Moskve" [1923], *Sovetskoe iskusstvo* 15 (1933), 126–143; my thanks to Lilia Grubisic of the Getty Center for the History of Art and the Humanities for her assistance in the translation of this passage (the published translation in Kenneth C. Lindsay and Peter Vergo, *Kandinsky Complete Writings on Art* [Boston: G. K. Hall, 1982], 455–472, refers [p. 467] to "Greek" rites, but it is clear that Kandinsky was alluding to pagan rituals generally).

In another proposal written in June 1921 for the Physicopsychological Department of the Russian Academy of Artistic Sciences, Kandinsky also emphasized the pressing need for "research into primitive art and into all the aesthetic concepts that give primitive art its style," including in his list the art of "primitive peoples" as well as "primitivism in modern art." Kandinsky's proposal was published in *Iskusstvo: Zhurnal Rossiiskoi Akademii khudozhestvennykh nauk* 1 (summer 1923), 415–416; translated in John Bowlt, *Russian Art of the Avant-Garde* (New York: Viking, 1976), 196–198.

22. *Lyrical* is reproduced in Weiss, *Kandinsky and Old Russia* (1995), 88.

23. See Edward Kimball and Peg Weiss, "A Pictorial Analysis of *In the Black Square*," *Art Journal* 43/1 (spring 1983), 37–40; see also Peg Weiss, "Kandinsky and the Symbolist Heritage," *Art Journal* 45/1 (summer 1985), 137–145. Both paintings are illustrated and discussed in Weiss, *Kandinsky and Old Russia* (1995), 141, 149, 146–150.

24. For more information on the importance of Saint George's Day both in Russia and in Kandinsky's personal self-myth, see Weiss, "Kandinsky and 'Old Russia' " (1987); and Weiss, *Kandinsky and Old Russia* (1995), xv, 97, 145, 148, 178, 249 n. 10, and passim.

25. For a reproduction of *Through-Going Line*, see Roethel and Benjamin, *Kandinsky Catalogue Raisonné*, 648.

26. For a discussion of Schoenberg and the directorship of the Weimar Musikhochschule, see Hans Heinz Stuckenschmidt, "Musik am Bauhaus," in *Vom Klang der Farben: Die Musik in der Kunst des 20. Jahrhunderts*, ed. Karin von Maur (Munich: Prestel, 1985), 408–413, esp. 409.

27. Kandinsky, *Über das Geistige in der Kunst*, 102–103.

28. For more information on the helmeted head of the Saint George motif and the Lapp shamanic myth of the *Ganfliege*, see Weiss, *Kandinsky and Old Russia* (1995), 183. For a reproduction of *Schwarz und Violett*, see Roethel and Benjamin, *Kandinsky Catalogue Raisonné*, 650.

29. Kandinsky, *Über das Geistige in der Kunst*, 98.

30. Kandinsky and Schoenberg passed each other in transit during this period, Schoenberg leaving Europe via Paris at the end of October 1933. Although Kandinsky had been in Paris in October, he had returned to Berlin at the end of that month in order to pack for his final move to Paris on 21 December.

31. See the catalog *Wassily Kandinsky: Die erste sowjetische Retrospektive* (Frankfurt am Main: Schirn Kunsthalle, 1989); also published in Russian.

32. See Weiss, *Kandinsky and Old Russia* (1995), 147. On the shaman-drum series, see Weiss, *Kandinsky and Old Russia* (1995), 153–167; on *Peevish*, 168–170.

33. Kandinsky to Schoenberg, *Schoenberg/Kandinsky Letters*, 83–85. Danz, who would later write enthusiastically on Schoenberg (see Louis Danz, "Schoenberg the Inevitable," in *Arnold Schoenberg*, ed. Merle Armitage [New York, 1937]), was also an admirer of Kandinsky, probably introduced to his work through their mutual friend Galka Scheyer, who was Kandinsky's dealer on the West Coast. At the time of this visit, Danz also delivered to Kandinsky a copy of his book *Zarathustra Jr. Speaks of Art* (New York: Brentano's, 1934), with a foreword by Merle Armitage, to which Kandinsky made reference in a letter to Galka Scheyer of 6 August 1936. Scheyer also knew Merle Armitage, with whom she was in touch by 1933. Of course, she also knew Schoenberg, who tried to interest her from time to time in selling his paintings.

34. For a reproduction of *Triangles*, see Roethel and Benjamin, *Kandinsky Catalogue Raisonné*, 962.

35. Evidence for the possible date lies in the fact that the verso of this sheet of drawings carries a sketch of the layout of the artist's exhibition at Jeanne Bucher's gallery in Paris in December 1936, and thus could have been conceived sometime prior to that exhibition. The drawing is reproduced in the catalog *Kandinsky: Oeuvres de Vassily Kandinsky 1866–1944*, ed. C. Derouet and J. Boissel (Paris: Collections du Musée National d'Art Moderne, 1985), no. 615 (lower left), 387. In Weiss, *Kandinsky and Old Russia* (1995), 183, no. 171, this figure is identified as a characteristic conflation of the Saint George/shaman/piebald horse images employed by Kandinsky in many of his later works; the shamanic ladder also appears often in Kandinsky's work.

36. Kandinsky had depicted Saint George in feathered headdress on the cover of *Der Blaue Reiter*. The ethnographic imagery and symbolism of these paintings has been explicated by this author in a series of public lectures as well as in *Kandinsky and Old Russia* (1995), 193–195, 200–204. *The Green Bond* and its preparatory drawings have also been illustrated and analyzed in Weiss, "Kandinsky and 'Old Russia' " (1987). I analyzed the shamanic dimensions of *Around the Circle* in the lecture "Kandinsky's Shamanic Emigrations," delivered at the 28th International Congress of the History of Art in Berlin, July 1992, and in "Interpreting Kandinsky's Iconography: Sources in Ethnography and Shamanism," in *Papers in Art History from the Pennsylvania State University*, vol. 9, ed. Susan C. Scott (University Park, Pa.: Pennsylvania State University, 1995). For a reproduction and discussion of *Around the Circle*, see Weiss, *Kandinsky and Old Russia* (1995), 194, 193–195.

FOUR

The Émigré Experience

Schoenberg in America

Alan Lessem

In 1935, some two years after arriving in the United States as a refugee from Hitler's Germany, Arnold Schoenberg delivered a short lecture to which, with characteristic irony, he gave the title "Driven into Paradise."[1] He told his listeners that he was not prepared to talk about the horrors he had left behind, since he had come here to forget them. Unlike the biblical snake, driven from paradise to crawl on its belly and eat dust, he announced, he had been driven *into* paradise: "I have come to a country where I am allowed to go on my feet, where my head can be erect, where kindness and cheerfulness dominate and where to live is a joy, where to be an expatriate of another country is the grace of God." Despite some initial setbacks—his less than satisfactory teaching position at the Malkin Conservatory, the bitter East Coast winters—he held out the highest hopes in this first period for a fresh start in the New World, as indeed did many of his fellow émigrés. Such expectations for his personal future were linked to a positive assessment of America's musical prospects; there is here, he affirmed, "an extraordinarily large amount of talent, inventive ability, and originality, which in my opinion justify the highest hopes."[2] The evidence around him, especially in regard to the spread of musical education and the proliferation of musical performances, led him so far as to believe that "hegemony" in music (as he called it) would shift westward, from Europe to America—a development that at the time he seemed to welcome.[3] Naturally, his influence and teaching would contribute significantly to that shift!

The belief that European culture could be rescued as cargo from a sinking political ship and transplanted to terra firma in America was, as one might expect, widespread among those who were now bringing it with them, but there were Americans of the same mind too. Roger Sessions, most notably, spoke of Europe's loss as America's gain, and called for a "genuine collaboration . . . in building gradually a real and profound musical tradition on our side."[4] Yet he also had his doubts: American culture was still far from having reached maturity, as could be seen most obviously in the absence of any integration of musical life with institutional functions;[5] similarly Mark Brunswick, though commending the universities for their leadership role in offering a haven to the émigrés, believed that America as a whole was not yet ripe enough to take advantage of what European musical culture was now bringing to its doorstep.[6] Brunswick spoke quite bluntly about the "commercial and artistic gangsterism which seems to pervade the radio and concert world,"[7] a complaint the émigrés soon began to voice themselves. Schoenberg, for one, was to make no bones about an all too typically American laissez-faire and the lack of principled leadership in the sphere of the arts. At the same time he proudly underlined his own resistance to such conditions: He himself "made no concessions to the market."[8]

Those émigrés who took a more realistic view of opportunities available to them—most obviously the Korngolds, Steiners, and Rozsas in Hollywood—as well as those who more reluctantly permitted the exploitation of their talents to tide them over difficult circumstances, can well be said to have made a more palpable contribution to American culture, or at least that part of it that is represented by the development of distinctive popular idioms. It was they who in effect created the music of the Hollywood motion picture. Yet by the same token it would be wrong to assume that those who refused the temptations of Mammon, and also insisted that transplantation in no way compromised their integrity as composers, were unaffected by an environment in which considerations of worldly and material success overruled all others. For one thing it is evident that a number of the émigrés, discouraged by the unresponsiveness of publishers, performers, and audiences alike—what Krenek called the *Echolosigkeit* of the American musical milieu—indeed composed significantly less than before and went through some quite lengthy periods of silence, especially during the war years. More significant than this quantitative falloff was the tendency of their work to become more sharply divided between public and private, practical and ideal, prosaic and poetic. Hanns Eisler wrote film music for money but for himself composed songs the texts of which express nothing but contempt for the values of Hollywood society. Schoenberg, too, presented a public face, identifying in his correspondence with conductors and performers what could be considered to be his "popular" works (among them *Verklärte Nacht, Pelleas und Melisande,* the First Chamber Symphony, and his various orchestral arrangements), and urging that at least they be heard so as to open the door to his overall oeuvre. In all, as Krenek wryly remarked,

America had a sobering effect on the Europeans: it sharpened their sense of reality, but at the cost of what Robert Musil had called the "sense of possibility."[9] In 1941 Schoenberg told Erwin Stein that his affairs as a composer were in a distressing state. He was receiving no income from Europe, and American publishers were interested only in a quick return on their investments. Performers, and in particular conductors (most of whom, of course, were émigrés themselves), were also part of what he called the "commercial racket." Taking stock a few years later, in 1944, Schoenberg lamented that Wallenstein in Los Angeles had performed nothing of his in six years, that Klemperer had ventured only some of his arrangements, and that Koussevitsky (ostensibly a champion of the moderns) had played only his accessible Variations, op. 43, and badly at that. After the war he became increasingly distrustful of the musical establishment, convinced by now of a conspiracy all around to suppress his music. He spoke of the "malice" directed against him by his "enemies," the New York critics, of decrees issued by public institutions against difficult music such as his own, of professional jealousies that isolated him even within the university. Above all, he saw himself as the victim of a cultural nationalism now given a renewed impetus by the Allied victory and the American presence in Europe. Although Schoenberg had from the beginning repeatedly declared his support for the cause of American music, he was inclined to see this latest development less as a legitimate nationalist aspiration than as yet another manifestation of political and economic opportunism: as he put it, less "an emotional necessity of the soul" than "an attempt to conquer a market."[10] Inevitably it was himself that he saw as having been dealt a particularly hard and unjust blow.

> Just like the racket of concert agents, there is now a racket in the making which intends to suppress gradually all European composers. Though I was probably the first European composer to speak and write publicly in favor of American composers, establishing their rightful claim to a place in American concert programs, the thanks for my attitude seems to be that I have been elected to be the first victim of the nationalistic movement, with others to follow.[11]

The origin of the postwar developments referred to by Schoenberg was the increasing prominence already given to American music during the war period itself, when Americans tended to turn inward and cultivate their own resources in answer to what Elliot Carter called the "brutalizing forces released by Europe's conflict."[12] Though most Americans naturally welcomed this external stimulus to the homegrown product, there were also those like Sessions who sympathized with the plight of the Europeans now suffering, as a result, comparative neglect. Sessions spoke of the "aggressive self-assertion" of Americans, which "at least for a time poisoned the musical atmosphere and made it one of exclusiveness."[13] Although such remarks may have been somewhat exaggerated, there was no question of the by then very considerable infiltration of American music and musical life by the new wave of immigrants, and the growing measure of suspiciousness and mistrust engendered by such a development. This is reflected, for instance, in public debates such as that published in the pages of the *Musical Courier* through several of its 1940–1941 issues. American participants in that debate argued that the foreign influx would "leaven" the substance of a national music; more generally, it was alleged that having to accommodate the émigrés would result in a neglect of obligations to home-trained musicians. One contributor went so far as to propose that we take into the country only a handful of the very best among the Europeans—that, after all, we have enough nonentities ourselves.

The influence of German and Austrian émigrés came to be looked upon with especial ambivalence: Did not, surely, the insidious traits of Teutonism lie at the very heart of the atonal idiom, more particularly of twelve-tone music? Regrettably enough, xenophobia clouded the judgment of many, including some of the country's most eminent composers and critics.

With the end of the war American cultural nationalism appeared to Schoenberg to have become more arrogantly self-assertive than ever. By way of retaliation he accused Americans of adopting an imperialist policy of cultural domination rivaling its Stalinist counterpart in Soviet Russia in its determination to colonize the entire civilized world. Ironically enough, the hopes he had earlier expressed for American hegemony in music had become, for him, a grim reality. Over the next few years Schoenberg attacked not only institutions and organizations but also individuals. American critics and conductors, and even composers, were forced to defend themselves against his allegations. A characteristic instance was the exchange with Aaron Copland, one that began in the press and then moved into a private correspondence that remains as yet unpublished. Virgil Thomson's column in the *New York Herald Tribune* of 11 September 1949 carried Schoenberg's "birthday blast" (as Thomson put it) against opponents of his music. Copland is not only counted among them but seen as the instigator of a policy of discrimination; as such he must be coupled with Stalin. In his reply to Thomson, published in the same newspaper two weeks later, Copland defends himself as in fact a Schoenberg supporter who helped disseminate some of Schoenberg's music, and he suggests that Schoenberg's linking him with the infamous Russian dictator may have had something to do with his photographed appearance with Shostakovich during the latter's recent visit to the United States. Copland now insists on dissociating himself from Shostakovich's attack, made during the Soviet composer's visit, on modernists such as Stravinsky, Hindemith, and Schoenberg. Replying a few months later, Schoenberg brushes all that aside and takes another tack altogether. He is distressed to learn that

> Mr Copland had given young students who asked for it the advice to use "simple" intervals and to study the masters. Much damage had been done to an entire generation of highly talented American composers, who . . . were taught to write a certain style. It will certainly take a generation of sincere teaching until this damage can be repaired.
>
> And only in this respect did I couple Mr Copland with Stalin: they both do not consider musical composition as the art to present musical ideas in a dignified manner, but they want their followers to write a certain style, that is to create an external appearance, without asking about the inside. This I must condemn.[14]

Copland responded with a personal letter to Schoenberg, in which he again defended himself against what he considered unfair charges, arguing that he had adopted pedagogical principles essentially no different from Schoenberg's, for he had never imposed compositional formulas or stylistic choices on his students but had rather let their own capacities and interests determine the directions they took.[15] The next letter from Schoenberg is, at last, conciliatory, declaring his admiration for Copland's music and conceding that he may have been the victim of "gossip" in respect to whatever Copland may have said about him.[16]

This particular peacemaking gesture aside, Schoenberg's long battle against the French neoclassical influence on American music and, more broadly, against nationalist aspirations as such must be taken seriously, since both were connected in his own mind with the American fixation on creating a product, the values and purposes of which were external to the process of developing musical ideas from the "inside"—that is, out of material that itself was rooted in and evolved uninterruptedly from tradition. As is well enough known, his antipathy toward neoclassicism, whether of Stravinskyan or more generally Latin derivation, dates back to the 1920s, when he felt that his influence was being challenged by the tonal (in his view, pseudotonal) music of composers who refused to acknowledge the importance of his advances into new territory. In the United States, subsequently, Schoenberg saw his position with regard to the enemy camp to have become even more tenuous; students there, lacking any deep sense of his tradition, were all the more susceptible to musical instruction given, as he put it, "in the manner in which a cook would deliver recipes."[17] Young Americans, in other words, were being encouraged to look to the means rather than the ends, and in so doing leaned too heavily on abstract precepts and theories. When provided with principles of musical composition, Schoenberg complained, these students "want to apply them too much 'on principle.' And in art that's wrong. . . . musical logic does not anwer to 'if—, then—,' but enjoys making use of the possibilities excluded by if-then."[18] Furthermore, it worried him that Americans demanded results too quickly, a visible return in short order on the money they invest in their education. They had neither the time nor the patience for the lengthy, slow process of learning by the emulation of model and example, which inevitably requires the discipline of steady practice. Schoenberg was to find this problem especially acute among professionals who sought to take advantage of his presence in Los Angeles. Oscar Levant described the situation succinctly at the time:

> There is hardly a period in Hollywood when all the orchestrators and most of the movie composers are not studying with one or another of the prominent musicians who have gone to live there recently. At one time the vogue was for Schoenberg, who came with a great reputation, of course, as a teacher. However, most of the boys wanted to take a six weeks' course and learn a handful of Schoenberg's tricks. They were sorely disappointed when they discovered that it was his intention to give them instruction in counterpoint, harmony and chorale, which meant that they would have to expend considerable effort themselves in doing assigned work.[19]

Not surprisingly, most of these seekers after quick fixes were to find themselves rejected by the master. "I am not one of those," he said, "who can teach . . . a number of effective tricks in a short time. I only teach the whole of the art."[20] And his concern with the whole of the art meant, in turn, a rejection of any hard and fast system or simplified method of teaching it.

In this regard it is interesting to compare his approach with that of fellow Europeans such as Toch and Krenek. For those two composers, transplantation sparked the desire for some fresh thinking about their musical heritage; moreover, the very different teaching conditions from those back home had them reconsider how students might best be instructed in that heritage. Toch began to look for ways of freeing instruction from fossilized "theory," and of linking it more closely to contemporary needs. The avowed aim of his *Shaping Forces in Music*[21] was to impose a focus on the past from a contemporary viewpoint and to lead from that to a "universal core of thought which would serve as a starting-off point for young composers of today."[22] Similarly, Krenek found that his teaching activity stimulated him to reflect, de novo, on the composer's relationship to the materials bequeathed to him by the past. Impatient to bring his students to the heart of the matter, he attempted to reduce older compositional criteria to a handful of general principles and then to proceed directly to contemporary means of expression. His twelve-tone counterpoint manual, which sprang from his own interpretation and drastic distillation of melodic elements in medieval music, was intended to provide the basis of a new métier. It was dismissed by Schoenberg precisely because, in making use of the past for the purposes of historical precedent, it took leave of tradition. Yet insofar as it suggested a specific method of composition, Krenek's pedagogy was perhaps better suited to American conditions than Schoenberg's, which was rooted nonsystematically in the idea of traditional practice.[23]

The spirit of Schoenberg's teaching was animated by a fervent belief in the crucial role that education would play in a country where a profusion of musical talent struggled with cultural immaturity. That endowment of, as it were, "resources" would require careful nurturing and guidance if it was not to be exploited and misused. For one thing, music lovers would have to be instructed in critical listening and their attention focused on strictly musical criteria and values rather than waylaid by the commercialized hype of the concert world and its performing "stars." For another, encouragement should be given to amateur music making, in order to counter the culturally damaging effects of excessive professionalism and the consumerism that went along with it. As far as the actual teaching of composition went, Schoenberg presented himself not as a theorist or pedagogue but as a master practitioner; he believed that his students would benefit most from acquiring a basic facility in generating simple musical ideas and elaborating upon them in ways appropriate to the character of those ideas and the kinds of demands made by them. For students, the majority of whom could not be expected to approach the heights of true creativity, the analysis of masterworks (to which Schoenberg gave much emphasis) would serve to point up the qualitative differences between the imaginative solutions of genius and their own modest exercises. Even more important, comprehension and appreciation of an ideal represented by great achievements of the past went beyond a training in composition to form part of a moral education that developed the whole personality. If successful, such an education would give students "the courage to express what they have to say."[24]

As Hindemith was brought to Yale, or Krenek to Hamline, Schoenberg was welcomed to UCLA in 1934 with the understanding that the appointment would lend prestige to the institution, and that the new faculty member could expect the university's assistance with major reforms and improvements in the music curriculum. Yet many of Schoenberg's proposals were rejected, and one suspects that the ruffling of professional feathers may have had as much to do with that as with any lack of funds needed for implementing the proposals. Moreover, those proposals, advanced with an aggressive bearing of authority that was hardly politic coming from a newcomer and foreigner to boot, were nothing less than sweeping. On finding that his teaching effectiveness was inhibited by large classes of students with very different levels of ability, he suggested a new structure that would divide courses into basic and advanced types of instruction. He insisted, at the same time, that those teaching the beginners be his own, more advanced students. Basic training must be "in the hands of an instructor who is entirely familiar with my system. It is literally impossible to work successfully with students who come to me without being trained in this system."[25] Not surprisingly, he was accused of attempting to set up what amounted to a school within a school, based on a European model. But so convinced was Schoenberg on this issue that, as an alternative, he considered setting up a private school, the "Arnold Schoenberg School of Composition," with himself as director and three of his pupils as associates, who would contribute from their earnings to meet expenses. The associates he had in mind were Hanns Eisler, Gerald Strang, and Leonard Stein; their function would be to prepare students for advanced study with him. As to the role of the director, Schoenberg was quite unambiguous. In all that pertained to the establishment, administration, and development of the school, the director was to have "dictatorial powers."[26]

Much has been made in the biographical and critical literature of Schoenberg's authoritarian and high-minded idealism. Less has been said, however, about some quite different and complementary character traits that provide a more balanced picture. Chief among these was a down-to-earth pragmatism, which his encounter with America seems to have called into particular prominence. Not that Schoenberg bowed to circumstances to the extent that many of his fellow émigrés did. Nevertheless, he did attempt to provide for what he saw to be the practical needs of American musicians; not only did he compose for the college orchestra and amateur wind band, he also provided harmony, counterpoint, and composition manuals suited to American students with little prior training. Striking, in these texts, is his adaptation to circumstances, reflected in the omission of the kinds of philosophical speculation that had characterized his European books, among them the *Harmonielehre* and the unfinished *Der musikalische Gedanke, und die Logik, Technik und Kunst seiner Darstellung.* Now theoretical matters are reduced to a minimum, and rules for writing music presented as a distillation of practice. It is the doing that counts; the rest will come later.

Nor, for all the contempt he felt for its rampant commercialism, does the practically minded Schoenberg entirely disregard his Hollywood milieu. Among his unpublished papers is a proposal, addressed to the Academy of Motion Pictures, under the title "School for Soundmen." In it he notes that American films are careful in their handling of visual detail but sloppy and insensitive in their treatment of music and the relationship between music and dramatic event. The proposed remedy is a training for "soundmen" that will give equal emphasis to studio techniques and the necessary musical rudiments, the latter to include ear training and the ability to read a score. Nothing appears to have come of this proposal.

Teaching from the ground up, so to speak, was a precept to which

Schoenberg adhered uncompromisingly throughout his American years. The majority of his students were treated by him, as he once admitted, in a manner that "showed them I did not think too much of their creative abilities"[27] but instead helped to give them the musical foundation they so sorely needed. Beyond that his overall bearing was to them an example of high moral principles, and this example did not go unappreciated, at least among the more gifted and perceptive of his students, to whom it served as a guiding light during artistically troubled times. Lou Harrison, who for a short period attended some of Schoenberg's classes at UCLA, later wrote him the following words of gratitude:

> No person has given me so much confidence in myself, and I have had much need since then, in the face of fads and fashions, of just that intense and real belief in the importance of honesty towards oneself and honesty towards the art which I profess that you seemed to give me.[28]

In his closing years such appreciation was joined by an awakening of genuine interest in Schoenberg the composer, rather than merely Schoenberg the inventor of a revolutionary "method" of composition. After the long years of neglect there began to be more performances of both recent and earlier works in New York and even in the until then recalcitrant Los Angeles. A small band of younger Americans began to write to Schoenberg about being won over to the music and about finding in it, as Sessions put it, "a source of deep comfort and faith . . . an immensely renewed faith in the relevance of one's own efforts, as well as renewed courage to be making them."[29]

A gratifying response, surely, even if coming to the composer at such a late stage. Yet it appears to have done little for the cloud of mistrust and suspicion that shrouded his relationship to his American environment and sat heavily upon him until the end. As late as 1950 he wrote a circular letter to several of his older pupils, asking them to protest what he considered official propaganda directed against him, in particular, a CBS ban on his music for being (so he had heard) too "controversial."[30] From the moment he set foot on American soil Schoenberg had applied himself to the task of helping to bring his adopted country to musical maturity, but it would seem that in the end, when all was said and done, he felt he was still far from having accomplished that goal. True enough, he could look back on an active and in some ways successful American career as an educator and publicist for his own musical values and ideas. He had given many American students the technical grounding they so sorely needed, and, beyond that, secure artistic and moral direction. To a variety of lay audiences he had spoken with extraordinary forthrightness on many of the leading issues—musical, aesthetic, and cultural—of his day. As a composer, moreover, loneliness and a deep sense of isolation had not prevented him from stepping into the limelight with music that addressed (or alluded to) contemporary sociopolitical concerns. The rhetoric of works such as the *Ode to Napoleon* and *A Survivor from Warsaw* brings them squarely into the realm of publicly oriented "protest" music.

Nevertheless, the gap between public and private could only widen with advancing age and the accumulation of disappointments. In late works such as the String Trio and the Fantasy for Violin with piano accompaniment, we find a retreat from the greater classicizing ambition of the first mature twelve-tone works and a return to the pithy, aphoristic, loosely structured manner of pre–World War I expressionism. Abandoned with such music is the attempt at an all-encompassing synthesis, and left unanswered, in the unfinished *Jakobsleiter* and *Moses und Aron*, are the fundamental questions raised by humanity's struggle with destiny. Schoenberg could only withdraw deeper into himself. With his last composition, the *Moderne Psalmen*, he conversed in music with his God, with whom he had been left alone.

NOTES

This essay was edited after Alan Lessem's death by Joan Evans; Alexander Ringer gave the oral presentation at the 1991 Schoenberg conference.

1. Arnold Schoenberg, unpublished manuscript (ASI). See Rufer, *Works of Arnold Schoenberg*, 149, where it is listed as B.16.: "Adress [*sic*]: Driven into Paradise. 9.10.1935."

2. Arnold Schoenberg, "Why No Great American Music?" (1934), in *Style and Idea*, 176–181, esp. 176.

3. Arnold Schoenberg, unpublished manuscript (ASI). See Rufer, *Works of Arnold Schoenberg*, 157, where it is listed as C.228.: "Some problems for the educator" (n.d.).

4. Roger Sessions, "Vienna—Vale, Ave," *Modern Music* 15/4 (May-June 1938), 203–208, esp. 206.

5. See Roger Sessions, "Schoenberg in the United States," *Tempo* 9 (December 1944), 2–7, esp. 2.

6. Mark Brunswick, "Refugee Musicians in America," *Saturday Review of Literature* 9 (26 January 1946), 50–51.

7. Ibid., 50.

8. In 1950 Albert Goldberg, a music critic for the *Los Angeles Times*, requested from a number of émigré composers their opinion regarding the effects of transplantation on their work. The responses appeared in the *Times* column "The Sounding Board," on 14, 21, and 28 May of that year. The column of 14 May contained Schoenberg's statement.

9. Ernst Krenek, "Amerikas Einfluss auf eingewanderte Komponisten," *Musica* 13 (December 1959), 757–761, esp. 761.

10. Arnold Schoenberg, "Folkloristic Symphonies," in *Style and Idea*, 161–166, esp. 166.

11. Schoenberg to K. Aram, 15 November 1947, *Schoenberg Letters,* no. 218, 249–250, esp. 250.

12. Elliott Carter, "The Changing Scene, New York, 1940," *Modern Music* 17/4 (May-June 1940); reprinted in *The Writings of Elliott Carter: An American Composer Looks at Modern Music,* ed. Else Stone and Kurt Stone (Bloomington: Indiana University Press, 1977), 81–85, esp. 81.

13. Roger Sessions, "Music in a Business Economy," *Berkeley: A Journal of Modern Culture,* July 1948; reprinted in *Roger Sessions on Music: Collected Essays,* ed. Edward T. Cone (Princeton, N.J.: Princeton University Press, 1979), 164–165.

14. Arnold Schoenberg, "An Answer to Aaron Copland's Reply," 23 December 1949, ASC/LC.

15. Copland to Schoenberg, 13 February 1950, ASI.

16. Schoenberg to Copland, 21 February 1950, ASI.

17. Arnold Schoenberg, "The Blessing of the Dressing," in *Style and Idea,* 382–386, esp. 386.

18. Schoenberg to Ernst Krenek, 1 December 1939, *Schoenberg Letters,* no. 183, 210.

19. Oscar Levant, *A Smattering of Ignorance* (New York: Doubleday, 1940), 125.

20. Schoenberg to Leonard Meyer, 5 December 1940, ASI.

21. Ernst Toch, *The Shaping Forces in Music* (New York: Criterion Music Corp, 1948).

22. Ernst Toch to Elizabeth Coolidge, 19 January 1942, Ernst Toch Collection, Library of Congress.

23. For more information about Schoenberg's approaches to teaching, see Alan Lessem, "Teaching Americans Music: Some Emigré Composer Viewpoints, ca. 1930–1955," *Journal of the Arnold Schoenberg Institute* 11/1 (1988), 4–22.

24. Arnold Schoenberg, interview with William Lundell (ASI). Listed in Rufer, *Works of Arnold Schoenberg,* as B.9.: "First American Broadcast. 19.11.1933."

25. Schoenberg to Leroy Allen, chair of the Department of Music at UCLA, 7 June 1934, ASI.

26. Schoenberg to Hanns Eisler, 20 August 1934, ASI.

27. Arnold Schoenberg, "The Blessing of the Dressing," in *Style and Idea,* 382–386, esp. 385.

28. Lou Harrison to Schoenberg, 4 November 1944, ASI.

29. Roger Sessions to Schoenberg, 30 October 1947. Published in *The Correspondence of Roger Sessions,* ed. Andrea Olmstead (Boston: Northeastern University Press, 1992), 349–350.

30. A copy of the letter, dated 28 April 1950, is in the Koldolfsky Collection, ASI.

Creations

FIVE

Schoenberg and the Origins of Atonality

Ethan Haimo

Seen from the vantage point of the 1990s, the birth of atonality is an accomplished and inarguable fact, one of the most significant events in the history of Western music. Placed as we are in time—after this complete transformation of musical thought—it is difficult to imagine that it could have been otherwise.

But, at least as far as the arts are concerned, I am no historical determinist. Atonality was not the ineluctable consequence of the development of musical style, not an inescapable historical necessity.[1] To be sure, by 1900 many composers felt that tonality as it had been understood was at the point of exhaustion and that substantive changes in musical language were in store. Nonetheless, it is by no means certain that, without Arnold Schoenberg, we would have seen the emergence of music that we would define as atonal. Rather, we probably would have seen (and did, in fact, see) new scales or modes, new definitions of dissonance or methods of dissonance treatment, new procedures for voice leading, new kinds of harmonic progressions, and so forth. Nevertheless, however sharply the pre–World War I music of Stravinsky, Bartók, Debussy, Scriabin, and others diverges from tonality as it had been understood before the turn of the century, their music retained many significant aspects of tonal organization. It is reasonable to wonder whether without Schoenberg we would ever have seen anything like the Klavierstücke, op. 11. And it should not be forgotten how seminal that opus was. As Reinhold Brinkmann pointed out, op. 11 was the first Schoenberg work that Bartók got to know,[2] and Stravinsky studied it while composing *Le sacre du printemps.*

If indeed the idea of atonality was not so much the product of anonymous historical forces as it was the specific notion of a single thinker, then we are faced with a basic problem in the epistemology of music: What was there in Schoenberg's thought that brought about the birth of atonality?

To answer this question, however, we must recognize that the birth of atonality was not sudden, did not emerge complete in all of its details. Schoenberg did not abandon all aspects of tonality between one composition and the next. Rather, there was an extended period in which the syntax and idioms characteristic of tonal music gradually disappeared and nontonal procedures began to take their place.[3] Recognizing that there was such an evolutionary process is important for the understanding of the birth of atonality, for it is my central contention here that Schoenberg's idea of atonality emerged from his conception of tonality. Therefore the question might be reformulated as, What was there in Schoenberg's view of tonality that motivated the birth of atonality?

It is tempting to consider approaching the reconstruction of Schoenberg's compositional thought in the years roughly between 1900 and 1909 simply by examining the compositions, preferably in chronological order. And although the chronology of the compositions in the period leading up to World War I is hardly ironclad, there is relatively reliable chronological information about almost all of the most significant compositions of this period.[4] But analysis of the compositions alone may not be completely satisfactory. It would be best if it were possible to support analytical observations with the composer's contemporaneous writings, diaries, letters, or polemics.

The problem is, however, that Schoenberg did not become an author until the period in question was already well under way. His first formal essays, a few short, angry responses to the ever intensifying tidal wave of criticism of his music, were not written until 1909, after the completion of opp. 11 and 15, and are in any event irrelevant to the topic under discussion.[5] Most of Schoenberg's later (and usually rather general) comments on the subject in the 1920s, 1930s, and 1940s are necessarily colored by the complete transformation that had taken place in his artistic thinking in the intervening years, not the least of which was the evolution of the twelve-tone method. Furthermore, these later articles, like "My Evolution," "Wie man einsam wird" ("How One Becomes Lonely"), and others, were written, at least in part, in response to the many violent assaults on the legitimacy of his music.[6] Slanted, as they necessarily were, by the exigencies of providing a defense for his musical style, these polemics may not be as reliable or useful as would testimony gathered during the period of Schoenberg's gradual turn toward a new kind of musical organization.

There is, however, one text from the period that has the potential to supply us with what is needed, though only if it is used carefully. I refer, of course, to Schoenberg's *Harmonielehre*.[7] As Jan Maegaard has shown,[8] Schoenberg began writing this massive theoretical/philosophical treatise in 1910 and finished and published it in 1911—that is, after the *George-*

Lieder, op. 15, the Piano Pieces, op. 11, the Five Orchestra Pieces, op. 16, and *Erwartung,* op. 17.

Having dismissed other post-1909 texts as unsuitable for revealing important features of Schoenberg's compositional thinking in the period of the birth of atonality, it might seem illogical that I now suggest examining a 1911 treatise for that purpose. But the *Harmonielehre* has some crucial differences from the other writings. If we except some of the later chapters and various scattered passages in which Schoenberg self-consciously attempts to describe and justify some of his latest compositional developments, the book is in no sense designed as a primer for Schoenberg's emergent style. Rather, it represents a species of music-theory textbook that fundamentally no longer exists: a text designed to teach a beginning pupil how to become a composer of tonal music.

The very fact that this is a textbook makes it particularly effective as a vehicle to help us re-create Schoenberg's compositional thinking. It can be used in much the same way that Walter Frisch used Schoenberg's pedagogical writings to good effect for the clarification of Schoenberg's concept of developing variation.[9] Because he is writing a text for a beginning student interested in learning how to compose tonal music, Schoenberg is forced to begin at the beginning, with fundamental principles. Examination of the practical details of his instructions for voice leading, chord formation, and harmonic progression enables a reconstruction of some of the most significant underpinnings of Schoenberg's idea of tonality. And it is in Schoenberg's conception of tonality that the most useful clues for the origins of atonality can be found.

I would like to preface my analysis of the evidence I believe to be most useful by describing some material from the *Harmonielehre* that contributes to the overall picture, though I suspect it may not be completely reliable. I refer to passages such as the extended discussion of consonance, dissonance, and the overtone system in chapter 3. This discussion includes Schoenberg's assertion that the difference between the closer and more remote overtones is a matter of degree, not of kind. If this view of the overtones was indeed a determinant of Schoenberg's thinking before circa 1908, it would be an obvious source for the origins of atonality. A compositional method grounded on the notion that the distinction between dissonance and consonance is artificial would provide much of the appropriate philosophical/acoustical background for the birth of atonality. And it would not be the first time that theories of consonance and dissonance—credible or not—had determined the direction of musical style.

But these remarks—and there are other, similar ones—seem suspiciously like ex post facto justifications, appeals to history and the laws of nature to justify a musical transformation that had already taken place, thus perhaps reflecting the concerns of the composer of 1910 rather than the composer of earlier tonal compositions.[10] Therefore I intend to restrict my discussion to the practical material of the *Harmonielehre,* of which there is more than enough for my purpose.

There are at the very least three basic ways in which Schoenberg's theory of tonality, as expressed in the practical sections of the *Harmonielehre,* can cast light on the origins of atonality: through his concept of harmonic progression, through his notion of the hierarchy of the diatonic collection, and through his procedures for chord formation.

In chapters 4 and 5—the first chapters in which he gets down to the nitty-gritty of practical musical, as opposed to philosophical or acoustical, details—Schoenberg shows the beginning student how to form all of the diatonic triads, seventh chords, and their inversions. After enunciating basic principles of voice leading, Schoenberg demonstrates how to connect chords one to another. It is quite remarkable that the emphasis is exclusively on connections from chord to chord. Absent from this extended discussion (which lasts nearly a quarter of the entire book and includes sixty-nine musical examples) is any systematic discussion of harmonic progression. This entire stretch of the book includes no theoretical framework to organize the successions of harmonies into progressions directed toward a tonic, as opposed to merely ending on the tonic. The omission is also reflected in the musical examples, many of which include harmonic successions that wander about rather aimlessly.[11] Moreover, although Schoenberg several times employs the useful pedagogical technique of introducing a new concept with an example containing an error, he defers until the beginning of chapter 7 any mention of the possibility that these aimless harmonic progressions need improvement.

When he finally does get around to this topic, he introduces his theory of harmonic progressions—a theory that, as Robert Wason has shown, is distantly related to Simon Sechter's (and Anton Bruckner's) theories of chord progression.[12] Schoenberg's theory is founded on three types of chord progressions: strong (or ascending), weak (or descending), and over-skipping (or superstrong). He formulates his theory of chord progressions as a dictum: "*in planning our root progressions we shall give absolute preference to the ascending progressions and shall use the descending ones primarily in those chord connections where the total effect is still that of ascent.*"[13]

The generally negative verdict that subsequent musical theorists have expressed regarding this theory of harmonic progressions is irrelevant here. I am interested in this theory not so much for its own sake but for what it reveals about Schoenberg's view of tonality. As a matter of fact, his theory is uncommonly revealing, for it does virtually nothing to address the issue of what other theories of tonality would consider to be the harmonic aimlessness of Schoenberg's progressions. Indeed, using Schoenberg's in-

structions one can readily produce progressions that express no functionally integrated, tonic-defining structure. As a result, his theory of strong/
weak/superstrong progressions is no different in kind or focus from the
ideas in the preceding one hundred pages of his text; just as chapters 4 and
5 placed their emphasis on chord-to-chord connections, so too is Schoenberg's theory of progressions, in the final analysis, largely a refinement of
that idea.[14]

In the next section of the chapter, when at long last he brings cadences
into the picture, Schoenberg's approach finally begins to yield harmonic
progressions that resemble those of more traditional theories of harmony.
When one limits the number of chords in a progression to a relatively small
number; when one begins and ends a phrase in the tonic, preparing the
close with one of the traditional cadential formulas; when one chooses chords
utilizing only tones of the diatonic collection; and when one follows Schoenberg's dictum that strong progressions are to be given absolute preference—
the resultant harmonic progressions, as shown in Schoenberg's examples,
are virtually indistinguishable from progressions one would find by theorists or figured-bass authors as diverse as Hugo Riemann and Paul Vidal.

But in Schoenberg's post-1900 music few of these restrictions hold. The
cadence was—in true late-Romantic style—unlikely to be found in unambiguous form at the end of every phrase or period. Rather, it was a device
of some rarity, avoided entirely or deferred to the very end of a composition
or important section. Similarly, the tonic triad (or dominant chord) was
not always clearly demarcated at the beginnings or endings of phrases. Nor
did Schoenberg limit himself to the diatonic tones of a scale or to relatively
short harmonic progressions. Therefore, even when Schoenberg gives absolute preference to strong progressions in his connections from chord to
chord, his harmonic progressions frequently lack any strong sense of tonal
identification. They become not tonic-defining *progressions* with a direc-
tional push toward the tonic but *successions* of chords, each of which is related most strongly to its immediate predecessor and successor, and absent
of any clear tonal goal—exactly as we might conclude from his theory of
progressions. Therefore, the tonic definition of a phrase or passage (if it
exists at all) is likely to be established not so much by the underlying harmonic progressions as by other factors—frequently by beginning or ending
a phrase or section on a chord that by agogic emphasis or temporal placement seems like the tonic, or sometimes by the melodic points of emphasis
in the outermost voices. This is not to say that Schoenberg never wrote
phrases whose progressions begin on the tonic, move to a dominant preparation chord, continue on to a dominant, and return to the tonic. But it is
clear that in his tonal thought, progressions of this sort were not regarded
as normative, nor even necessary for what he saw as tonic definition.

Given the unique character of virtually every one of his works, it is a risky business to cite examples and present them as representative of Schoenberg's compositions. There is the real danger that whatever examples one chooses might be—at least in some dimension—representative only of that work and of no others. With this caution in mind, I would like to cite an example that I believe is illustrative of the view of tonic definition that emerges from Schoenberg's *Harmonielehre*.

The song "Mädchenlied," op. 6, no. 3 (1905), begins with a fairly clear expansion of an E-minor triad in measure 1 (see example 1). By virtue of its placement as the first chord of the composition and its comparative agogic emphasis, we can—even on first hearing—take E to be the tonic, a judgment that is confirmed by the song's conclusion. Schoenberg begins the second stanza of the poem (measure 9) again in E minor, reestablishing E by the same temporal and agogic emphases that were used at the beginning of the song. Between these two comparatively unambiguous tonal reference points there is a plethora of identifiable triads, seventh chords, augmented triads, and so forth. And the successions from chord to chord are invariably structured to move primarily by strong or superstrong progressions, faithfully following the principles of chord progression and voice leading outlined in the *Harmonielehre*.

If, however, one were presented with only measures 2 through 7, it would be impossible to identify E minor (or any other sonority) as the tonic of this passage, or to anticipate the return of E minor at the beginning of measure 8. Nothing in the intervening harmonic progressions defines E minor as the tonic, nor does any other tone suggest a tonic lasting beyond one chord.

Although this is but a single example, I believe it to be highly representative of Schoenberg's approach to tonality. It is frequently the case in his works that the tonic is neither established by, nor deducible from, the harmonic progressions. Instead Schoenberg normally establishes the tonic by temporal placement or agogic emphasis. Without such emphases or placement it is difficult or impossible to identify the tonic.

The theory of harmonic progressions in the *Harmonielehre* is not a fluke, not an error, not even a pedagogical simplification. Rather, it represents an essential aspect of Schoenberg's thinking. As such it is one of the most significant clues in our search for the origins of atonality, for it yields a musical style employing the traditional vocabulary of tonality (triads and seventh chords) and traditional syntax (no parallel fifths, proper resolution of sevenths, and so forth) without defining or establishing the tonic as the referential sonority by means of harmonic progression.

A further source of the idea of atonality can be found in a second basic aspect of Schoenberg's view of tonality. In most other theories of tonality, both before and since Schoenberg, the diatonic scale is accorded a special hierarchical standing. The diatonic collection is normally considered to be

Example 1. Arnold Schoenberg, "Mädchenlied," op. 6, no. 3, mm. 1–8

potentially key defining, and thus relatively stable. It follows that the remaining five tones of the chromatic scale are less stable; they must normally resolve to, be seen as elaborators of, or be heard in reference to one of the seven diatonic tones. In the beginning stages of his treatise Schoenberg restricts himself to chords built only on the diatonic degrees, and it might appear that he too is respecting the hierarchical standing of the diatonic collection. However, in a telling passage from chapter 10, Schoenberg reaches back to the church modes as the justification to explain the presence of tones outside of the referential diatonic collection. In so doing, he draws a distinct line in the sand between his theories and those of his contemporaries and predecessors:

> I have already mentioned that peculiarity of the church modes wherein variety was produced in the harmony through accidentals (sharps, flats, naturals, which momentarily and incidentally alter diatonic tones of a scale). Most textbooks commonly try to replace this richness with a few instructions pertaining to chromaticism. That is not in itself the same thing, however, nor does it have the same value for the pupil since it is not sufficiently systematic. What took place in the church modes happened without chromaticism, so to speak, diatonically, as we can still see in our minor mode. . . . Now, should our major and minor actually contain the entire harmonic wealth of the church modes, then we must include these characteristics in a manner consistent with their sense. It becomes possible thereby to use in a major key all the nondiatonic tones and chords that appeared in the seven church modes.[15]

To be sure, had Schoenberg recommended forming specific passages solely with the elements of a given church mode, there would not necessarily have been a challenge to tonality. But that is not what he is suggesting. Rather, he is justifying the use of the five chromatic tones as functionally equivalent replacements for any of the seven diatonic tones at any time and in any place, a procedure that—if employed freely—would make it impossible to identify a specific seven-tone diatonic collection as the referential collection.

This is not Schoenberg's only justification for extensive chromaticism. In another passage, where he shows how to connect distantly related chords to one another, he remarks:

> There is a means that is always appropriate for making such chord connections smoothly and convincingly: chromaticism. Formerly, when we were dealing with simpler connections, with the most immediate relationships, a diatonic scale segment from the fundamental key or a related key assumed the responsibility for what happened harmonically. Here, more and more, a single scale assumes all such functions: the chromatic scale.[16]

The potential consequences that these two approaches have for tonality should be clear. Schoenberg's view of the modes, and of the voice-leading

Example 2. Arnold Schoenberg, "Traumleben," op. 6, no. 1, mm. 1–7

connections necessary to connect distantly related harmonies, encourages both equal standing for and the constant circulation of all twelve tones. That being so, a key cannot be defined by its collection, nor can a move from key center to key center be effected through changes in the referential collection: all "keys" have the same basic collection, all twelve tones.

Although the previously cited Schoenberg passage about modes might be read to imply that free use of the chromatic (that is, "modal") tones was normative, such an interpretation is not entirely borne out by Schoenberg's tonal music, at least not by his early tonal music. Initially—that is, before about 1904–1905—he tended to use chromatic tones more in the way he describes in the second passage cited earlier: as segments of chromatic scales. For instance, the four-measure phrase that begins the song "Traumleben," op. 6, no. 1 (1903), even concludes with the tonic chord, prepared by a root-position dominant-ninth chord (see example 2). As is often the case, all twelve tones appear within this phrase, mostly as segments of chro-

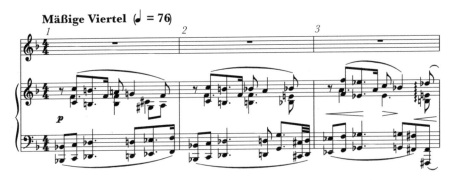

Example 3. Arnold Schoenberg, "Jane Grey," op. 12, no. 1, mm. 1–3

matic scales. One could certainly argue that the referential collection of E major is deducible from this phrase, thus permitting us to describe the nondiatonic tones not as tones of equivalent standing (as the first quotation would suggest) but as chromatic elaborators of relatively stable diatonic tones, originating from the connection of distantly related chords.

Nonetheless, the virtually constant use of chromatic segments in all of the voices, both in this example and in many others like it, makes it very difficult to identify a referential diatonic collection and, consequently, to establish a clear tonal hierarchy. It might be possible to make such distinctions if a clear diatonic collection at the beginning were the norm, or if the tonic could easily be inferred from the harmonic progressions. But that is rarely the case in Schoenberg's tonal music.

Another example shows how difficult it is to decipher which are the diatonic tones; it also serves to demonstrate what Schoenberg might have meant in justifying the chromatic tones through recourse to the modes. Example 3 presents the first three measures of the 1907 ballad "Jane Grey," op. 12, no. 1. Although the tonality with which the work concludes is D, the first measures are difficult to reconcile with D minor or, for that matter, with any key. In these first three measures all twelve tones appear. Unlike the example cited from op. 6, no. 1, here the chromaticism is not the product of chromatic-scale segments within the strands of polyphony. But the very complexity of the formations makes it impossible to identify a referential diatonic collection that is stable. Is the B-natural in the right hand a chromatic tone or a diatonic tone? Is it B-natural or C-flat? Which of the two tones, D-flat or D-natural, is the structural tone in the bass?

Passages of this sort are hardly atypical in Schoenberg's tonal music, and they reflect precisely what his theories suggested we would find—twelve tones being used in free circulation, without any firm hierarchy or even distinction between the seven diatonic tones and the remaining chromatic tones.

Another source for atonality that I can trace to ideas in the *Harmonielehre* concerns Schoenberg's method and procedures for chord formation. A substantial proportion of the book is devoted to identifying and classifying chords—hardly unusual for a book on harmony, to be sure, but I know of no other treatise that is more exhaustive in its search for all possible variants.

Schoenberg is careful in the initial stages of the book to make a clear distinction between chordal types—consonant chords and those that contain a dissonance. When he introduces the VII-chord, for example, he makes it clear that unlike the other diatonic chords, this one contains a dissonance, and chords with dissonances have special voice-leading requirements. In this respect Schoenberg's approach, for all of its philosophical musings about dissonance, is rather traditional. In regarding sevenths, for instance, as essential dissonances that need resolution and demand a change of harmony, he is following a well-trodden path that can be traced back to Kirnberger. In the simpler chords—the diatonic sevenths, for example—it is of course a relatively trivial matter to identify the dissonance, and as a result Schoenberg's instructions for voice leading do not differ appreciably from previous approaches.

However, the more complex the chromaticism and the more alterations in the chord, the greater the difficulty in discriminating between dissonance and consonance, and the greater the possibilities for ambiguous results. It is not that it is impossible to identify whether a chord is (or is not) dissonant according to the rules of tonal theory. It simply becomes difficult or impossible to determine which of the tones in the chord is the unstable tone, and which are the stable ones. When the dissonance cannot be identified, its resolution cannot be directed. And when that happens the emancipation of the dissonance is at hand—not as the result of theoretical speculation about the more remote overtones of the harmonic series but as a consequence of the extension of the methods of chordal formation to include multiple altered and elaborative tones.

Here, too, the theories implicit in the practical sections of the *Harmonielehre* are amply reflected in Schoenberg's music. Dissonance treatment in Schoenberg's post-1900 music is not suddenly abandoned; rather, it is gradually made so complex as to cease to have a functional role. The conjunction of two chords both of which contain dissonances but in neither of which it can be ascertained which of the tones are the dissonances eventually leads to the nonfunctionality of dissonance. "Emancipation of the dissonance" is a marvelous slogan, carrying subtle undertones of a kind of musical-liberation theology. The practical facts were probably far more

Example 4. Arnold Schoenberg, First String Quartet, op. 7, mvt. 1, mm. 8–10

mundane: Schoenberg was not searching for stable intervals when he reached toward the more remote overtones of the harmonic system; instead, his principles of chord formation made it impossible to identify which tones needed resolution. The consequences of this are profound. If dissonance cannot be identified, it cannot be resolved. And if it cannot be resolved, then the very notion of consonance and dissonance becomes moot.

One example can stand for many. In the First String Quartet, op. 7 (1904–1905), a succession of complicated sonorities appears in measures 8 through 10 (see example 4). On the last beat of measure 8 the chord consists of the tones E-flat, A, C-sharp, and F. This chord is followed on the first beat of measure 9 with a chord that includes A-flat, C, F-sharp, and (eventually) E-flat, and on the second beat with the sonority C, B-flat, F-sharp, and D. All three of these chords contain dissonant intervallic relationships—in some cases, many such dissonant intervals. But which tone is the dissonance? In the first chord the orthography might suggest that the E-flat is the seventh of the chord and C-sharp the raised fifth, and that those tones might be identified as the dissonances in the harmony. But this is belied by the part-writing connections to the next chord. In any event, Schoenberg stated clearly that in complicated chords he would choose his spelling for the convenience of the performer, not the analyst.[17] But even respelling this sonority in various ways does not produce an unambiguous harmonic structure with both clearly defined stable tones and identifiable dissonances.

The same situation obtains for the remaining chords in this phrase, up to and including the chord that, introducing a dramatic pause, closes the phrase (F-sharp, D, B-flat, G-sharp). One after another, the chords seem to be composed of four elements—that is, they seem to be types of seventh chords. But each of these chords is so constructed as to make it impossible to determine which tone might be the root, seventh, ninth, raised fifth, lowered fifth, or other traditional dissonance.

This, in conjunction with the two previous concepts, reveals that some of the essential pillars of tonality have been pulled down: the lack of directed harmonic progressions throws the existence of a tonic into doubt; the lack of hierarchy abolishes the diatonic scale as a referential collection; the inability to identify the dissonance erases the distinction between consonance and dissonance. Indeed, the challenges to tonal coherence posed by the three concepts are, in many senses, interrelated. If it were possible to identify an unambiguous referential collection, it might be possible to determine which tones in a chord were structural and which elaborative. If the tonic could be identified from the harmonic progressions, it might be possible to identify a referential collection. If the chords could be deciphered, perhaps the tonic could be identified. Rarely in Schoenberg's tonal music is any one of these steps possible, let alone all three together.

I have identified three important technical features in Schoenberg's view of tonality that I believe were essential in providing the conceptual basis for his idea of atonality. Of course, these features in and of themselves would not have led to atonality were it not for some other very important aspects of his intellectual makeup. Let me conclude by briefly sketching some of these features.

Schoenberg was, as is readily seen in both his compositions and his writings, very much taken with the idea of progress in the arts. He saw artistic value not merely residing in immanent aesthetic qualities, but also stemming from the historical importance of the work, which, in his thought, is often tied up with chronological precedence; witness Schoenberg's controversy with Hauer over the twelve-tone system,[18] and with Webern over *Klangfarbenmelodie*.[19] Because he was so concerned that his compositions be at the cutting edge of modernity, it was essential that each new composition be in some manner innovative. It is no wonder that each new composition had the effect of pushing back the frontiers of what was possible in tonal organization.

The second essential character trait relates to Schoenberg's commitment to organicism. Schoenberg, like many late-nineteenth-century German composers and theorists, was strongly influenced by the idea that in order to have merit, a composition must be constructed so that all events are derived from a fundamental idea stated at the beginning of the work; in Schoenberg's case this was seen primarily in motivic terms. One consequence of organicism in his late tonal music was to make normative within a composition whatever harmonic/motivic event was the first to occur in the work. Thus when, as in the case of op. 14, no. 1, a composition began with two chords, neither of which was a stable, classifiable, tonal sonority, the concept of organicism dictated that this harmonic succession become the structural foundation of the entire composition. The consequences of this for the destabilization of tonality are clear.

Finally, the consequences of Schoenberg's pedagogical background for the idea of atonality should not be underestimated. It was not, as one wag has suggested, that the problem with autodidacts is that they have such terrible teachers. In Schoenberg's case it might be more accurate to say that the advantage of autodidacts is that they do not have overbearing teachers. Because he was largely self-trained, Schoenberg was capable of seeing possibilities that might have been suppressed had he had a more traditional education.

The birth of atonality was the result of a single composer's intellectual and artistic makeup. It was not alone the fact that Schoenberg was an organicist, or that he believed in and acted upon the notion of progress in the arts, or that his training was informal. Rather, the combination of all of these factors—together with a view of tonality in which harmonic progressions no longer aimed for a tonic, hierarchical distinctions disappeared between diatonic and chromatic tones, and dissonances could no longer always be identified and resolved—resulted in the possibility of a new and unprecedented idea of musical organization.

NOTES

1. Carl Dahlhaus asserts both that the rise of atonality was not a historical necessity and that it is "impossible to give a reason for Schoenberg's decision" to cross the frontiers of tonality; see Carl Dahlhaus, "Schoenberg's Aesthetic Theology," in *Schoenberg and the New Music,* trans. Derrick Puffett and Alfred Clayton (Cambridge: Cambridge University Press, 1987), 81–93, esp. 88. I agree with the first assertion; my reasons for disagreement with the second are the substance of this paper.

2. Reinhold Brinkmann, *Arnold Schönberg: Drei Klavierstücke op. 11: Studien zur frühen Atonalität bei Schönberg* (Wiesbaden: Fritz Steiner Verlag, 1969), 40. László Somfai, however, asserts that the first work of Schoenberg that Bartók studied was the String Quartet op. 7; see his article on Bartók in *New Grove Dictionary of Music and Musicians,* ed. Stanley Sadie (London and Washington: Macmillan, 1980), 2:207.

3. There remains much disagreement about when tonality disappeared from Schoenberg's music, with some authors questioning whether it ever completely disappeared. It is my belief that some residual aspects of tonality remained in Schoenberg's music until approximately op. 23.

4. See Jan Maegaard, *Entwicklung des dodekaphonen Satzes*, vol. 1. The most significant remaining lacunae in the chronology are the unreliable chronological ordering for the individual songs of op. 15, and the questionable dating of "Am Strande."

5. Three essays, written in 1909, apparently represent Schoenberg's first literary forays: "Eine Rechtsfrage" ("A Legal Question," in *Style and Idea*, 185–189); "Ein Kunsteindruck" ("An Artistic Impression," in *Style and Idea*, 189–191); and "Über Musikkritik," *Der Merker* 1/2 (1909), 59–64 ("About Music Criticism," in *Style and Idea*, 191–197).

6. Among the pertinent essays are "Gesinnung oder Erkenntnis" (1925) ("Opinion or Insight?" in *Style and Idea*, 258–264); "Neue Musik: Meine Musik" (c. 1930) ("New Music: My Music," in *Style and Idea*, 99–106); "Wie man einsam wird" (1937) ("How One Becomes Lonely," in *Style and Idea*, 30–53); and "My Evolution" (1949), in *Style and Idea*, 79–92.

7. Schoenberg, *Harmonielehre* (Vienna: Universal Edition, 1911). Schoenberg revised his treatise rather extensively for the third edition, published in 1922, which served as the principal basis for the English translation by Roy E. Carter, *Theory of Harmony*. Carter's translations will be used throughout this article because for every passage case cited, the 1911 and 1922 texts coincide either exactly or very closely. Further, for the sake of convenience, reference will be made throughout the text to chapter numbers as they appear in Carter's translation, even though there were none in the 1911 edition.

8. Maegaard, *Entwicklung des dodekaphonen Satzes*, 1:68–69.

9. Walter Frisch, *Brahms and the Principle of Developing Variation* (Berkeley and Los Angeles: University of California Press, 1984), 9–18.

10. For a similar reading of Schoenberg's motivations, see Carl Dahlhaus, "Schoenberg and Schenker," in *Schoenberg and the New Music*, 134–140, esp. 137–138.

11. For instance, example 30b (1911 ed., 94; *Theory of Harmony*, 80) has the following harmonic progression: I VI II IV$_4^6$ VII III I.

12. See Robert Wason, *Viennese Harmonic Theory from Albrechtsberger to Schenker and Schoenberg* (Ann Arbor, Mich.: UMI Press, 1985), 136–139.

13. Schoenberg, *Theory of Harmony*, 120. For the original German, see Schoenberg, *Harmonielehre* (1911), 138 (very similar in the 1922 edition, 146).

14. It is highly revealing to compare the *Harmonielehre* with Schoenberg's later treatise on harmony, *Structural Functions of Harmony*, ed. and rev. Leonard Stein (New York: W. W. Norton & Company, 1969), where in the opening chapter, "Structural Functions of Harmony," he distinguishes between "successions" that are "aimless" and "progressions" that have the "function of establishing or contradicting a tonality."

15. Schoenberg, *Theory of Harmony*, 175. For the original German, see Schoenberg, *Harmonielehre* (1911), 199–201 (very similar in the 1922 edition, 213–215).

16. Schoenberg, *Theory of Harmony*, 229. For the original German, see Schoenberg, *Harmonielehre* (1911), 250 (very similar in the 1922 edition, 278).

17. Schoenberg, *Harmonielehre* (1911), 174–175 (1922 edition, 188); Schoenberg, *Theory of Harmony*, 426.

18. See, for instance, Bryan R. Simms, "Who First Composed Twelve-tone Music, Schoenberg or Hauer?" *Journal of the Arnold Schoenberg Institute* 10/2 (1987), 109–133.

19. See Schoenberg's 1951 essay "Anton Webern: Klangfarbenmelodie," in *Style and Idea*, 484–485.

SIX

The Refractory Masterpiece

Toward an Interpretation of Schoenberg's Chamber Symphony, op. 9

Walter Frisch

It has often been remarked that in the early part of this century Schoenberg forged his path to the new music not primarily in the modern genres of music drama or symphonic poem, but in the tradition of chamber music.[1] The series of works he composed mainly in Vienna between 1899 and 1908 dramatically rerouted the mainstream of Austro-German music. *Verklärte Nacht*, op. 4; the First String Quartet, op. 7; the First Chamber Symphony, op. 9; the Second String Quartet, op. 10: each of these pieces brings to the fore—problematizes, one might now say—fundamental questions of genre, form, harmony, and thematic style in ways that were decisive not only for Schoenberg himself but also for much of the music that followed in the twentieth century.

The Chamber Symphony is arguably the key work, and the most dialectical, within this group. The tensions embodied in it may be represented broadly as follows:

symphony—chamber music
public—private
communal—individual
homophonic—polyphonic
objective—subjective

These oppositions must be explored in order to develop an appropriate understanding of how the Chamber Symphony fits into Schoenberg's musical, intellectual, and cultural world.

I

Schoenberg was not the first to use the title "Kammersinfonie." In 1905 a composer in Berlin, Paul Juon, had published with that title a work for

strings, woodwinds, and piano.[2] Several more similarly named pieces were
to appear over the next decade or so.[3] But unlike the chamber symphonies
of his contemporaries, Schoenberg's may be said to have created a new
genre, in which two previously separate traditions, those of chamber and
symphonic music, merge—or, more precisely, collide. Reinhold Brinkmann
has aptly called op. 9 a "*gepresste Sinfonie*," a compressed symphony;[4] it might
be equally considered a piece of "*explodierte Kammermusik*." The best way to
get a sense of this dialectic of chamber/symphonic, which in turn incorpo-
rates some of the others mentioned above, is through the interpretive
frameworks developed by Paul Bekker, Theodor W. Adorno, and Carl
Dahlhaus, upon which I draw in the following discussion.

From the late eighteenth century the two streams of chamber and symphonic music, though independent in many respects, had tended to share
instrumental structures such as the sonata form. Over the course of the
nineteenth century they began to diverge both sociologically and compositionally. Symphonic music, especially as embodied in the symphonies of
Beethoven, tended to address a large public audience. Beethoven's symphonies were conceived, Bekker asserted, in the spirit of human liberation
and brotherhood—*Menschheitsbefreiung* and *Menschheitsverbrüderung*.[5] As
such, they are authentically *gesellschaftsbildend*, community forming. For
Adorno, the Beethoven symphonies were "orations to mankind."[6] Chamber
music, on the other hand, was aimed at a more select, sophisticated audience—at first, from the Renaissance through the late eighteenth century,
an aristocratic one; then, after the late eighteenth century, an educated,
musically cultivated bourgeoisie.

These social aspects had compositional ramifications. As a public genre,
and like a public oration, the symphony tended toward bolder, blunter effects. This is not to suggest any lack of compositional sophistication in the
symphonies of Beethoven, but, as Adorno says, "in principle, they are simpler than chamber music despite their substantially more lavish apparatus."[7] Chamber music—and here the late quartets of Beethoven are probably the paradigms—has a more inward and intricate compositional
language. Adorno defines chamber music as being characterized by the
principle of "*motivische-thematische Arbeit*," or motivic-thematic working.[8]
Dahlhaus adds to this definition the technique of "obbligato accompaniment," in which ostensibly secondary parts take on great thematic importance. He asserts also that chamber music became "intimately bound up
with" a further compositional principle, that which Schoenberg called *developing variation*, the procedure of spinning out large, continuous spans
from the constant transformation or reinterpretation of very reduced thematic or motivic material.[9]

As exploited by German composers from Haydn to Schoenberg, all three
of these principles—motivic-thematic working, obbligato accompaniment,

and developing variation—led to increasing compositional sophistication and, concomitantly, greater technical and interpretive demands on players. The result was a radical, perhaps even paradoxical, transformation of the status of chamber music. As it became too demanding both intellectually and technically for the private amateur player, chamber music was forced out into the public concert hall and into the hands of professional ensembles. String quartets—from the Schuppanzigh in Beethoven's day, down through the Hellmesberger in Brahms's, to those of Rosé and Kolisch in Schoenberg's (and now the Arditti and Kronos in our own)—were formed in large part to bring the music of modern composers before the concertgoing public.

From Beethoven's late quartets through the works of Brahms and Schoenberg, chamber music became a kind of refuge for the most advanced compositional techniques. In the case of Brahms, the complexity of the music and the comprehension of the public seemed still to coexist in a delicate balance. But with Schoenberg's early chamber works, a crisis point in this development was reached. In Adorno's words: "The requirements of Schoenberg's chamber music could not be reconciled any more with Hausmusik, with the ambience of domesticity. They were as explosive in content as in technique. They obliged chamber music to make its definitive move to the concert hall."[10] And as is well known, the public reaction to Schoenberg's early chamber music was mainly hostile. Dahlhaus captures the paradox: "The isolation into which Schoenberg fell is to be understood primarily as the distancing of the chamber-music composer from the chamber-music listeners, from the musically cultivated audience."[11]

II

Schoenberg's First Quartet, op. 7, and First Chamber Symphony, op. 9, were premiered within a few days of each other in Vienna, on 5 and 8 February 1907, respectively. The report filed in a local paper on 11 February by a critic identified only as "rbt" is characteristic of much of the public and critical response:

> Still more painful than the String Quartet was the Chamber Symphony for 15 solo instruments. Just think: Schoenberg and 15 solo instruments! Oh, when they are let loose! Each of them plays away frantically, with no concern for the other. Schoenberg deliberately avoids the natural consequences of individual voices coming together at a harmonic resting point. He sees it openly and earsplittingly as true counterpoint, which refrains completely from harmonic consideration, and he believes that the true harmony is that which places itself above all laws of euphony and musical logic. The new harmony instruction, which he has figured out, knows only one rule: *consonances* are to be used only in passing and then only seldom. Not one in ten listeners

can endure even for a moment compositions based on this maxim, and thus a portion of the public fled during the cacophonies of the Chamber Symphony without awaiting the end.[12]

On one level, these remarks, with their condemnation of unbridled polyphony and harsh dissonance, are just a vivid example of the kind of critical fustian heaped upon so much new music at the turn of the century. But the conjunction of the Chamber Symphony and the comments of "rbt" can also open a broader window onto cultural-intellectual aspects of the period.

In his fine article from 1977 on what he calls the *geschichtlicher Gehalt*, the historical content, of the Chamber Symphony, Brinkmann has suggested that the polyphonic density that disturbed listeners and critics is representative of the crisis of subjectivity felt throughout Austro-German culture around 1900.[13] Many leading artists and intellectuals felt it was no longer easy, or even possible, to perceive (and thus project) a comfortable or reassuring unity in the world around them. Brinkmann persuasively adduces passages from two of the best-known Viennese writers of the period, Hermann Bahr and Hugo von Hofmannsthal. Bahr, who always had his finger on the pulse of his age, saw contemporary literature dissolving by 1891 into the communication of "sensation, nothing but sensation, unconnected and momentary imprints on the nerves of rapidly occurring events."[14] Hofmannsthal, in the famous *Lord Chandos Letter* of 1902, describes the fragmentation of thought and language that became known at the turn of the century as the *Sprachkrise*. The implied author of the letter confesses that he can no longer engage in creative writing: "I have utterly lost my ability to think or speak coherently about anything at all." He describes how he came to this point, how the world around him crumbled perceptually: "Everything fell into fragments for me, the fragments into further fragments, until it seemed impossible to contain anything at all within a single concept."[15]

For both Bahr and Hofmannsthal, experience and art are characterized by a lack of coherence and continuity. They share with other writers of the *Jahrhundertwende* a strong sense of isolation and individualism.[16] Brinkmann sees these attitudes and circumstances trickling down to Schoenberg's Chamber Symphony:

> The historical position of the First Chamber Symphony is evident in the renunciation of an epic worldview and in the withdrawal into the subject. The artistic subject of this symphony no longer sees itself in the position to experience reality as a unity, to perceive its broad outline, and to transcend it. Rather, the subject seeks to preserve its identity exclusively through an extreme submersion in the self, through the location of the source of artistic production solely in the isolated subject.[17]

The sonic manifestation of this subjectivity is, for Brinkmann, precisely the intense profiling of the individual voices in the Chamber Symphony that "rbt" identified.

One might argue that the analogy of polyphony and subjectivity is too simple, too essentialist. What about the dense counterpoint and independence of voices in the music of J. S. Bach? Are these technical features necessarily reflective of an *Identitätskrise* in eighteenth-century Saxony? Caution is always necessary when relationships between notes and people are being proposed. Yet there can be little question that both "rbt" and Brinkmann are onto something: there *is* an air of crisis and urgency about Schoenberg's Chamber Symphony, however we may wish to define it.

Another name has often been attached to the musical traits identified by "rbt" and Brinkmann: expressionist, which we normally take to mean a style prevalent in the arts primarily in Germany and Austria in the two decades after 1900, and in which an individual artist's expression and representation of some "inner necessity" (Kandinsky's term, also taken up by Schoenberg) takes precedence over traditional formal-structural considerations. Brinkmann suggests that "if any work in the realm of music should be called expressionistic, it is this Chamber Symphony, op. 9, by Arnold Schoenberg."[18]

This view has intriguing consequences for traditional music historiography. In standard accounts, the Chamber Symphony is seen as part of a group of works by Schoenberg (and other early-twentieth-century composers) that retain strong ties to late-Romantic forms and styles, especially those of Liszt and Strauss. It is Schoenberg's atonal works of 1908–1909— the Three Piano Pieces, op. 11; the Five Orchestral Pieces, op. 16; and especially the monodrama *Erwartung*, op. 17—that are normally considered the "classic" expressionist compositions, in which outward form is (or seems) completely determined by the content. Identifying the Chamber Symphony of 1906 as "expressionist," a position not without merit, can cast a rather different light on music at the turn of the century. Above all, what the attachment of such a label reveals is that our conventional historical-stylistic categories for music around 1900 (as for many other musics) are largely arbitrary, and they are inadequate to the task of representing the powerful crosscurrents that constituted musical "reality" at the time.[19]

There is a further perspective on the Chamber Symphony that construes its subjectivity in a much less extreme or drastic fashion than does Brinkmann or "rbt." This viewpoint emerges from a remarkable review published by Elsa Bienenfeld on 12 February 1907 in the *Neues Wiener Journal*. Bienenfeld, a musicology student of Guido Adler, taught music history at the same Schwarzwald School in Vienna where Schoenberg had given lessons in harmony and counterpoint in 1903. Bienenfeld's reviews of Schoenberg's works from this period are consistently the most balanced and thoughtful. Unlike most critics, who are a priori hostile, she starts from the belief that Schoenberg's works are serious, expressive contributions to a tradition. In her review, which covers both the Chamber Symphony and First Quartet and merits quotation at length, she grapples with the relationship between these works and the past:

> The gap that separates Schoenberg from his forebears consists not in the content of what he is representing. Sorrow, repentance, longing remain always the same emotions and will always constitute the problems of art. Rather, the distinction lies in their outward form, in the possibility of their representation. Longing for peace can be incorporated in poetry such that only the charm of valleys, only the loveliness of a gentle evening is depicted: Eichendorff's poetry or the style of Mörike. Others, though, in ways that neither elevate nor diminish the value of their work, are obliged to represent the struggle and the conflicting ecstasies that precede peace and have it as their goal. He who loves Goethe, he who reads Knut Hamsun, will long since have recognized that. But there is still a third possibility open: to represent feelings in persons each of whom has different character traits yet all of whom experience equally sorrow that is unfortunate, different, but for each inevitable. Each [sorrow] is itself both goal and necessity; and only he who sees all the characters at once will perceive a harmony that gives all these passionate figures a common middle point and a common compassion. This is the manner of representation that Dostoyevsky, living in a more confused emotional state, employed in order to convey the single essential and sublime aspect of his ideas out of the multiplicity of characters and the momentary quality of situations. Schoenberg, working in a different art, with other means, seems to me to want to attain the same thing. Whether the public wants to grant him the achievement of this goal remains up to the pleasure of each individual listener.[20]

Like her contemporaries Bahr and Hofmannsthal, Bienenfeld seems to acknowledge a crisis of subjectivity in her culture, or at least within the culture that art represents. But for her the crisis is able to be overcome, and indeed is so in Schoenberg's works. It is striking that Bienenfeld compares Schoenberg with a novelist like Dostoyevsky or Goethe, who must manipulate many different characters. For Bienenfeld, the extreme subjectivity of Schoenberg's piece, as represented by the different "characters," must be perceived as a collective whole in order to be understood properly.

What is also interesting about Bienenfeld's remarks is that they present the Chamber Symphony as an essentially Romantic work, one in the tradition of the great novelists. For her, the piece occupies an expressive sphere in which reconciliation and closure are real possibilities. For Brinkmann and the critic "rbt," as we have seen, the Chamber Symphony inhabits a very different world, where no such transcendence or unity is achievable.

III

Still another historical-critical perspective on the Chamber Symphony is that offered by Adorno in his 1955 essay on Schoenberg in *Prisms*. This passage, to my mind the most stimulating (but also the most difficult) written on the piece, merits citation and consideration at some length:

> Yet the compulsion to purge music of everything preconceived leads not only to new sounds like the famous fourth chords, but also to a new expressive dimension beyond the depiction of human emotions. One conductor has felicitously compared the area of resolution at the end of the big development section to a glacier landscape. For the first time a break is made in the Chamber Symphony with what had been a basic stratum of music since the age of the *basso continuo*, from the *stile rappresentativo*, from the adjustment of musical language to the significative aspect of human language. For the first time Schoenberg's warmth turns around into the extreme of coolness, whose expression consists in the absence of expression. Later he polemicized against those who demand "animal warmth" of music; his dictum, which proclaims that what music has to say can only be said through music, suggests the idea of a language unlike that of human beings. The brilliant, dynamically reserved and yet barbed quality which increases throughout the First Chamber Symphony, anticipated almost fifty years ago the later objectivity, without any preclassical gestures. Music which lets itself be driven by pure, unadulterated expression becomes irritably sensitive to everything representing a potential encroachment on this purity, to every intention to ingratiate itself with the listener as well as the listener's reciprocal effort, to identification and empathy. The logical consequence of the principle of expression includes the element of its own negation as that negative form of truth which transforms love into the power of unremitting protest.[21]

If for Bienenfeld the Chamber Symphony was essentially a Romantic work and for Brinkmann a protoexpressionist one, for Adorno it is proleptically neoclassical in its anticipation of the new "objectivity" or *Sachlichkeit* associated with Hindemith and others in the 1920s.[22] What Adorno identifies as "objective" in the Chamber Symphony is the work's brittle, almost anti-expressive quality. The path by which he arrives at this characterization is intriguing and—for this listener, at any rate—leads to real insights about op. 9.

For Adorno, expression in the Chamber Symphony is so extreme, so naked ("pure, unadulterated"), that it short-circuits (my metaphor, not his) and thus becomes transformed into its opposite, the lack of expression. This is the "coolness" he identifies, "whose expression consists in the absence of expression." As he says, summing up the dialectic or the paradox, the principle of expression contains within itself the element of its own negation. For Bienenfeld the musical language of the Chamber Symphony, like that of a nineteenth-century novel, clearly manifests the "animal warmth" that

Example 5. Arnold Schoenberg, Chamber Symphony no. 1, op. 9, mm. 355–359; 364

allowed for communication with and about human beings. But for Adorno the human element is stripped away from the language of the Chamber Symphony.

Adorno's language may be extreme, but his characterization (by way of an unnamed conductor) of the end of the development section of op. 9 as a "glacier landscape" seems particularly apt. Here the principal fourths-theme of the work is presented in a dizzying series of crisscrossing, inter-locking statements that eventually "freeze" at measure 364 into a six-part simultaneity of stacked fourths (see example 5). At the outer extremes of this chord are the pitches E and F, which as key areas have played a crucial role in the Chamber Symphony to this point. This remarkable chord, which is repeated *fff* over four measures and utterly resists being perceived tonally as related to a key, is indeed without human warmth. It is a sonority with which a listener cannot easily identify or empathize, to use Adorno's terms. The chord can be said to embody a dialectic between the tonalities of E and F that is as central to the piece as those tensions listed at the outset of this article.

IV

Although compelling, Adorno's vision of the Chamber Symphony requires some adjustment. The piece does not, of course, end on the frozen chord at the end of the development section: that sonority thaws into a series of ascending fourths, which then set the recapitulation in motion. Eventually, in an exhilarating coda, E major is confirmed as the tonic. Schoenberg probes one last time the E-F tonal dialectic that framed the frozen six-part chord. The tonalities of E and F had already been juxtaposed at the very outset of the Chamber Symphony, where a cadence to F major (measures 1 through 4) is followed by one in E major (measures 8 through 11).[23] The

Example 6. Arnold Schoenberg, Chamber Symphony no. 1, op. 9, mm. 582–584; 593

central pitches of these keys are then, as we have seen, superimposed at the climax of the development section. At the very end of the piece, Schoenberg pits the two tonalities against each other, and the conflict is now resolved decisively in favor of E, to which F or an F-major chord moves again and again (see example 6).

What these resolutions suggest is that for all its dialectical rhetoric, the Chamber Symphony is ultimately an affirmatory work; it reasserts the power of tonality to unify, organize, make coherent. In this sense Bienenfeld's interpretation of an overarching "harmony" that brings together the different "characters" is closer to the mark than either Brinkmann's or Adorno's more pessimistic interpretations, in which subjectivity prevents any *Welterfassung.* One might say that the oppositions set out above are resolved in favor of the first element: symphony, public, communal, homophonic, objective.

Schoenberg's own remarks of 1937 on the Chamber Symphony suggest that at the time of composition he very much shared the optimistic viewpoint:

> After having finished the composition of the *Kammersymphonie* . . . I believed I had now found my own personal style of composing and that all problems which had previously troubled a young composer had been solved and that a way had been shown out of the perplexities in which we young composers had been involved. . . . It was as lovely a dream as it was a disappointing illusion.[24]

These comments imply that what followed in Schoenberg's development represented a significant break. And indeed, the works of 1907–1909 differ radically in style from the Chamber Symphony.

Immediately after completing op. 9 in the summer of 1906, Schoenberg began another chamber symphony, for a slightly larger ensemble (eighteen

instruments). Progress was slow and sporadic. Although Schoenberg managed to complete most of the first movement by the fall of 1908, the Second
Chamber Symphony was to remain a fragment until 1939, when it was published (in two movements) as op. 38. The portion written in 1906–1908,
which makes up most of the first movement, is a lyrical masterpiece in an
advanced and very subtle tonal idiom.[25] But there is little engagement with
the intense dialectics of the First Chamber Symphony. Perhaps for this reason—because there was more to say about the issues raised in op. 9—the
Second Chamber Symphony failed to advance and became displaced in
Schoenberg's workshop in 1907 by the Second String Quartet, op. 10.[26]

This quartet, which was to be the last of the early series of chamber
works, revisits some of the dialectics set out in the First Chamber Symphony.
In the remarkable finale to op. 10 the pull is again between individuality
and collectivity, now cast much more specifically than in op. 9 in terms of
atonality versus tonality. The opening of the movement, in which the four
different instruments successively take up the main melody, is resolutely—
and famously—polyphonic. The linear independence then gives way after
a few minutes to the very harmonically, even triadically, conceived setting
of "*ich fühle luft von anderem planeten.*"

The individual/collective dialectic also forms the premise of the George
poem "Entrückung" that is sung in the movement: the persona floats alone,
set free from his earthly context. Yet this liberation, representing apparently
the ultimate degree of subjectivity, soon turns into its opposite, as he dis-
solves his identity into music's collectivity: "*ich löse mich in tönen.*" At the
end, in the last line, he becomes "*ein funke nur vom heiligen feuer. . . . ein
dröhnen nur der heiligen stimme*" (only a spark of the holy fire, only a roar of
the holy voice). The individual is thus completely subsumed or absorbed
by a greater force.

This paradoxical negation or reversal—liberation becoming enslave-
ment—is analogous to that posited by Adorno for the expressive (or anti-
expressive) world of the Chamber Symphony. But in the Second Quartet,
as in the Chamber Symphony, the process can be given a positive spin:
transcendence *is* possible, and in this case brings with it a sweeping, indeed
interplanetary, worldview.

It could be argued (though it is not possible to do so here) that Schoenberg never lost the goal of transcendence articulated musically in the
Chamber Symphony and the Second Quartet, that he never succumbed to
the pressures of subjectivity so prevalent in his Viennese culture (and in
his music) at the beginning of this century. Throughout numerous *Kultur-
krisen,* geographic displacements, and two world wars, he might be said to
have retained the affirmatory vision and found different ways of communicating it in his compositions for half a century.

NOTES

1. See, for example, Carl Dahlhaus, "Brahms und die Idee der Kammermusik," *Brahms-Studien* 1 (1974), 48. Of course, lieder also formed an integral part of Schoenberg's development at this time.

2. Juon's work, op. 27 in B-flat, appeared from the firm of Schlesinger.

3. Among the *Kammersinfonien* were those by Kurt Striegler (pub. 1912); Ferdinand Kollmaneck, op. 373 (pub. c. 1914); Richard Stöhr, op. 32 (c. 1920); and the better-known one by Franz Schreker (pub. 1916).

4. Reinhold Brinkmann, "Die gepresste Sinfonie: Zum geschichtlichen Gehalt von Schönbergs Opus 9," in *Gustav Mahler: Sinfonie und Wirklichkeit*, ed. Otto Kolleritsch (Graz: Universal, 1977), 133–156.

5. Paul Bekker, *Die Sinfonie von Beethoven bis Mahler* (Berlin: Schuster & Loeffler, 1918), 17, 24–25.

6. Theodor W. Adorno, *Einleitung in die Musiksoziologie* (Frankfurt am Main: Suhrkamp, 1962), 105.

7. Ibid.

8. Ibid., 97.

9. Dahlhaus, "Brahms und die Idee der Kammermusik," 47–48.

10. Adorno, *Einleitung in die Musiksoziologie,* 108.

11. Dahlhaus, "Brahms und die Idee der Kammermusik," 49.

12.

Noch schmerzhafter als das Streichquartett wirkte die "Kammersinfonie für 15 Soloinstrumente." Man denke: Schönberg und 15 Soloinstrumente! Wehe, wenn sie losgelassen. Jedes von ihnen spielt wie toll drauf los, unbekümmert um das andere. Schönberg zieht geflissentlich gar nicht die natürlichen Konsequenzen aus dem Zusammentreffen der Einzelstimmen zum harmonischen Ruhepunkt. Er hält augenscheinlich und ohrenverletztend den für den wahren Kontrapunkt, der von der harmonischen Rücksicht völlig absteht und glaubt, die wahre Harmonie wöre die, welche sich über alle Gesetze des Wohlklanges und der musikalischen Logik hinwegsetzt. Die neue Harmonielehre, die er sich zurechtgelegt hat, kennt eine einzige Regel: *Konsonanzen* dürfen bloss im Durchgang und selbst da nur selten angewendet werden. Kompositionen, welche nach dieser Maxime entstanden sind, hält vorläufig freilich noch der zehnte nicht aus, und so verliess denn schon während der Kakaphonien der "Kammersymphonie" ein Teil des Publikums fluchtartig den Saal, ohne den Schluss abzuwarten.

This review comes from a collection held at the Arnold Schoenberg Institute in Los Angeles. At this time Schoenberg subscribed to a service that clipped and sent him reviews of his works. Unfortunately, in this case the newspaper from which the review comes is not identified.

13. Brinkmann, "Die gepresste Sinfonie," esp. 146–154.

14. Cited in Brinkmann, "Die gepresste Sinfonie," 149.

15. Hugo von Hofmannsthal, *The Lord Chandos Letter,* trans. Russell Stockman (Marlboro, Vt.: Marlboro Press, 1986), 19, 21. A portion of this work is cited in German in Brinkmann, "Die gepresste Sinfonie," 149.

16. For a useful anthology of, and introduction to, turn-of-the-century thought

in Austria and Germany, see *Literarische Manifeste der Jahrhundertwende, 1890–1910,*
ed. Erich Ruprecht and Dieter Bänsch (Stuttgart: Metzler, 1970).

17.

> In der Absage an epische Welterfassung und in der Zurücknahme ins Subjekt ist der
> geschichtliche Ort der 1. Kammersinfonie deutlich. Das künstlerische Subjekt dieser
> Sinfonie sieht sich nicht mehr in der Lage, die Wirklichkeit als Einheit zu erfahren und
> sie in einem grossen Entwurf zu umfassen und zu transzendieren, sondern allein aus
> extremer Versenkung ins Ich, in der Fundierung der künstlerischen Produktion allein
> vom isolierten Subjekt her, versucht es, seine Identität zu bewahren.
>
> Brinkmann, "Die gepresste Sinfonie," 148.

18. Brinkmann, "Die gepresste Sinfonie," 146. For an elaboration of these ideas,
see also Reinhold Brinkmann, "Schönberg und das expressionistische Ausdruckskonzept," in *Bericht über den 1. Kongress der Internationalen Schönberg-Gesellschaft,* ed. Rudolf Stephan (Vienna: Lafite, 1978), 15–16. A useful recent survey of
the phenomenon of expressionism in music is John and Dorothy Crawford, *Expressionism in Twentieth-Century Music* (Bloomington: Indiana University Press, 1993).

19. The term *musical reality* is used, and pondered, with reference to this period
by Carl Dahlhaus in *Nineteenth-Century Music,* trans. J. Bradford Robinson (Berkeley
and Los Angeles: University of California Press, 1989), 381–382.

20.

> Die Kluft, die Schönberg von seinen Vorgängern trennt, liegt nicht im Inhalt des
> Dargestellten—die Trauer, die Reue, die Sehnsucht bleiben immer dieselben Gefühle
> und immer die Probleme der Kunst—, sondern nur in ihrer Gestaltung, der Möglich-
> keit ihrer Darstellung. Die Sehnsucht nach Frieden kann in der Poesie so verkörpert
> werden dass nur die Anmut der Täler, nur die Lieblichkeit des sanften Abends gebildet
> wird: Eichendorffs Gedichte oder der Stil Mörikes. Andere freilich, ohne dass dadurch
> der Wert des Werkes erhöht oder verringert würde, sind genötigt, den Kampf darzustel-
> len und die sich bekämpfenden Ekstasen, die dem Frieden vorausgehen und ihn als
> ihr Ziel haben. Wer Goethe, wer Knut Hamsun liebt, wird dies längst erkannt haben.
> Aber noch ist eine dritte Möglichkeit offen: die Gefühle in Personen darzustellen, die,
> jede von andern Charakteranlagen, doch alle gleich unglücklich, verschiedene, aber
> für jeden notwendige Leiden erleben, so dass jeder sich selbst Zweck und Notwen-
> digkeit ist; und nur wer alle Personen zugleich betrachtet, begreift eine Harmonie die
> allen diesen leidenschaftlichen Gestalten einen gemeinsamen Mittelpunkt gibt und ein
> gemeinsames Mitleid erweckt. Dies ist die Art der Darstellung, die Dostojewski, in
> einem verwirrteren Seelenzustande lebend, anwandte, um das Eine Wesentliche und
> Erhabene seiner Ideen aus dem Vielen der Charaktere und dem Augenblicklichen der
> Situationen darzustellen. Dasselbe scheint mir Schönberg, in einer anderen Kunst
> wirkend, durch andere Mittel, erreichen zu wollen. Ob ihm das Publikum die Er-
> reichung dieses Zieles zuerkennen will, das steht in jedes einzelnen Hörers Gefallen.
>
> Elsa Bienenfeld, *Neues Wiener Journal,* 12 February 1907.

21. The translation is adapted (with tacit corrections of small mistranslations)
from Adorno, "Arnold Schoenberg," 158–159. The original:

> Der Zwang jedoch, Musik vom Vorgedachten zu reinigen, führt nicht nur auf neue
> Klänge wie die berühmten Quartenakkorde, sondern auch auf eine neue, der Ab-
> bildung menschlicher Gefühle entrückte Ausdrucksssphäre. Ein Dirigent hat das
> Auflösungsfeld am Ende der grossen Durchführung mit Glück einer Gletscherland-

schaft verglichen. Die Kammersymphonie sagt sich zum erstenmal von einer Grund-schicht der Musik seit dem Generalbasszeitalter los, dem stile rappresentativo, der An-passung der musikalischen Sprache an die meinende der Menschen. Zum erstenmal schlägt die Schönbergsche Wärme ins Extrem einer Kälte um, deren Ausdruck das Aus-druckslose ist. Später hat er polemisch gegen die sich verwandt, die von der Musik "animalische Wärme" verlangen; sein Diktum, dass Musik ein nur durch Musik zu Sagendes sage, entwirft die Idee einer Sprache, die der der Menschen nicht gleicht. Das Helle, beweglich Spröde und gleichsam Stachliche, ein Charakter, der sich im Fortgang der ersten Kammersymphonie verstärkt, antizipiert vor fast fünfzig Jahren die spätere Sachlichkeit ohne alle vorklassische Gebärde. Musik, die sich treiben lässt von der reinen und unverstellten Expression, wird gereizt empfindlich gegen alles, was diese Reinheit antasten könnte, gegen jegliche Anbiederung an den Hörer wie jegliche des Hörers an sie, gegen Identifikation und Einfühlung. In der Konsequenz des Express-ionsprinzips selbst liegt auch das Moment von dessen Verneinung als jene negative Form der Wahrheit, welche die Liebe in die Kraft des unbeirrten Protests versetzt.

Adorno, Prismen, 194–195.

22. German *neue Sachlichkeit* and Stravinskian neoclassicism, while not identical, share many traits, including the revival of baroque and classical forms and tech-niques, and the stripping away of what was deemed Romantic excess. Stravinsky's comment of 1924 on his Octet is characteristic: "My *Octuor* is not an 'emotive' work but a musical composition based on objective elements which are sufficient in them-selves." This remark is cited in Richard Taruskin, "Back to Whom? Neoclassicism as Ideology," *19th Century Music* 16 (1993), 287. Taruskin's review-essay presents a helpful discussion of many issues (especially the political ones) surrounding neo-classicism and *neue Sachlichkeit.*

23. For a fuller explication of the E-F conflict and its working out in op. 9, see Walter Frisch, *The Early Works of Arnold Schoenberg, 1893–1908* (Berkeley and Los Angeles: University of California Press, 1993), 236–246. A recent study of the Chamber Symphony, which came to my attention too late to be included in my essay, is Claus-Steffen Mahnkopf, *Gestalt und Stil: Arnold Schönbergs Erste Kammersym-phonie und ihr Umfeld* (Kassel: Bärenreiter, 1994).

24. Arnold Schoenberg, "How One Becomes Lonely," *Style and Idea,* 49.

25. For an analysis, see Frisch, *Early Works of Arnold Schoenberg,* 251–258.

26. For a chronology of the intertwined geneses of the Second Chamber Sym-phony and the Second String Quartet, see Frisch, *Early Works of Arnold Schoenberg,* 248–251.

SEVEN

Whose Idea Was *Erwartung?*

Bryan R. Simms

Schoenberg's *Erwartung* is a paradigm of modernism. Its conception, both of musical language and of dramatic form, has no direct or immediate antecedent. Its text anticipates by several years the style of German expressionist drama, and its music is experimental to a degree that Schoenberg never surpassed. Yet despite an originality that has long attracted the attention of specialists in twentieth-century music, *Erwartung* continues to guard its secrets. One of these prompts the title of this article. Did the dramatic content of *Erwartung* originate with Schoenberg, which he then asked Marie Pappenheim to flesh out? Or was Pappenheim responsible for the libretto's initial concept as well as its execution? These questions presuppose others. Is there one essential idea underlying the work, and did the librettist and composer proceed from a common starting point? And, finally, does Schoenberg's music conform to the objectives of Pappenheim's text, or does it carry the listener along a fundamentally different path?

Schoenberg believed that the basic idea for the opera was his. Shortly after beginning to compose the music on 27 August 1909 he wrote to Ferruccio Busoni:

> I have started on a new composition; something for the theater; something quite new. The librettist (a lady), acting on my suggestions, has conceived and formulated everything just as I envisaged it. More news shortly; for at present I am head over heels in work and hope to be finished in 14 days.[1]

Schoenberg's view of the origins of the opera was transmitted by Egon Wellesz in his 1921 biography of the composer, and it has been accepted by most later writers. What is known about the temporary rupture in Schoenberg's marriage and the circumstances leading to the suicide of Richard Gerstl—events that transpired shortly before the opera was written—seems to support the assumption that the tale of infidelity and violent death was based on an outline that originated with the composer and reflected his own experiences and innermost feelings. Also identifying Schoenberg with the text is the line near the end of *Erwartung* that reads "tausend Menschen ziehen vorüber"; this is virtually identical to the first line of John Henry Mackay's poem "Am Wegrand," which Schoenberg had set to music in 1905 and later included in his Eight Songs, op. 6.

But Marie Pappenheim told a very different story about the origins of the opera. In an interview with Dika Newlin in 1951 she flatly denied having received any suggestions regarding the opera's subject or content,[2] and she reiterated this in a letter to Helmut Kirchmeyer in 1963, three years before her death:

> I received neither directions nor hints about what I should write (I would not have accepted them anyway). When Zemlinsky or Schoenberg spoke about libretti, it was about Schreker's, about *Pelléas et Mélisande*, etc.[3]

Before addressing the contradictions between these two accounts, it will be useful to review the history of the work. *Erwartung* was composed during Schoenberg's vacation retreat in Steinakirchen, in lower Austria, during the summer of 1909, when the composer joined Alexander Zemlinsky, Erwin Stein, Marie Pappenheim, and others for a customary summer period of work, discussion, and relaxation. It was a productive time, for in addition to composing all of *Erwartung* Schoenberg completed the Five Orchestra Pieces, op. 16, and the last of the Three Piano Pieces, op. 11. Pappenheim, an acquaintance and possibly distant relative of the Zemlinskys, joined the gathering in Steinakirchen after completing her medical studies at the University of Vienna in June.[4] Although her arrival in Steinakirchen marked her first meeting with Schoenberg, she may already have been known to him by reputation, since four of her poems had been published in 1906 in Karl Kraus's journal *Die Fackel.*[5]

Pappenheim told Kirchmeyer in 1963 that Schoenberg asked her to write an opera text for him. She had agreed and then left to visit other friends in Traunkirchen, where within three weeks she drafted a "lyric poem" for what she termed a monodrama. Fully anticipating that Schoenberg would demand many changes, she was surprised to find that he asked for very few revisions and had indeed begun to compose the music virtually upon receipt of the first draft. Apparently there was no further personal contact between them before Schoenberg completed the score on 12 September 1909.[6]

Pappenheim's previous literary efforts were closely related to her profession as a physician. In two of the poems published in *Die Fackel,* "Seziersaal" and "Prima graviditas," she wrote from the perspective of a clinician who probes the emotional as well as the physical constitution of her patients. In

"Seziersaal" (autopsy room), the lifeless features of a corpse still betray emotions, which the narrator sympathetically describes:

> His mouth is pale and his eyes weary,
> as one who stares nightly into the darkness.
>
> . . . .
> How sadly his desire wafts about me,
> so much that my own heart betrays its torture.[7]

In "Prima graviditas," too, the subject is the emotions, now associated with pregnancy. In these poems a clinical or pathological condition stimulates an outburst of feelings both from the patient and from the observer, a point of view to which Pappenheim would return in *Erwartung*.

Pappenheim later specialized in dermatology, but like her intellectual and artistic Viennese contemporaries she was aware of the emerging study of psychoanalysis.[8] The writings of Sigmund Freud and his associates projected a scientific model for a deeper understanding of the workings not only of the mind but also of the emotions, a special interest of Pappenheim's. She had yet another reason to be interested in psychology: her kinswoman Bertha Pappenheim, who had suffered from hysteria in the 1880s, was the subject of the first celebrated case history of psychoanalysis.[9] Bertha's physician, Josef Breuer, gave her the pseudonym "Anna O." in the 1895 *Studien über Hysterie*, which he wrote in collaboration with Sigmund Freud.[10]

According to Breuer and Freud, hysteria can result when an individual responds to a traumatic event by channeling its memory into the unconscious mind. The trauma can persist in the form of physical ailments— among them amnesia, hallucinations, and disorders of vision and speech— for which there is no pathological basis. In the case of Anna O., hysteria was brought on by the illness and subsequent death of her father. Her symptoms were especially severe and, in addition to anorexia and paralysis of the limbs, included hallucinatory visions of snakes, periodic loss of recent memory, and a speech defect. Breuer's treatment was ingenious. During periods of self-induced hypnosis—states that Breuer termed *conditions secondes*—he led her through a "talking cure." She was coaxed to relive the painful memories and emotions associated with her father's death, thus exposing them to her rational mind, where they could be coped with, dispelled, or worn away. Following this cathartic process her abnormal symptoms disappeared.

The Woman in *Erwartung* exhibits classical symptoms of hysteria as they were defined by Breuer and Freud in the *Studien über Hysterie*. Her ailments stem from the loss of her beloved to another woman, a disturbance all the more unbalancing because she had become totally dependent upon him. In a jealous rage she murders him in the vicinity of the house of her rival.

Like Anna O. she thereupon experiences amnesia, partially banishing the murder from her conscious mind while beset at the same time by a speech impediment and hallucinations involving imaginary slithering or crawling animal forms.

The Woman's wistful recollections of her lover indicate that her hysteria is also associated with a frustrated sexual relationship. In this Pappenheim followed Freud's distinctive analysis of the disease rather than Breuer's. Breuer had determined that Bertha Pappenheim's hysteria had no sexual origin; according to him "sexuality was astonishingly undeveloped in her."[11] But for Freud hysteria almost always stemmed from sexual causes; in the *Studien* he wrote: "In so far as one can speak of determining causes which lead to the *acquisition* of neuroses, their aetiology is to be looked for in *sexual* factors."[12]

The clinical model that underlies *Erwartung* would have been plain to the many readers of the *Studien über Hysterie* around the year 1909. But Pappenheim's underlying message in *Erwartung* goes beyond scientific models or case studies of neurotic disease. Eva Weissweiler has argued persuasively that Pappenheim's *Erwartung* is essentially an attack upon the Viennese upper class, of which she sees the Woman as representative.[13] According to this interpretation, the crucial message in Pappenheim's text is to be found not in the details of the Woman's hysteria or in her jumbled emotions but in the circumstances that led to the acquisition of her symptoms. And here Breuer's analysis is again influential.

Breuer concluded his study of Anna O. by speculating that her hysteria resulted ultimately from her upbringing, one typical of upper-class Viennese girls. She had been assiduously protected from life, kept in a monotonous, sheltered family routine. But her intellect and curiosity about the world could not be suppressed, and her only outlet was through daydreaming, which became a regular and prolonged habit with her. This daydreaming, according to Breuer, began to dissociate her conscious from her unconscious faculties, inviting traumatic events and emotions in her life to be repressed into the unconscious.

Susceptibility to neurosis is the central subtext in Pappenheim's libretto. The Woman's predisposition to hysteria, Pappenheim tells us through the Woman's words, was caused by an excessive reliance upon her partner, by having yielded her independence: "My one and only love. . . . How much, oh how much I loved you. . . . What am I to do here alone? . . . My boundary was where you were. . . . I lived isolated from everything. . . . All I knew was you."[14]

It is very unlikely that Schoenberg interpreted the text of *Erwartung* as Pappenheim had intended, as a realistic study of hysteria with feminist overtones. Instead his own reading of the poem focused directly on the jumble of emotions that the Woman experiences. In his comments on the opera

Schoenberg stated explicitly that the subject of *Erwartung* was the emotions in a heightened state of intensity. His viewpoint was first made public in a 1920 article by Egon Wellesz, who no doubt drew on information received from the composer when he wrote:

> The poem of the monodrama *Erwartung* sets out to give a dramatic portrayal of the problem of what transpires in a person in a moment of greatest tension and intensity of feeling. Marie Pappenheim, to whom Schoenberg communicated this idea, attempted to solve the problem in such a way as to disperse the tension throughout a succession of scenes.[15]

Schoenberg restated this interpretation himself in a marginal annotation to a 1924 review by Paul Bekker, in which Bekker postulated a close relationship between *Erwartung* and Wagner's operas, especially their concluding love scenes. Common to all, Bekker had written, is

> the idea of a music of womankind, of sounds representing erotic feelings, of a music that forces its way out of the conscious over into the unconscious, of a music of liberation, transfiguration, and redemption.[16]

In his copy of Bekker's review Schoenberg dismissed this interpretation:

> Not at all. It [the opera] is, as I have often explained, the slow representation of things that go through the mind in a moment of great anxiety. What does *Erwartung* have to do with redemption? The Woman may have been wrong in her fearful states of mind, or not (this is not clear, but, all the same, these are only fearful imaginings and they become manifest). She is not at all redeemed by them.[17]

Schoenberg asserts, in other words, that the basic subject of the opera is the nature of an individual's mental condition when the emotions are heightened, in this case by fear. Whereas the physician Pappenheim was concerned with the Woman in *Erwartung* as an individual, a "patient" whose tortured emotions are symptoms of an illness she could have avoided by taking possession of her emotional life, the musician Schoenberg dealt in *Erwartung* with the emotions per se; for him, the Woman's individuality and psychology were secondary, even arbitrary.

Schoenberg's intention to paint an operatic portrait of the emotions rather than to create a work with psychological or sociological implications is apparent in the changes that he made in Pappenheim's original text.[18] Relatively few in number, they are limited almost entirely to deletions. But in addition to deleting minor redundancies and references to sounds, Schoenberg made a significant change in Pappenheim's text by deleting the disjointed references that the Woman makes to the murder of her beloved. In one passage, for instance, the Woman, lying beside the corpse, in the original version utters these lines, all subsequently removed by the composer:

> What are they [your eyes] staring at in the trees . . . The moon is consumed, as from horror . . . open as though crying for help . . . What have they done to you . . . Oh you . . . you . . . I wasn't here . . . The evening was so peaceful . . . The leaves trembling against the sky . . . your hair is bloody . . . your soft brown hair . . . And blood on my hands . . . and blood on the ground . . . Who did this . . . Who did this to you? . . . You are the only thing here, you must know . . . You spiteful face of stone . . . How your lips are pressed together . . . Don't you smirk . . . The shadowy hollows . . . the den of thieves . . . Here he backed against the tree trunk . . . And then the shot . . . [19]

In this passage Pappenheim reveals clearly enough that the Woman murdered her beloved, although she blurts out memories of the crime in a disjointed manner amid denials and a tangle of other memories and conflicting emotions. Schoenberg's elimination of the passage, so crucial for the coherence of Pappenheim's narrative, indicates that he did not wish the poem to be construed as a realistic or objective study but instead as a hallucination. "The whole drama *can* be understood as a nightmare," Schoenberg remarked later.[20] Pappenheim was of course well aware that such deletions changed the emphasis of her text, and she later confided to Kirchmeyer:

> One of these changes was for a long time very disagreeable to me—namely, deletions in the scene where she sees the dead body. With these deletions, which I have long forgotten, the mystical or, as it were, the hallucinatory quality became strengthened, while I was by no means sure that it was not a realistic occurrence. But perhaps the change made the overall effect more powerful after all.[21]

Schoenberg's focus in *Erwartung* upon the emotions is symptomatic of his broader interest in the human psyche as the source of artistic creativity and of his own atonal musical language. His writings from 1909 and 1910 return repeatedly to the role of intuition and unconscious mental activity in the creative process. In a letter to Ferruccio Busoni, written only days before beginning to compose *Erwartung*, Schoenberg spoke of emotions as the gateway to the unconscious mind and the very basis of expressivity in his new music:

> And the [musical] results I wish for:
> no stylized and sterile protracted emotion.
> People are not like that:
> it is *impossible* for a person to have only *one* sensation at a time.
> One has *thousands* simultaneously. And these thousands can no more readily be added together than an apple and a pear. They go their own ways.

And this variegation, this multifariousness, this *illogicality* which our senses demonstrate, the illogicality presented by their interactions, set forth by some mounting rush of blood, by some reaction of the senses or the nerves, this I should like to have in my music.

It should be an expression of feeling, as our feelings, which bring us in contact with our unconscious, really are, and no false child of feelings and "conscious logic."[22]

Despite Schoenberg's use of concepts that were shared with psychoanalysis, his understanding of emotions and their role in the psyche is only partly true to Freudian theory. Freud and Breuer had described the unconscious as a turbulent realm of painful, repressed memories and emotions that spoke to an individual through dreams and neurotic symptoms. But for Schoenberg it was the source of creativity, communicating to an artist through emotion and instinct rather than reason: "It is only unconscious creative strength that has creative power," he wrote to Busoni.[23]

Schoenberg was closer to the Freudian model in his statements concerning the compulsive nature of artistic instincts. A great composer, he believed, was compulsively driven to adopt a certain musical language. "The artist *must*," he wrote in 1911 in "Problems in Teaching Art." "He has no say in the matter, it is nothing to do with what he wants."[24] This often repeated statement seems to suggest Schoenberg's belief in a predetermined mode of development for music, a course through which music must progress. But in light of his statements about the origins of creativity in the unconscious mind, his dictum takes on an entirely different meaning. If music must express the feelings and thus "bring us in contact with our unconscious" rather than with our rational faculties, then the artist can no more control the musical outcome than the hysterical patient can control the symptoms of her ailment.

Schoenberg's theory of emotions that erupt incoherently and irrationally from the unconscious mind and provoke a composer's work must surely have been discussed at the gathering in Steinakirchen in 1909, and in all likelihood it is at the heart of what he thought he had communicated to Pappenheim at that time. Schoenberg had good reason to assume that Pappenheim had taken his meaning; after all, the emotions of the Woman in *Erwartung* conform exactly to Schoenberg's prescription for what the feelings "really are": irrational, highly divergent, and jumbled one upon the other. Schoenberg's theory of emotion is also a key to understanding the highly experimental musical language of *Erwartung*, which deviates so strikingly from his music prior to 1909. The opera was composed rapidly, with virtually no sketching, no conventional motivic work, and no use of traditional formal archetypes. It is concise, free in expression, and highly diversified in its motivic content—indeed, an embodiment of just those qualities that he told Busoni he wanted in his music.

Schoenberg's study of the emotions in *Erwartung* is carried to a more universal level by its conjunction with its companion work, *Die glückliche Hand*. Although he never insisted that the two one-act operas be performed as a pair, he conceived of them as such and hoped to see them staged together: "It is my burning desire to have [*Die glückliche Hand*] performed with the monodrama," he wrote to Albertine Zehme.[25]

Schoenberg began to conceive *Die glückliche Hand* even before the monodrama was completed. In an undated letter from Pappenheim to Schoenberg, probably written in early September 1909, in which Pappenheim asks about revisions, she also self-effacingly comments upon the second opera:

> In Vienna it is rumored that you are writing an opera with Kokoschka. Maybe he would have been better after all. I don't like my monodrama much.[26]

She must have been more than a touch bemused to hear that the companion opera to *Erwartung* might use a text by Kokoschka, in whose writings female characters were often drawn as distorted types. In his play *Mörder, Hoffnung der Frauen*, for example, which had been performed publicly in Vienna in July 1909, women are violent, sex-crazed warriors who plunge into a life-and-death battle with any men who happen by. Although his collaboration with Kokoschka never came to pass, Schoenberg's own text for *Die glückliche Hand* was decisively influenced by Kokoschka's use of gender types as dramatic symbols.

The Man in *Die glückliche Hand* symbolizes the creative individual, whose other attributes include generosity, naïveté, and persistence in the face of mundane failure and the antagonism of society. The Woman is his opposite: she possesses no trace of intellect or creativity, and she is also faithless, weak, and cunning. Her character is derived from the unflattering female image that was common in such turn-of-the-century German literature as Otto Weininger's *Geschlecht und Charakter* and writings by Frank Wedekind, Karl Kraus, and August Strindberg, all of which Schoenberg admired.

But *Die glückliche Hand* is ultimately a drama about the Man alone: the other characters are mere projections and personifications of his inner aspirations and destiny. This is the interpretation Erwin Stein expressed in a 1928 article whose content was probably received directly from the composer, in which Stein asserts that all the constituent elements of the opera—text, music, and staging—contribute directly to an "inner experience" that embodies the idea of the work. "And this experience," he concludes, "is precisely the experience of a single person, the Man. It is his drama, which is projected outward by the staging."[27]

Die glückliche Hand forms the complement to *Erwartung*. One is the opera of a man whose nature it is to be creative; the other is the opera of a woman who suffers from an emotional condition then thought common among women. Given Schoenberg's view of emotion and creativity as both opposites and complementary, it is not surprising that he should have turned to a significantly contrasting musical language for his second opera. The music of *Die glückliche Hand* represents a far more structured and systematic approach to composition than is evident in *Erwartung*. *Die glückliche Hand* contains examples of themes shaped according to classical forms, motivic and sectional recurrences, counterpoint, and regular rhythm and meter, all formulated through extensive sketching.[28] The image of a systematically composed music reinforces and symbolizes the drama of the creative man, just as a music that rises "in a stream of unconscious sensations"—Schoenberg's description to Busoni of his music at the time of *Erwartung*—symbolizes the drama of emotions beyond rational control.

Following *Die glückliche Hand* Schoenberg did not return to a music of the emotions as it existed in *Erwartung*. His future direction was steadily on the path of an ever more systematic approach to composition, a course that led him eventually to the twelve-tone method. *Erwartung* and *Die glückliche Hand* were destined to stand on opposite sides of a peak in his lifelong quest for new musical resources. On one side the peak was approached through ever greater freedom from existing formal principles; on the other side was a return to a classical conception of music reformulated for the twentieth century.

NOTES

1. Schoenberg to Busoni, n.d., *Busoni Letters,* 398–399, esp. 399.

2. Dika Newlin, *Bruckner, Mahler, Schoenberg,* rev. ed. (New York: W. W. Norton & Company, 1978), 239 n.

3.

> Ich bekam weder einen Hinweis noch eine Angabe was ich schreiben sollte (hätte ihn auch nicht angenommen). Wenn bei Zeml. oder Schönberg von Texten geredet wurde, sprach man von Schreker, von "Pelleas und Melisande" etc.

Pappenheim's letter to Kirchmeyer is reprinted in Peter Naumann, "Untersuchungen zum Ton-Wort Verhältnis in den Einaktern Arnold Schönbergs" (Ph.D. diss., University of Cologne, 1988), 2:1–7, esp. 3. Unless otherwise noted, all translations are by the author.

4. See Diane Hollaway Penney, "Schoenberg's Janus-Work *Erwartung:* Its Musico-Dramatic Structure and Relationship to the Melodrama and Lied Traditions" (Ph.D. diss., University of North Texas, 1989), 62.

5. "Seziersaal," "Trennung," "Vor dem Konzert," and "Prima graviditas" were published under Pappenheim's pseudonym Marie Heim in *Die Fackel,* no. 202 (30 April 1906), 23–25.

6. In her letter to Kirchmeyer, Pappenheim wrote:

> I . . . thought that Schönberg would read it, change it, make suggestions (I didn't know him very well at that time). Then I never got the manuscript back at all, Schönberg just

told me which things he was going to change. . . . He seemed to want to compose it at the same "white heat" in which I had written it.

(Ich . . . glaubte, Schönberg werde es lesen, ändern, Vorschläge machen (ich kannte ihn damals noch nicht sehr gut). Dann bekam ich das Manuskript überhaupt nicht mehr zurück, Schông sagte mir nur, was er ändern wolle. . . . Er schien es eben so "rasendschnell" komponieren zu wollen wie ich es geschrieben.)

Naumann, "Ton-Wort Verhältnis," 2:1–2.

7.

Sein Mund ist bleich und seine Augen müd',
Wie einem, der des Nachts ins Dunkel sieht.

. . . .

Wie traurig sein Verlangen mich umweht,
Dass mein gequältes Herz sich selbst verrt.

"Seziersaal," Die Fackel,
no. 202 (30 April 1906), 23.

8. See Michael Worbs, *Nervenkunst: Literatur und Psychoanalyse im Wien der Jahrhundertwende* (Frankfurt am Main: Europäische Verlagsanstalt, 1983); and Lewis Wickes, "Schoenberg, *Erwartung,* and the Reception of Psychoanalysis in Musical Circles in Vienna until 1910/1911," *Studies in Music* 23 (1989), 88–106.

9. Concerning the kinship between Bertha and Marie Pappenheim, see Penney, "Schoenberg's Janus-Work *Erwartung,*" 94.

10. Josef Breuer, "Case 1: Fräulein Anna O.," in Josef Breuer and Sigmund Freud, *Studies in Hysteria,* trans. James Strachey et al., in vol. 2 of *The Standard Edition of the Complete Psychological Works of Sigmund Freud* (London: Hogarth Press, Institute of Psycho-Analysis, 1955), 21–47. A second edition of the *Studien über Hysterie* appeared in 1909.

11. Breuer, "Fräulein Anna O.," 21.

12. Sigmund Freud, "The Psychotherapy of Hysteria," in Breuer and Freud, *Studies in Hysteria,* 257.

13. Eva Weissweiler, " 'Schreiben Sie mir doch einen Operntext, Fräulein,' " *Neue Zeitschrift für Musik* 145 (1984), 4–8.

14.

Mein einzig Geliebter. . . . Wie lieb, wie lieb ich dich gehabt hab'. . . . Was soll ich allein hier tun? . . . Meine Grenze war der Ort, an dem du warst. . . . Allen Dingen ferne lebte ich. . . . Ich wusste nichts als dich.

As Weissweiler has observed, Pappenheim returned to the theme of women's social and psychological independence in later works, especially in her novel *Der graue Mann* (1949). Here a woman achieves a productive and fulfilling existence only after asserting her independence from a husband who is all too insensitive to her needs and abilities.

15.

Die Dichtung des Monodrams "Erwartung" setzt sich das Problem, dramatisch darzustellen, was in einem Moment höchster Spannung und Intensität der Empfindung in einem Mensch vorgeht. Marie Pappenheim, der Schönberg diese Idee mitteilte, hat das

Problem dergestalt zu lösen versucht, daßß die Spannung in einer Folge von Szenen auflöst.

> Egon Wellesz, "Arnold Schönbergs Bühnenwerke,"
> *Anbruch* 2/18 (November 1920), 604–608, esp. 604.

16.

[Es] ist die Idee der Musik des Weibes, des erotischen Gefühlslautes, der Musik, die aus dem Bewussten hinüber drängt zum Unbewussten, der Musik als Befreiung, Verklärung, Erlösung.

> Paul Bekker, "Schönberg: 'Erwartung,' " *Anbruch* 6/8–9
> (August/September 1924), 275–282, 277.

17.

In keiner Weise. Es ist, wie ich oft erklärt habe, die langsame Darstellung der Dinge, die einem im Moment einer Hochspannung durchs Hirn gehen. Was hat die Erwartung mit Erlösung zu tun? Die Frau hat sich in ihren Angstvorstellungen geirrt, oder nicht (darüber wird nicht entschieden—aber es sind eben nur Angstvorstellungen und die waren gezeigt)—sie ist nicht einmal davon erlöst.

> ASI

18. Schoenberg's changes are reproduced in José Maria Garcia Laborda, *Studien zu Schönbergs Monodram "Erwartung," op. 17* (Laaber: Laaber Verlag, 1981), 122–141.

19.

Was sie in die Bäume starren . . . Der Mond ist verzerrt wie vor Schreck . . . offen wie im Hilferuf . . . Was haben sie dir getan . . . Oh du . . . du . . . ich war nicht hier. . . . Der Abend war so friedlich . . . Die zitternden Blätter vor dem Himmel . . . dein Haar ist blutig . . . dein weiches braunes Haar . . . Und Blut an meinen Händen . . . und Blut auf dem Boden . . . Wer hat das getan? . . . Wer hat das getan du? . . . Du bist das Einzige hier du musst es wissen . . . Du boshaftes Steingesicht . . . Wie es die Lippen zusammen-presst . . . Grinse nicht du..[. . .] Die Schattenhöhlen . . . das Räubernest . . . Hier drückte er sich an den Stamm . . . Und dann der Schuss . . .

> Laborda, *Schönbergs Monodram "Erwartung,"* 134–135.

20. Schoenberg to Ernst Legal, 14 April 1930, *Schoenberg Letters*, no. 114, 139–141, esp. 139.

21.

Eine dieser Änderungen war mir in Gedanken noch lange Zeit unangenehm, nämlich Striche in der Szene da sie den toten Körper sieht. Durch diese Striche, die ich längst nicht mehr weiss, wurde das Mystische oder sagen wir Halluzinatorische verstärkt, während ich gar nicht so sicher war, dass es nicht eine wahre Begebenheit sei. Vielleicht ist es aber wirklich dadurch in der Wirkung stärker geworden.

> Naumann, "Ton-Wort Verhältnis," 2:2–3.

22. Schoenberg to Busoni, n.d., *Busoni Letters*, 387–390, esp. 389.

23. Schoenberg to Busoni, 20 July 1909, *Busoni Letters*, 383.

24. Schoenberg, "Problems in Teaching Art," in *Style and Idea*, 365–369, esp. 365.

25. "Es ist mein 'heisser' Wunsch es mit dem Monodram zusammen aufgeführt zu bekommen." Schoenberg to Zehme, 13 September 1913, ASC/LC.

26.

In Wien kursiert, dass Sie mit Kokoschka eine Oper schreiben. Vielleicht wär's doch besser gewesen? Mein Monodr. gefällt mir wenig.

> Pappenheim to Schoenberg, n.d., ASC/LC.

27. "Und zwar des Erlebens eines einzigen, des 'Mannes.' Es ist sein Drama, das bühnenmässig nach aussen projiziert wird." Erwin Stein, "Schönbergs 'Glückliche Hand,' " *Die Oper: Blätter des Breslauer Stadttheaters* 16 (1927–1928), 4.

28. For more on Schoenberg's compositional approach in the opera, see Joseph Auner, "Schoenberg's Aesthetic Transformations and the Evolution of Form in *Die glückliche Hand*," *Journal of the Arnold Schoenberg Institute* 12/2 (November 1989), 103–128, as well as Auner's contribution to the present volume.

EIGHT

"Heart and Brain in Music"

The Genesis of Schoenberg's *Die glückliche Hand*

Joseph Auner

In the 1946 essay "Heart and Brain in Music" Schoenberg challenges the "misconception . . . that the constituent qualities of music belong to two categories as regards their origin: to the heart or to the brain."[1] He argues that the so-called cerebral aspects of his musical language such as intricate counterpoint and "sophisticated form" were in fact often the products of spontaneous inspiration, whereas "beautiful melodies" that appeared to be pure emotional outpourings were produced by "deliberate calculation." Referring to the rapid composition of many of his works and the frequent lack of sketches or revisions, Schoenberg acknowledges that "it often happens to a composer that he writes down a melody in one uninterrupted draft and with a perfection that requires no change and offers no possibility of improvement."[2] But many compositions required hard work. Of the First Chamber Symphony, for instance, he notes that his "perfect vision" of the whole work included only the "main features";[3] the details had to be worked out in the course of the composition. In language he had used in several previous essays he concludes:

> But one cannot pretend that the complicated ones required hard work or that the simple ones were always easily produced. Also, one cannot pretend that it makes any difference whether the examples derive from a spontaneous emotion or from a cerebral effort.
>
> . . . But one thing seems to be clear: whether its final aspect is that of simplicity or of complexity, whether it was composed swiftly and easily or required hard work and much time, the finished work gives no indication of whether the emotional or the cerebral constituents have been determinant.
>
> . . . everything of supreme value in art must show heart as well as brain.[4]

No doubt this essay was in part a response to the frequent charge that twelve-tone composition was a purely cerebral exercise.[5] More important, however, I believe the essay addressed a fundamental conflict in Schoenberg's mind about the relationship between compositional process, structure, and expression.

The intensity with which Schoenberg in 1946 argued for the interdependence of inspiration and intellect was matched by his insistence on their incompatibility in the years leading up to the First World War. With the completion of that remarkable series of works in the summer and early fall of 1909—the Three Piano Pieces, op. 11; the Five Orchestra Pieces, op. 16; and *Erwartung*, op. 17—Schoenberg felt he was on the threshold of a new intuitive art unmediated by the intellect and convention. Music, he wrote to Ferruccio Busoni in 1909, "should be an expression of feeling, as our feelings, which bring us in contact with our subconscious, really are, and no false child of feelings and 'conscious logic.' "[6] Anticipating the language of his later critics, Schoenberg wrote in even stronger terms to Kandinsky in 1911:

> art belongs to the *unconscious!* One must express *oneself!* Express oneself *directly!* Not one's taste, or one's upbringing, or one's intelligence, knowledge or skill. Not all these *acquired* characteristics, but that which is *inborn, instinctive.* And all form-making, all *conscious* form-making, is connected with some kind of mathematics, or geometry, or with the golden section or suchlike.[7]

Such revolutionary pronouncements have understandably been treated with skepticism. It is difficult to reconcile Schoenberg's claims of unconscious, instinctive expression with the elaborate organizational strategies in many of his atonal works.[8] Moreover, Schoenberg's remarks are themselves full of ambiguities; alongside his most radical utterances he often hints at underlying continuities with the past.[9] In fact, increasingly in his later writings Schoenberg contradicted or repudiated many of his earlier statements, stressing instead the evolutionary features of his development and his continuity with tradition.

Nonetheless, a study of Schoenberg's writings and works from the prewar years suggests that the ideal of direct emotional expression continued to have a profound impact on his compositional process and his approach to musical structure in the works he composed from the end of 1909 to early in 1912, when he began *Pierrot lunaire*, op. 21. These works include op. 11, no. 3; op. 16, no. 5; *Erwartung;* the unfinished Three Pieces for Chamber Orchestra (1910); the Six Little Piano Pieces, op. 19 (1911); and *Herzgewächse*, op. 20 (1911).[10] But at the same time that he sought to make his vision of spontaneous, intuitive creation a reality, he found that composition was becoming increasingly problematic. In his writings he began to question his ability to live up to the demands of his creative ideal, and whether the path might be an error. With *Pierrot lunaire* and the works that followed, he began to distance himself from his most radical stance.

Die glückliche Hand, op. 18, provides unique insight into this crucial turning point in Schoenberg's attitude toward the "heart and brain." In contrast to the rapid composition of most of the atonal works, Schoenberg wrote this "drama with music" in a number of stages between 1910 and 1913. The work thus bridges a period of tremendous diversity in his creative output. Vestiges of these stylistic transformations remain in the opera. In its dramatic content, musical structure, and what can be traced of its creation it provides a record of Schoenberg's painful acceptance of the distance between inspired vision and attainment. Whereas some passages resemble *Erwartung*'s constant change and diversity, other sections are closer to *Pierrot*'s thematic development, clearly defined form, and use of contrapuntal devices. Scholars have noted the differences between *Die glückliche Hand* and *Erwartung,* but insufficient knowledge about the genesis of the work has made it difficult to fit the opera into a comprehensive view of the period.[11] Examined in the light of a new compositional chronology, the sketches document that in the course of the work's evolution Schoenberg's approach to musical organization and the creative process changed as he began grudgingly to acknowledge a role for the "conscious intellect."[12]

Schoenberg left little direct information about the composition of *Die glückliche Hand.* The libretto bears a June 1910 date of completion, and the composition's beginning and ending are indicated on the draft as 9 September 1910 and 18 November 1913, respectively. Through references in Schoenberg's correspondence it is possible to establish at least five separate stages during which Schoenberg worked on *Die glückliche Hand,* and the many surviving compositional materials for the work suggest chronological layers in the score corresponding to these five stages. On the basis of these sources the chronology of *Die glückliche Hand* may be summarized as follows: only the libretto, some of the artwork for the staging, and a few musical sketches originated in 1910;[13] the earliest portion of the draft, starting at measure 58 and extending to the end of scene 2 and possibly the beginning of scene 3, dates from the second period of composition, in the summer of 1911; the bulk of the score, including the third and fourth scenes as well as much of the first two scenes, was composed in 1912–1913, after *Pierrot lunaire.*[14]

In "Heart and Brain in Music" Schoenberg maintained that it made no difference whether a work was composed quickly or with great effort, but in 1910 he believed that the true artist was defined by the ability to compose spontaneously. The central climax of *Die glückliche Hand* occurs when the main character, the Man, outrages a group of artisans by forging a jeweled diadem with a single hammer stroke. The polarity between a craftsman's repetitive labor and the miraculous creation of genius reflects Schoenberg's conviction that a work of art must be created fully formed, not assembled from component parts. In 1912 he wrote:

For the work of art, like every living thing, is conceived as a whole—just like a child, whose arm or leg is not conceived separately. The inspiration is not the theme, but the whole work. And it is not the one who writes a good theme who is inventive, but the one to whom a whole symphony occurs at once.[15]

It followed that Schoenberg regarded sketching, planning, and revision as unwanted intrusions of the conscious intellect, and in fact in the period leading up to *Die glückliche Hand* he sketched very little and the draft manuscripts show few revisions.[16] *Erwartung* is perhaps the culmination of this tendency: the 426 measures of the draft were written in seventeen days, and the only sketches for it are a few brief ideas jotted down in the text manuscript. But the compositions that followed—the Six Little Piano Pieces, the unfinished pieces for chamber orchestra, and *Herzgewächse*—were also composed very rapidly and without sketching. And, although more sketches are preserved for *Die glückliche Hand* than for any of the other atonal works, there are few sketches for the early stages of its composition.

The sketches consist of six pages bound in a typed copy of the libretto, which Schoenberg labeled *Compositions Vorlage,* and a collection of nineteen pages.[17] These two sources differ in many ways, most importantly in what they reveal about Schoenberg's creative process. Although all the sketch material is undated, a number of factors suggest that many of the *Compositions Vorlage* sketches represent Schoenberg's earliest thoughts on the score; most of these sketches correspond to passages at the end of scene 2 and the beginning of scene 3. Other sketch pages from the *Compositions Vorlage,* which relate primarily to the second half of scene 3 and scene 4, appear to date from the later stages of the composition in 1912–1913. Figure 10 reproduces two facing pages from the *Compositions Vorlage,* showing the libretto and adjacent musical sketch that correspond to measures 58 through 61. Like the sketches in the text manuscript of *Erwartung,* these notations do not record Schoenberg actively working with material in various forms; rather, they represent small autonomous passages that he incorporated into the final score with few changes.[18] This kind of sketch is associated with a particular point in the text and does not serve as a source for themes or motives that are subsequently developed in the score. This is in sharp contrast to Schoenberg's approach in the later stages of the work or in *Pierrot lunaire,* where sketched material is developed over substantial passages.[19]

The idea of eliminating "the conscious will in art" had a profound impact on Schoenberg's organization of musical structure as well. Increasingly he had come to regard the "craftsmanly deftness, technique, and play with material" of traditional developmental procedures with suspicion. Schoenberg in 1911 makes a sharp distinction between intellect and feeling, talent and genius, craft and art:

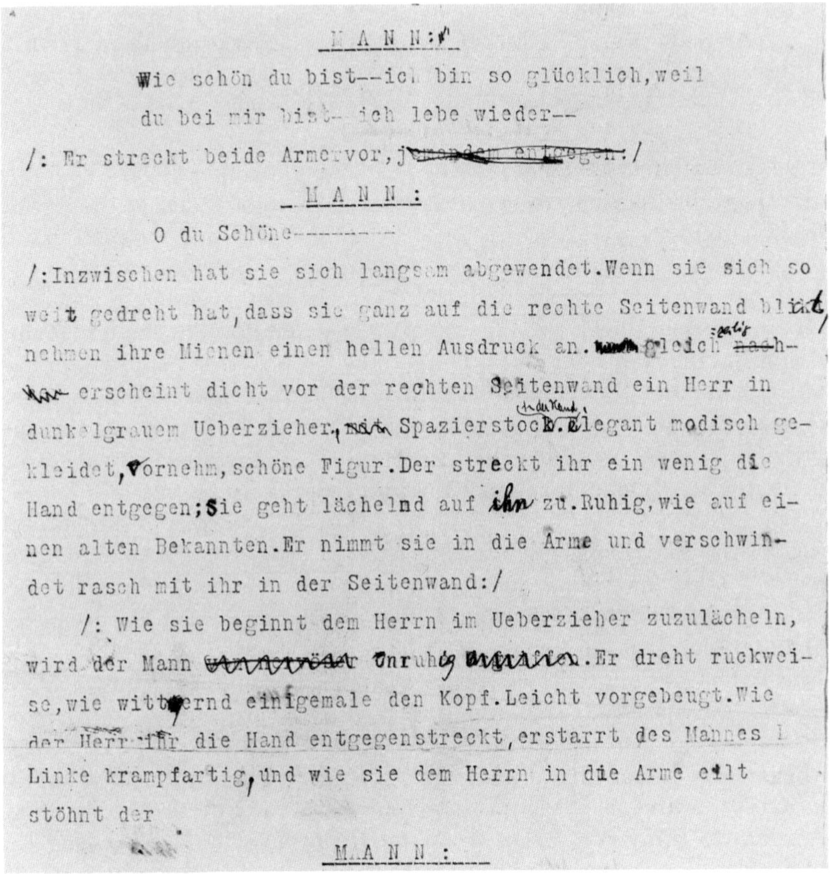

_M A N N :_

Wie schön du bist--ich bin so glücklich,weil
du bei mir bist- ich lebe wieder--
/: Er streckt beide Arme vor, ~~jmeinder entgegen~~ :/

_M A N N :_

O du Schöne----------

/:Inzwischen hat sie sich langsam abgewendet.Wenn sie sich so
weit gedreht hat,dass sie ganz auf die rechte Seitenwand blickt,
nehmen ihre Mienen einen hellen Ausdruck an. ~~und~~ gleich ~~nach-~~
~~her~~ erscheint dicht vor der rechten Seitenwand ein Herr in
dunkelgrauem Ueberzieher, ~~mit~~ Spazierstock.Elegant modisch ge-
kleidet,vornehm, schöne Figur.Der streckt ihr ein wenig die
Hand entgegen;Sie geht lächelnd auf *ihn* zu.Ruhig,wie auf einen alten Bekannten.Er nimmt sie in die Arme und verschwindet rasch mit ihr in der Seitenwand:/

/: Wie sie beginnt dem Herrn im Ueberzieher zuzulächeln,
wird der Mann ~~xxxxxxxxx~~ unruhig ~~xxxxxx~~.Er dreht ruckwei-
se,wie witternd einigemale den Kopf.Leicht vorgebeugt.Wie
~~der Herr ihr~~ die Hand entgegenstreckt,erstarrt des Mannes
Linke krampfartig,und wie sie dem Herrn in die Arme eilt
stöhnt der

_M A N N :_

Fig. 10. Schoenberg, *Die glückliche Hand, Compositions Vorlage,* sketch for mm. 58–61. Reproduced courtesy of Lawrence Schoenberg.

Mathematics and mechanics cannot produce a living being. Inspired by a true feeling, a rightly functioning intellect brought this form to completion. But a rightly functioning intellect almost always does the opposite of what is appropriate to a true feeling. A true feeling must not let itself be prevented from going constantly down, ever and anew, into the dark region of the unconscious, in order to bring up content and form as a unity.[20]

Schoenberg was of course aware that his works did not fully live up to this ideal. Writing to Busoni of the challenge of allowing "nothing to infiltrate which may be invoked either by intelligence or consciousness" he ac-

knowledged that "perhaps this is not yet graspable. It will perhaps take a long time before I can write the music I feel urged to, of which I have had an inkling for several years, but which, for the time being, I cannot express."[21] Intuitive expression was thus not a free reverie in which the results would be accepted without critique but involved editing out any aspects of musical language that he regarded as impurities.[22] The works of 1908–1911 show a gradual elimination of what he described to Busoni as the "architectural values and . . . cabalistic mathematics" of tonality,[23] and conventional structural elements such as thematic statements and development, form based on repetition, and imitative counterpoint. As he wrote in the 1911 essay "Problems of Teaching Art":

There is no style to carry one through, no ornament to give a lift; pomposity is out of the question, and fraud too. This is morality; an idea makes its appearance for what it is worth—no less, but no more either.[24]

Perhaps no concepts are more frequently linked to Schoenberg's music and thought than logic, construction, and comprehensibility. Looking back in 1941 to the period before World War I, Schoenberg wrote of the inevitable emergence in a composer of the "desire for conscious control" and the quest for knowledge of the "laws and rules which govern the forms which he has conceived 'as in a dream.' "[25] But at the time of *Erwartung* his reliance on intuition was accompanied by a deep ambivalence about the value of order and logic in composition. In his 1911 *Harmonielehre* he wrote: "It should not be said that order, clarity, and comprehensibility can impair beauty, but that they are not a necessary factor without which there would be no beauty; they are merely an accidental, a circumstantial factor."[26] Although Schoenberg did not renounce "all symbols of cohesion" in even his most radical works, there the unifying elements are attenuated to an unprecedented degree as a result of pursuing an image of composition as the transcription of the constantly changing and irrational unconscious. He described this to Busoni in 1909:

[I]t is *impossible* for a person to have only *one* sensation at a time. One has *thousands* simultaneously. . . . And this variegation, this multifariousness, this *illogicality* which our senses demonstrate, the illogicality presented by their interactions, set forth by some mounting rush of blood, by some reaction of the senses or the nerves, this I should like to have in my music.[27]

As Robert Morgan has suggested, the mysterious quality of music was for Schoenberg one of its most distinguishing features.[28] In a letter to Kandinsky from 1912 he objected to the painter's notion of a higher order standing behind apparent disharmony, adding, "We must be conscious that there are puzzles around us. And we must find the courage to look these puzzles in the eye without timidly asking about the 'solution.' "[29]

•   •   •   •   •

Works like *Erwartung, Herzgewächse,* and the early compositional stages of *Die glückliche Hand* show that Schoenberg attempted to carry out his vision of an intuitive art in the years 1909–1911. Despite his achievements during these years, the initial feelings of liberation soon gave way to anxiety and doubt as composition became increasingly difficult. In 1910, after making only a few isolated sketches, he set *Die glückliche Hand* aside and completed no other work that year. In 1911 he completed only the Six Little Piano Pieces and *Herzgewächse,* both composed in just a few days. In all of his writings from the prewar years Schoenberg stressed the necessity for abso-

lute self-confidence for the composer who would abandon theory and elimi-
nate the conscious will, but Schoenberg's own courage was faltering, and
his writings during 1910–1911 reflect his preoccupation with the themes of
failure, doubt, error, and a loss of faith.[30]

In a program note to the January 1910 performance of parts of *Gurre-lieder* and *Das Buch der hängenden Gärten* Schoenberg proclaimed his breakthrough into a new art free from "every restriction of a bygone aesthetic,"
but acknowledged at the same time that

> though the goal toward which I am striving appears to me a certain one, I
> am, nonetheless, already feeling the resistance I shall have to overcome; I feel
> how hotly even the least of temperaments will rise in revolt, and suspect that
> even those who have so far believed in me will not want to acknowledge the
> necessary nature of this development.[31]

Schoenberg's self-doubt was certainly motivated in part by the outrage and
incomprehension his works had encountered. Nevertheless, rejection was
not something new in the period after *Erwartung*. I believe that a more
significant cause for Schoenberg's creative crisis was his inability to live up
to the uncompromising demands of his own aesthetic beliefs, as well as a
growing sense that his exclusive reliance on intuition was an error. In contrast to the bold pronouncements about eliminating the conscious will in
art, Schoenberg increasingly characterized the relationship between heart
and brain as a struggle in which, as he wrote in "Franz Liszt's Work and
Being," "one must avoid the disturbing intervention of the constantly worried frightened intellect";[32] he describes an "undissolved residue" between
the artist's "expressive urge and his powers of depiction," and the resultant
need to rely on technique to unify "the outward phenomena to disguise
the gaps and deficiencies of the inner."[33] In the *Harmonielehre* Schoenberg
wrote that although what really matters is the ability "to look deep into
oneself[,] . . . [t]he average person seems to possess this ability only in a
few sublime moments, and to live the rest of the time, not according to his
own inclinations, but according to principles."[34]

Schoenberg's changing attitude toward an art free from tradition and
technique is also reflected in his involvement with painting. He had started
to paint around 1907 and continued to do so sporadically throughout his
life, but in 1910–1911 painting assumed a central place in his creative life.
For a time he considered pursuing it as a second career.[35] Like many of his
contemporaries, especially Kandinsky and Kokoschka, Schoenberg's turn
to an art form other than that in which he had been trained was motivated
by the desire to liberate himself from the constraints of inherited technique. He was a gifted painter, and many of his portraits show considerable
technical ability,[36] but that aspect held little interest for him; he explained
his point of view to the painter Carl Moll, who had discouraged him from

showing his paintings because of what he perceived as their primitive level of achievement.

> At first glance it must seem strange that I assume that someone who can do nothing is suddenly capable of doing something. However, I do not consider this unusual; it is with me, in any event, routinely the case. *I have always been able to do only that which is suited to me—absolutely, immediately* and almost without any *transition* or preparation. On the other hand, the things that others can do—that which passes for "education"—have always caused me difficulties.[37]

However, despite promising developments in his painting career, as he began to question the intuitive ideal, his enthusiasm for painting also waned. Just before beginning *Pierrot* he wrote to Kandinsky:

> I do not believe that it is advantageous for me to exhibit in the company of professional painters. I am surely an "outsider," an amateur, a dilettante. Whether I should exhibit *at all* is almost already a question. Whether I should exhibit with a group of painters is almost *no longer a question.*[38]

It is not that he could no longer produce paintings like the intuitive "gazes" or "visions," but rather that he no longer felt that this approach to painting—without technique or training—was valid. By denying that his paintings were legitimate, by calling himself an "amateur, a dilettante," Schoenberg called into question the basic premise of intuitive art and reaffirmed the traditional conception of art as dependent on acquired skills and "artistic methods."

To admit this in connection with his painting, however, was much easier than to accept the resurrection of craft and technique in his composition. Schoenberg had invested so much in the moral-religious-aesthetic nexus of the intuitive aesthetic that abandoning it meant losing all foundations for his thought.[39] If faith in oneself is the main prerequisite for the creative genius, any lack of conviction or faltering of courage becomes an admission of both creative and spiritual failure. Schoenberg's creative ideal allowed no compromise, as he wrote in the *Harmonielehre:*

> *The artist who has courage submits wholly to his own inclinations. And he alone who submits to his own inclinations has courage, and he alone who has courage is an artist.*[40]

Composition of *Pierrot lunaire* between March and July of 1912 provided a temporary release from Schoenberg's aesthetic quandary. The fact that the work resulted from a commission gave him a feeling of detachment from the project, as he described to Kandinsky:

> perhaps no heartfelt necessity as regards its theme, its content (Giraud's "Pierrot lunaire"), but certainly as regards its form. In any case remarkable

for me as a preparatory study for another work, which I now wish to begin: Balzac's *Séraphita*.[41]

It is revealing of his state of mind that he was able to complete the "preparatory study," while the more heartfelt work remained a fragment. As he began *Pierrot* Schoenberg still clearly aspired toward a spontaneous, intuitive expression. After completing the first of the melodramas, "Gebet an Pierrot," no. 9, he wrote: "The sounds here truly become an animalistically immediate expression of sensual and psychological emotions. Almost as if everything were transmitted directly."[42] Yet, although the twenty-one pieces that make up *Pierrot* exhibit an enormous range of approaches, the work shows the return of many traditional formal and developmental techniques. As Theodor W. Adorno noted, the ironic character of the work allowed Schoenberg to establish links to tradition without subjecting them to the intense scrutiny of aesthetic legitimacy.[43]

In contrast to his experience with preceding works, Schoenberg here felt less constrained in his compositional process as well; he considered different orderings of the cycle and made sketches for several movements.[44] Although most of the sketches, like those for *Erwartung*, are brief marginal notes in the text manuscript, they represent a very different working method and consequently a different attitude toward musical structure. Unlike the sketches for *Erwartung* or the early stages of *Die glückliche Hand*, which represented a single point in the completed score, many of the *Pierrot* sketches contain thematic and motivic material explicitly developed over the entire movement.

While he was completing *Pierrot lunaire* in the summer of 1912 Schoenberg again took up the score of *Die glückliche Hand*, but despite the relative ease and rapidity with which he had composed *Pierrot*, the opera still proceeded slowly. Again he set the work aside. It was completed only after a fourth period of composition at the end of 1912 and a final stage in the summer and fall of 1913. At each successive stage of work on the music drama, both compositional process and musical structure reflect the ongoing transformation of Schoenberg's aesthetic stance. Unlike the early stages from 1910–1911, the work Schoenberg did on it in 1912–1913 shows that he depended increasingly on thematic and motivic development, imitative counterpoint, and a clearly defined form based on large- and small-scale repetition. Though aspects of parody undoubtedly remain, all of the traditional techniques and procedures that had been reintroduced as ironic references in *Pierrot lunaire* were now used as legitimate, "genuine" features. The new structural approach was paralleled by a transformation in Schoenberg's working method, as is clear from the large number of sketches for the later compositional stages, including multiple sketches for several sections.

The thematic clarity and developmental logic of the end of the third scene, measures 166 through 202, strikingly demonstrate the distance Schoenberg had come. This passage is based on the contrapuntal development of a nine-measure theme first presented in the horns in measures 166 through 174, and repeated five times in complete and partial statements. More sketches survive for the horn-theme section than for any other part of *Die glückliche Hand,* and they record Schoenberg's experimentation with the horn theme and various canonic treatments of it, and culminate with a fully worked-out particell for measures 166 through 200.

Sketch page 2,440 contains sketches for the horn theme and the contrapuntal continuation (see figure 11). At the letter *B* he copied a version of the theme from a preceding sketch, then crossed out the final two measures of the theme at "2." Lower on the page at *D* he subsequently sketched a new conclusion that corresponds very closely to the final version. A significant addition to this revision is the sixteenth-note passage inserted before the concluding gesture, which recapitulates in order the first eleven pitches of the horn theme. The insertion prepares the cadence of the theme by returning to the pitch material of the opening. In a similar procedure, the diminution of the horn theme returns near the end of the passage, measures 193 and 194, to provide closure for the entire horn-theme section.

Schoenberg began with the intention of following the horn theme with a fairly strict canon-in-inversion based on the theme. This is worked out in detail in another sketch, but also hinted at here and at *A,* which presents the first two measures of the untransposed inversion of the horn theme (D-flat—C—A). At *E* he introduces a new countertheme, which appears with a whole-step transposition of the horn theme. While freer than the first version, this countertheme is closely related to the inversion, beginning with the same interval pattern and following the same general developmental process. Although Schoenberg did not ultimately use the literal inversion of the horn theme as the countertheme, he does refer to it in the oboe and chordal accompaniment in the winds of measures 174 and 175, which are sketched at *C.* In the second half of the measure, the first three pitches of the inversion of the horn theme (D-flat—C—A) are stated melodically along with D. These same four pitch classes are also stated harmonically at the first of the descending gestures, exemplifying his growing interest in equating horizontal and vertical presentations.

Schoenberg applied the clarity and logic of *Die glückliche Hand* in a still more refined way in the unfinished symphony he drafted in 1914–1915. His comment to Zemlinsky that the symphony would be a "worked composition," in contrast to the preceding "purely impressionistic works," could be taken to describe both the extensive sketching and planning, and his experimentation with protoserial structures.[45] Nevertheless, the conflict be-

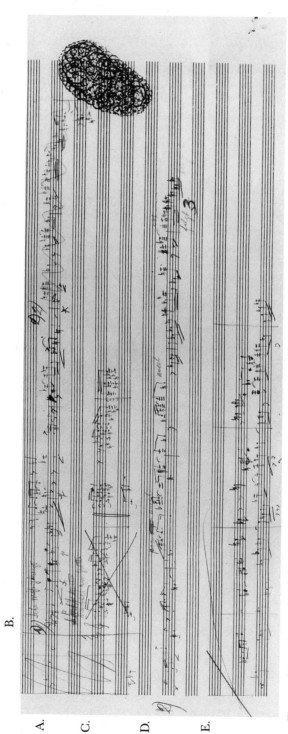

Fig. 11. Schoenberg, sketch for *Die glückliche Hand* (ASI microfilm 2440, box 18). Reproduced courtesy of Lawrence Schoenberg.

tween heart and brain was by no means resolved. There was a clear tension in *Die glückliche Hand* between the rigorous structures worked out in the sketches and the less systematic realizations of these passages that made their way into the final score. And although the symphony remained fragmentary, Schoenberg did complete the Four Orchestra Songs, op. 22 (1913–1916), which are in large measure consistent with his earlier structural ideals.

•　•　•　•　•

In his later writings Schoenberg minimized the differences in both style and aesthetic foundations between his twelve-tone works and his earlier tonal and atonal music. In his interpretation of his own development he focused on the continuity of his later works with tradition and on demonstrating that "the method of composing with twelve tones grew out of a necessity."[46] In 1928, for example, he wrote: "To be quite precise, I have been saying the same thing for about 25 years (if not more), only I am constantly saying it better."[47] Although there are undoubtedly significant continuities throughout his many stylistic transformations, the reintroduction in *Pierrot lunaire* and *Die glückliche Hand* of the conventional structural means he had systematically eliminated or suppressed between 1909 and 1911, and the solidification of the new compositional procedures, reflect Schoenberg's fundamental redefinition of the nature of art. And it is clear from his writings and the various compositional materials that this redefinition—in the course of which he had to abandon the Romantic image of the godlike artist and turn from an aesthetic ideal of "illogical" variegation to one of creation based on cohesion and logic—represented a profound crisis in his creative and spiritual life.

When he emerged from the most intensive period of self-examination early in 1912, he acknowledged to himself that he had passed a major turning point. As he began *Pierrot*, he wrote:

> And maybe this is the reason why I suddenly, for two years, no longer feel as young. I have become strangely calm! This is also evident when I conduct. I am missing the aggressive in myself. The spontaneous leaving of all [physical] constraints behind oneself and attacking, taking over.[48]

The impossibility of "leaving all constraints behind," of bridging the gulf between the material and spiritual through near-miraculous creative feats, became a central theme in his writings and compositions after *Erwartung*. Whereas the George texts for the Second String Quartet of 1908 describe crossing "endless chasms" with ease to merge with the "holy fire," by the time of *Die glückliche Hand* the rift between vision and worldly attainment had become unbridgeable. The central two scenes of *Die glückliche Hand* play out this pessimism in the recurrent drama of deception by the false lures of creative and personal fulfillment, symbolized by the "beautiful vision" of the Woman that cannot be captured but will "only slip away from you when you grasp it."[49] At the beginning of the work, the chorus laments:

> Be still, won't you? You know how it always is, and yet you remain blind. Will you never be at rest? . . . Will you not finally believe? . . . Once again you trust in the dream. Once again you fix your longing on the unattainable. Once again you give yourself up to the sirens of your thoughts, thoughts that roam the cosmos, that are unworldly but thirst for worldly fulfillment![50]

Despite his many remarkable achievements, Schoenberg never lost this sense of defeat. Indeed, in the essay "Composition with Twelve Tones" he describes human creativity as a "long path between vision and accomplishment" where "driven out of Paradise even geniuses must reap their harvest in the sweat of their brows."[51]

It was with the completion of *Die glückliche Hand* that Schoenberg laid the aesthetic and structural foundations for his subsequent compositional development, yet the bitter struggle and sense of loss that accompanied this transition still resonated with him more than thirty years later. It is surely not a coincidence that Schoenberg begins "Heart and Brain in Music" with a reference to Balzac's novel *Séraphita,* the work that in 1912 he intended to use as the basis for a massive oratorio describing the angelic Séraphita's ascent into heaven. By 1946, however, Schoenberg identified more with the mortal earthbound character Wilfred; he begins the essay by quoting Balzac's description of Wilfred "as a man of medium height as is the case with almost all men who tower above the rest. His chest and his shoulders were broad and his neck was short, like that of men whose heart must be within the domain of the head."[52]

NOTES

1. Schoenberg, "Heart and Brain in Music," in *Style and Idea,* 53–75, esp. 54.
2. Ibid., 57.
3. Ibid., 58.
4. Ibid., 74–75.
5. The comments of the Berlin critic Fritz Ohrmann about the Variations for Orchestra, op. 31 (which appeared in *Signale für die musikalische Welt* in its issue of 12 December 1928), are typical of such attacks: "Arnold Schoenberg's latest work . . . is calculated and excogitated musical mathematics dictated by intellect alone to one obsessed with a single eccentric idea." (*Arnold Schönbergs neuestes Werk, Variationen für Orchester, ist eine errechnete und erklügelte nur vom Intellekt diktierte musikalische Mathematik eines von einer verstiegenen Idee Besessenen.*) Translated and quoted in

Nicolas Slonimsky, ed., *Lexicon of Musical Invective: Critical Assaults on Composers since Beethoven's Time* (Seattle and London: University of Washington Press, 1965), 161.

6. Schoenberg to Busoni, n.d. [August 1909], *Busoni Letters,* 387–390, esp. 389.

7. Schoenberg to Kandinsky, 24 January 1911, *Schoenberg/Kandinsky Letters,* 23.

8. His description of the Orchestra Pieces, op. 16, in a letter of 14 July 1909 to Richard Strauss as "completely unsymphonic, devoid of architecture or construction, just an uninterrupted change of colors, rhythms and moods" clearly does not adequately characterize the first three movements, which he had by then completed, with their thematic organization, recurring harmonies, and pervasive contrapuntal devices. Letter translated and quoted in Nicolas Slonimsky, ed., *Music Since 1900,* 4th ed. (New York: Charles Scribner's Sons, 1971), 207.

9. See, for example, his letter to Busoni of 24 August 1909: "Yes indeed, when a new art seeks and finds new means of expression, almost all earlier techniques go hang: seemingly at any rate, for actually they are retained but in a different way (to discuss this would lead me too far)." *Busoni Letters,* 391–397, esp. 393.

10. Jan Maegaard has established that whereas the early movements of opp. 11 and 16 dated from the winter and spring of 1909, the last movements of both pieces were composed in August, shortly before Schoenberg began *Erwartung;* see Maegaard, *Entwicklung des dodekaphonen Satzes,* 1:63–76.

11. Important earlier studies of op. 18 include John Crawford, *"Die glückliche Hand:* Schoenberg's *Gesamtkunstwerk,"* *Musical Quarterly* 60/4 (1974), 583–601; Alan Lessem, *Music and Text in the Works of Arnold Schoenberg: The Critical Years 1908–1922,* Studies in Musicology, no. 8 (Ann Arbor, Mich.: UMI Research Press, 1979); Siegfried Mauser, *Das expressionistische Musiktheater der Wiener Schule,* Schriftenreihe der Hochschule für Musik, München, vol. 3 (Regensburg: G. Bosse Verlag, 1982); and Michael Mäckelmann, *"Die glückliche Hand:* Eine Studie zu Musik und Inhalt von Arnold Schönbergs 'Drama mit Musik,' " in *Musiktheater im 20. Jahrhundert,* Hamburger Jahrbuch für Musikwissenschaft, vol. 10, ed. Constantin Floros (Laaber: Laaber Verlag, 1988), 7–36.

12. The present study draws upon my dissertation, "Schoenberg's Compositional and Aesthetic Transformations 1910–1913: The Genesis of *Die glückliche Hand"* (Ph.D. diss., University of Chicago, 1991); and my article "Schoenberg's Aesthetic Transformations and the Evolution of the Form in *Die glückliche Hand,"* *Journal of the Arnold Schoenberg Institute* 12/2 (November 1989), 103–128. My account of Schoenberg's aesthetic development has been influenced in particular by John Crawford, "Schoenberg's Artistic Development to 1911," in *Schoenberg/Kandinsky Letters,* 171–186; Robert P. Morgan, "Secret Languages: The Roots of Musical Modernism," *Critical Inquiry* 10/3 (1984), 442–461; and Glen Alan Bauer, "A Contextual Approach to Schoenberg's Atonal Works: Self-Expression, Religion, and Music Theory" (Ph.D. diss., Washington University, 1986), 77–115, 166–189.

13. Many of the materials for the staging are reproduced in *Schoenberg/Kandinsky Letters,* plates 20–28.

14. For a further description of the sources and the compositional chronology, see Auner, "Schoenberg's Compositional and Aesthetic Transformations," 36–149.

15. Schoenberg, "Gustav Mahler," in *Style and Idea,* 449–472, esp. 458.

16. An exception is the Second String Quartet, op. 10 (1907–1908), for which a considerable number of sketches survive, especially for the second and third movements. More typical is *Das Buch der hängenden Gärten*, op. 15 (1908–1909), where preliminary materials survive for only three songs. Rudolf Stephan has pointed out that when Schoenberg ran into difficulties with a composition he was more likely to set aside the first draft and start again from the beginning. For the later works of 1909 there are even fewer sketches. No sketches are preserved for op. 11, and with the exception of the deletion of a section of eight measures in the final movement, the draft manuscript is virtually free of changes. Fragmentary sketches survive for the first four movements of the Five Orchestra Pieces, but significantly, there are no sketches for the final and longest movement. See also Maegaard, *Entwicklung des dodekaphonen Satzes*, 1:55–66; and Rudolf Stephan, "Über Schönbergs Arbeitsweise," in *Arnold Schönberg, Gedankaustellung 1974*, ed. Ernst Hilmar (Vienna: Universal Edition, 1974), 119.

17. With the exception of the draft manuscript (ASC/LC) and the fair copy of the full score in the archives of Universal Edition in Vienna, all sources are in the archives of the ASI. The sketch pages are identified by their microfilm numbers (2,432–2,452); sketches in the *Compositions Vorlage*, by their position in the manuscript. The sketches are described in detail in Auner, "Schoenberg's Compositional and Aesthetic Transformations," 463–469. See also Maegaard, *Entwicklung des dodekaphonen Satzes*, 1:66–68; and Harald Krebs, "New Light on the Source Materials of *Die glückliche Hand*," *Journal of the Arnold Schoenberg Institute* 11/2 (November 1988), 123–143.

18. The alterations primarily involve extending the two-and-a-half measure sketch into four and a half measures in the score. A number of other *Compositions Vorlage* sketches represent a similar compositional approach. Only the sketches for the beginning of the third scene show Schoenberg modifying his original idea. Other sketches in the *Compositions Vorlage* were abandoned when he rewrote passages in the later stages of the composition. See Auner, "Schoenberg's Compositional and Aesthetic Transformations," 236–267, 321–342.

19. This is obviously not to say that there are no similarities between melodic shapes in the finished score of this section. For example, the figure in the second half of measure 58 in the double bass is clearly a variation of the initial gesture in the sketch, yet already the variation is significantly different in intervallic content and rhythm. More important, the material introduced in this gesture—marked *Nebenstimme*—does not continue in the bass and is not taken up in its original form by other voices. Instead of conventional motivic references, Schoenberg creates more tenuous relationships by pitch class and pitch-class set recurrences; see Auner, "Schoenberg's Compositional and Aesthetic Transformations," 260–265.

20. Schoenberg, "Franz Liszt's Work and Being," in *Style and Idea*, 442–447, esp. 444.

21. Schoenberg to Busoni, n.d. [August 1909], *Busoni Letters*, 388.

22. Bauer makes this point in "Schoenberg's Atonal Works," 163.

23. Schoenberg to Busoni, 24 August 1909, *Busoni Letters*, 393.

24. Schoenberg, "Problems in Teaching Art," in *Style and Idea*, 365–369, esp. 368.

25. Schoenberg, "Composition with Twelve-Tones (1)," in *Style and Idea*, 214–245, esp. 218.

26.

Es soll nicht gesagt sein, dass Ordnung, Klarheit und Verständlichkeit die Schönheit beeinträchtigen können, aber sie sind nicht ein notwendiger Factor, ohne den es keine Schönheit gäbe, sondern ein zufälliger.

Schoenberg, *Harmonielehre* (1911), 31.

This passage from the first edition was substantially revised in the third edition of 1922; it is translated and quoted in Roy E. Carter's translator's preface to *Theory of Harmony*, xvii–xviii.

27. Schoenberg to Busoni, n.d. [August 1909], *Busoni Letters*, 389.

28. Morgan, "Secret Languages," 461.

29. Schoenberg to Kandinsky, 19 August 1912, *Schoenberg/Kandinsky Letters*, 54–55.

30. Toward the end of 1911 Schoenberg wrote to Berg: "I am unusually depressed. . . . I'm not composing anything at all right now. At any rate: I've lost interest in my works. I'm not satisfied with anything any more. I see mistakes and inadequacies in everything." 21 December 1911, *Berg-Schoenberg Correspondence*, 59–60.

31. Schoenberg, program notes from 14 January 1910; quoted in translation in Reich, *Schoenberg: A Critical Biography*, 49. Charles Rosen writes of this passage: "To speak of an inner compulsion is to recognize one's own unwillingness to yield, to feel the weight of the opposition and even partially to admit its validity"; see Rosen, *Schoenberg*, 7.

32. Schoenberg, *Style and Idea*, 444.

33. Ibid., 442.

34. Schoenberg, *Theory of Harmony*, 413. The *Harmonielehre*, written in 1910–1911, is deeply marked by Schoenberg's ambivalence about the interaction of the intellect and intuition, and the relationship of composition to theory and tradition. Written at the request of Emil Hertzka, the director of Universal Edition, the theory book served many functions for Schoenberg beyond the much needed one of immediate financial reward, and these contradictory goals are reflected in some of the book's peculiarities. Undoubtedly Schoenberg's efforts to secure a teaching position made it important to demonstrate his theoretical knowledge. Beyond the practical aims of the book, the *Harmonielehre* can be seen as part of an attempt to examine and articulate his own compositional philosophy. See also Auner, "Schoenberg's Compositional and Aesthetic Transformations," 288–295.

35. In October 1910 Schoenberg mounted a one-man exhibit of his works, and the following year his works were included in the first of Kandinsky's *Der Blaue Reiter* exhibitions. The importance that Schoenberg attached to his paintings, and the extent to which this affected how he was viewed, is indicated by the emphasis on his paintings in the special Schoenberg issue of *Der Merker* 2/17 (1911), which included the libretto of *Die glückliche Hand*, and the 1912 testimonial volume prepared by Berg and Schoenberg's other students, *Arnold Schönberg* (Munich: R. Piper & Co., 1912; facsimile ed., Wels, Austria: Druckerei Welsermühl, 1980). For reproductions of Schoenberg paintings, see Thomas Zaunschirm, ed., *Arnold Schönberg: Das bildnerische Werk* (Klagenfurt: Ritter Verlag, 1991).

36. Schoenberg viewed as his most significant works the series of paintings called "gazes" and "visions," which deemphasized traditional representation; he identified his more realistic paintings and portraits—favored, incidentally, by Kandinsky—as "finger exercises, scales" (*Fingerübungen, Skalen*), as he writes in a letter to Kandinsky of 14 December 1911; see *Schoenberg/Kandinsky Letters*, 40.

37. Schoenberg to Carl Moll, 16 June 1910, translated and quoted in Jane Kallir, *Arnold Schoenberg's Vienna* (New York: Galerie St. Etienne and Rizzoli, 1984), 44. The relationship between professional artistic or musical training and intuitive expression is the subject of considerable ambivalence in Schoenberg's writings throughout this period. In the essay "Über Musikkritik" ("About Music Criticism"), first published in *Der Merker* in 1909, Schoenberg insisted that intuition must be based on first mastering the technical aspects of a craft and then dispensing with them; see Schoenberg, *Style and Idea*, 191–197, esp. 191–192. See also Schoenberg, *Theory of Harmony*, 410–417.

38. Schoenberg to Kandinsky, 8 March 1912, *Schoenberg/Kandinsky Letters*, 48.

39. Carl Dahlhaus traces Schoenberg's mingling of religious and psychological imagery to nineteenth-century ideas; see Carl Dahlhaus, "Schoenberg's Aesthetic Theology," in *Schoenberg and the New Music*, trans. Derrick Puffett and Alfred Clayton (Cambridge: Cambridge University Press, 1987), 81–93.

40. Schoenberg, *Theory of Harmony*, 400.

41. Schoenberg to Kandinsky, 19 August 1912, *Schoenberg/Kandinsky Letters*, 54. Schoenberg commented on the commission, from Albertine Zehme, at several points in his diary. See, for example, the entry of 18 February 1912 in "Schoenberg, Attempt at a Diary," trans. Anita Luginbühl, *Journal of the Arnold Schoenberg Institute* 9/1 (June 1986), 7–51, esp. 30; for the original text, see *Arnold Schönberg, Berliner Tagebuch*, ed. Josef Rufer (Frankfurt am Main: Propyläen Verlag, 1974).

42. "Schoenberg, Attempt at a Diary," entry of 13 March 1912, 41.

43. Adorno, "Arnold Schoenberg," 163.

44. See Reinhold Brinkmann, "What the Sources Tells Us . . . A Chapter of *Pierrot* Philology," *Journal of the Arnold Schoenberg Institute* 10/1 (June 1987), 11–27.

45. Schoenberg to Alexander Zemlinsky, 9 January 1915, partially quoted in translation in Oliver Neighbour, "Arnold Schoenberg," in *The New Grove Second Viennese School* (New York: W. W. Norton and Co., 1983), 47.

46. Schoenberg, "Composition with Twelve Tones (1)," in *Style and Idea*, 216.

47. Schoenberg, "Das Tempo der Entwicklung," quoted in Jean Christensen, "The Spiritual and Material in Schoenberg's Thinking," *Music and Letters* 65/4 (1984), 344.

48. "Schoenberg, Attempt at a Diary," 39.

49. He later characterized the meaning of the title with this phrase, borrowed from the concluding chorus: "*Glückliche Hand, die zu packen sucht, was ihr nur entschlüpfen kann, wenn sies hält.*" Schönberg, "Die glückliche Hand," in Schoenberg, *Gesammelte Schriften*, 1:239.

50.

Still, o schweige; Ruheloser! Du weisst es ja; du wusstest es ja; und trotzdem bist du blind? Kannst du nicht endlich Ruhe finden? . . . . Willst du nicht endlich glauben? . . . . Immer wieder glaubst du dem Traum; immer wieder hängst du deine Sehnsucht ans

Unerfüllbare; immer wieder überlässt du dich den Lockungen deiner Sinne, die das Weltall durchstreifen, die unirdisch sind, aber irdiches Glück ersehnen!
  Schönberg, *Die glückliche Hand,* Drama mit Musik (Wien: Universal Edition, 1917), 1–5; trans. David Johnson in *Schoenberg/Kandinsky Letters,* 91–92.

51. Schoenberg, "Composition with Twelve Tones (1)," in *Style and Idea,* 215.

52. Schoenberg, "Heart and Brain in Music," in *Style and Idea,* 53.

NINE

Schoenberg's Incomplete Works and Fragments

Jan Maegaard

Incomplete works and fragments may form quite a substantial portion of a composer's entire output. Together with completed works that were either withdrawn or never considered for publication, this body of works cannot be expected to contribute much to an author's image. But a closer examination may well contribute considerably to an understanding of the composer's creative development and perhaps even influence the evaluation of the completed and published works. The main purpose of this article is to give a survey of Arnold Schoenberg's incomplete works and fragments and attempt to group them into categories, with the hope that this may encourage further investigation. Because there are far too many incomplete works to allow a detailed consideration of each, only the larger fragments will be discussed more fully.

The materials Schoenberg left unfinished range from a few notes jotted down in haste to extended passages. At times it is difficult to distinguish clearly between the ways in which the items are unfinished. In an attempt to provide some provisional order in the wilderness, I propose a division into three categories: sketch, outline, and fragment.

A *sketch* shall be defined as a brief notation of a musical idea at any point within a work. It is often monophonic and shows the composer at work on some detail. There are numerous sketches, not included here, that pertain to finished works, as well as those that do not seem related to any identifiable work. Such cursory notations may be very hard to identify, and an unidentified sketch may, upon closer examination, turn out to belong to a known composition.

An *outline* shall be defined as a musical trajectory of some length. It transcends the shortness of the sketch and is focused not on details but rather on a comprehensive view of a part or several parts of a composition.

A *fragment* shall be defined as a piece of music, of any length, that starts at the beginning and is worked out in detail but not concluded. A large number of fragments contain only the first five to twenty measures of a composition. Normally such a fragment will be identical with what Schoenberg called an *Einfall*—a spontaneous idea, hastily notated in full or almost full detail, that was intended to be worked out and developed. This concept plays a crucial role in Schoenberg's compositional practice as well as in his teaching. On one of the first pages of his posthumously published textbook on composition he states:

> The *motive* generally appears in a characteristic and impressive manner at the beginning of a piece. The features of a motive are intervals and rhythms, combined to produce a memorable shape or contour.[1]

In 1911, immediately following the completion of the *Harmonielehre*, Schoenberg conceived another textbook, *Das Komponieren mit selbständigen Stimmen*. It exists in the form of two outlines, which show several subject headings and their chapters and subchapters. In part 1, under the heading "Das Wesen des Satzes mit selbständigen Stimmen" (The essence of the texture of independent parts), Schoenberg concludes:

> Homophony and polyphony are just two different manifestations of the same matter, two principles of style—the same matter of art, the same matter of music, therefore identical laws, but different applications of them.[2]

He goes on to say that in homophony, harmony is form creating and restricted by melody, whereas in polyphony, melody is restricted by harmony. This explanation—which pertains to very short bits of music—makes explicit what kind of texture Schoenberg had in mind as a primary goal in his teaching of composition. It conforms with what he demanded from the *Einfall*. Twenty years later, in 1931, in a commentary on Ernst Kurth's 1917 *Grundlagen des linearen Kontrapunkts*, he stated this even more clearly:

> "Whatever happens in a piece of music is nothing but the endless reshaping of a basic shape." . . . [T]here is nothing in a piece of music but what comes from the theme, springs from it and can be traced back to it; to put it still more severely, nothing but the theme itself.[3]

Such beginnings of just a few measures are conspicuous among Schoenberg's fragments. Out of the total of 111 fragments, which span every stage of his creative career, 77 are twenty-five measures long or less; 41 of these are twelve measures long or less.

In the following tables, the sketches, outlines, and fragments are listed by category. Each item is identified by title (or, if untitled, by an indication of genre or instruments) and date (in editorial brackets if the date is derived from internal evidence); items whose date cannot be established are listed separately under "Undated." Titles in italics are by Schoenberg, those in square brackets by the author. Similarly titled works from the same year are distinguished by Roman numerals following the year. Most of the material is located in the archives of the Arnold Schoenberg Institute, Los Angeles (abbreviated as ASI), in which case the microfilm, sketch, or sketchbook number is given. If the item is located or cited elsewhere, it is identified as follows:

Belmont	Belmont Music Publishers, Los Angeles
Maegaard	Jan Maegaard, *Studien zur Entwicklung des dodekaphonen Satzes bei Arnold Schönberg*, vol. 1 (Copenhagen: Wilhelm Hansen, 1972)
Nachod	J. A. Kimmey, *The Arnold Schoenberg—Hans Nachod Collection*, Detroit Studies in Music Bibliography, no. 41 (Detroit: Detroit Information Coordinators, 1979)
Pierpont	Pierpont Morgan Library, New York
Schott	B. Schott's Söhne, Mainz
Steiner	Ena Steiner, "Schoenberg's Quest: Newly Discovered Works from His Early Years," *Musical Quarterly* 60 (1974), 401–420

Whereas the sketches that do not pertain to previously known music add little to our insight into Schoenberg's composing, other outlines and fragments reveal important details about his life and creativity. The fragments, for instance, illustrate Schoenberg's concentration on the initial motive as the starting point of a composition. This motive tended to come to him spontaneously in a moment of inspiration. His term for it, *Einfall*, and *inspiratio*, the Latin root of *inspiration*, actually have identical meanings— something that comes from outside one, that "falls" or "is blown" into one's mind. On several occasions Schoenberg stressed the importance of inspiration, as in a letter to the conductor Fritz Reiner regarding the Band Variations, op. 43, in which he wrote: "I know it is inspired. Not only because I cannot write even 10 measures without inspiration, but I really wrote the piece with great pleasure."[4] Many, if not all, of the fragments document just such moments of inspiration.

Schoenberg's dependence on inspiration is also documented by the fragment of an early piano piece in A-flat major (see dated fragment no. 13). At the point where Schoenberg broke off, after bar 46, he wrote:

Continuation follows . . . If only I knew how the continuation should be!— Twice I have been mistaken about it. Now I dare not hope, or fear, anything any more. Will continuation follow?—Arn. Sch. February 1901.[5]

This illustrates how Schoenberg set out, hoping from the beginning that the initial inspiration would carry him through. It also illustrates how such

TABLE 1   Fragments (Dated)

	Source	Number of bars
1. *Klein Vögelein* (1893)	Steiner 417	10
2. *Gute Nacht* (1893–1894)	Nachod 91	5
3. *Das gefärbte Osterei* (1893–1894)	Nachod 94	4
4. *Das Unglück* (1893–1894)	Nachod 92	20 + 2
5. *Serenade* [Scherzo, Finale] (1896)	ASI U199–231	63 + 198
6. *Wenn weder Mond* (1897)	ASI 976–978	54
7. *Vorfrühling* (1897)	Nachod 96	10 + 1
8. *Dank* [prelude] (1898)	ASI 2333	12
9. *Frühlings Tod* (1898)	ASI U232–260	15
10. *Gethsemane* (1899)	ASI U71–74	88
11. *Schmerz* (1899)	ASI 221	14
12. Symphony (1900)	ASI U261–264	73 + 7
13. [for piano] (1900–1901)	ASI U1–2	46
14. *Wir müssen* (1901)	Pierpont	17 + 1
15. *Darthulas Grabgesang* (1903)	ASI U352–370	38
16. string quartet (1904)	ASI U122–130	79 + 1
17. [for string quintet] (1904–1905)	ASI Sk45	22
18. *Dümmer ist* (1905)	ASI Sk71	11
19. *Gutes thu* (1905)	ASI Sk69–70	21 + 3
20. *Ein Stelldichein* (1905)	ASI U158–164	90
21. *Wer geboren* (1905)	ASI Sk71	21
22. *Wie das Kriegsvolk* (1905)	ASI U439–440	21 + 12
23. *O süsser Blick'* (1905)	ASI Sk86	8 + 4
24. [for piano] (1905–1906)	ASI Sk159	26
25. *Die Kürze* (1905–1906)	ASI Sk149	15
26. *Heilig Wesen* (1906)	ASI Sk182	6
27. *Still so ist mein Tag* (1906)	SI 187–188	23 + 6
28. *Am Himmelsthor* (1906–1907)	ASI Sk215	6
29. *Pippa tanzt* (1906–1907)	ASI U423–425	6
30. *Aus schwerer Stunde* II (1906–1907)	ASI U87	16
31. *Greif aus* (1906–1907)	ASI Sk214	13

Continued on next page

TABLE 1 *(continued)*

	Source	Number of bars
32. *Jeduch* (1907)	ASI Sk244–246	82
33. *Mignon* (1907)	ASI Sk276	54
34. *Friedesabend* (1908)	ASI U77	28
35. [for chamber ensemble] (1910)	ASI 1301	8
36. *Seraphita* (1912)	ASI U426	13
37. [for chamber ensemble] (1913)	ASI U270	8
38. [for chamber ensemble] (1914 I)	ASI U170	10
39. [for chamber ensemble] (1914 II)	ASI U171	2
40. *Die Jakobsleiter* (1917–1922)	Belmont	700
41. [for piano] (1918)	ASI U46	9
42. [for string septet] (1918)	ASI U175–177	25
43. *Ich fühle* (1919)	ASI U192	11
44. [for chamber ensemble] (1922 I)	ASI U156–157	4 + 1
45. *Gerpa* (1922)	Maegaard 114	127
46. [for piano] (1925)	ASI U57–58	41
47. [for string quartet] (1926 I)	ASI U133–136	12
48. [for strings II] (1926 II)	ASI U137–141	3 + 4
49. [Violin Concerto] (1928)	ASI U296–301	43
50. [for violin/piano] (1930)	ASI U108	12 + 4
51. *Moses und Aron* [1930—]	Schott 2106	
52. [for piano] (1931 I)	ASI U5–11	35
53. [for piano] (1931 II)	ASI U12–13	25
54. Piano Phantasy, four-hand (1937)	ASI U14–15	24
55. [for orchestra] (1939)	ASI U313	14 + 2
56. [Organ Sonata; Scherzo and Moderato] (1941)	ASI U18–35	57 + 25
57. [for orchestra] (1946)	ASI U315–321	28
58. *Nachspiel I* (1947)	ASI U322	5
59. [for orchestra] (1948)	ASI U323–330	25
60. *Israel Exists Again* (1949)	ASI U399–418	64
61. *I Got an A* (1951)	ASI U178–182	15
62. *Moderne Psalmen* (1951)	Schott	86

TABLE 2   Fragments (Undated)

1. *Auf den Knien*	ASI U67–68	18
2. *Aus schwerer Stunde* I	ASI U87	4
3. [for chamber ensemble I]	ASI U173–174	5 + 6
4. [for chamber ensemble II]	ASI U172	6
5. [for chamber ensemble III]	ASI U154–155	12
6. [for chamber ensemble IV]	ASI U110	10
7. [for chamber ensemble V]	ASI U290	6 + 2
8. [for chamber orchestra]	ASI U265–267	30 + 4
9. [Chamber Symphony]	ASI U268–269	22
10. [for clarinet quintet]	ASI U150–153	32
11. *Glaub mir*	ASI U85–86	39
12. *Hans im Glück*	ASI 2343	13
13. *Ein Harfenklang*	ASI U190	21
14. *Im Reich der Liebe*	ASI U65–66	21
15. *In langen Jahren*	ASI U69–70	32
16. *Der Jünger*	ASI U92	6
17. *Lausch mein Herz*	ASI U191	6 + 2
18. *Lied*	ASI U105	10
19. *Mannesbangen*	ASI Sk471	10
20. *Noch ahnt man*	ASI U430	5
21. [for orchestra I]	ASI U153	35
22. [for orchestra II]	ASI U331	6
23. [for piano I]	ASI U38–40	76
24. [for piano II]	ASI U54–55	20
25. [for piano III]	ASI U42–43	5
26. [for piano IV]	ASI U56	13
27. [for piano V]	ASI U41	15
28. [for piano VI]	ASI U45	21
29. [for piano VII]	ASI U44	13
30. [for piano VIII; op. 23A]	ASI U47	9
31. [for piano IX; op. 23B]	ASI U48	12

Continued on next page

TABLE 2 *(continued)*

32. [for piano X]	ASI U60	3
33. [for piano XI]	ASI U61	22
34. [for piano XII]	ASI U62	2
35. [for piano XIII]	ASI U63	5 + 1
36. [for piano XIV]	ASI U64	2
37. *Rosenglaube*	ASI U90	7 + 1
38. Scherzo [for piano]	ASI U3–4	79
39. *Die Stille*	ASI U91	5
40. *Die stille Wasserrose*	Nachod 77	9
41. [for string quartet I]	ASI U142	13 + 24
42. [for string quartet II]	ASI U119–120	11 + 6
43. *Toter Winkel*	ASI U167–169	31
44. Trio	Nachod 76	15
45. *Die tröstende Nacht*	ASI U88–89	11
46. [Walzer no. 11]	Maegaard 152	9
47. *Wanderlied*	ASI 453	20
48. *Zweifel*	ASI U441–442	31 + 1

an attempt could fail, even at times when composition of other works—in this case, *Gurrelieder*—was proceeding successfully. Furthermore, it reveals Schoenberg's own doubts as to whether he would be able to get back on track once he had lost the inspiration. Later developments, such as the 1900 symphony fragment, *Die Jakobsleiter,* and *Moses und Aron,* show that his doubts were well founded.

Among the outlines, two of Schoenberg's attempts to write a symphony (not his first attempts at the genre) are of particular interest. One is a fragment of a symphony dating from February 1900 (dated fragment no. 12), that is, a little earlier than the piano piece just mentioned; the second is a sketch from 1905 (dated sketch no. 6). The first manuscript shows a complete introduction of seventy-three bars in G minor followed by a short sketch of the beginning of the main part of the movement, an Allegro moderato in G major. There it stops abruptly. It is unlikely that Schoenberg would have composed such an extended introduction, and even written one page of it out in full score as a fair copy, as he did, without having had

TABLE 3   Outlines (Dated)

1. *Wie kommt's* (1903)	ASI U75–76
2. *Die Poesie* (1905)	ASI Sk115
3. *Lied eines Sünders* (1905–1906)	ASI Sk142–144
4. *Nächtlicher Weg* (1906)	ASI Sk200–201
5. *Über unsre Liebe* (1906–1907)	ASI Sk213
6. *Patrouillenritt* (1906–1907)	ASI Sk226
7. [Lied] (1907 II)	ASI Sk267–268
8. *Symphonie* (1914–1915)	ASI U100, 371–398; Sk326–333
9. [for chamber ensemble] (1917)	ASI Sk334–341
10. [Violin Concerto] (1922)	ASI U292–295
11. *Die du vor dir* (1927)	ASI U93
12. *Prozessionsmusik* (1927)	ASI U93
13. [for piano] (1931)	ASI U59
14. [Piano Concerto] (1933)	ASI U308–310
15. *The Good Earth* (1935)	ASI Sk Good Earth
16. *Symphonie* (1937)	ASI U311–312

TABLE 4   Outlines (Undated)

1. *Adagio*	Maegaard 165
2. *Geuss nicht*	ASI Sl751–752
3. [Lied; no text]	ASI U101–102
4. [for orchestra III]	ASI U332–333
5. *Ständchen*	ASI 979–981
6. *Who is like*	ASI U433–438

a notion of what it was to be an introduction to. Nonetheless he abandoned the Allegro after those first seven bars and never returned to it. We do not know why, but can only surmise that it was put aside in favor of the composition of *Gurrelieder,* which he had begun in March of that year. And after that he may have felt that his orchestral and compositional technique had developed too far in another direction.

TABLE 5   Sketches (Dated)

Title	Source
1. *Ach lieber* (1901)	ASI Sk707–708
2. *O wär mein Herz* (1904)	ASI Sk6
3. *Was thust, was denkst du* (1904)	ASI Sk6
4. *Ich weiss nicht* (1904–1905)	ASI Sk41
5. *Sonnenuntergang* (1905)	ASI Sk158
6. *Symphonie* (1905)	ASI Sk108
7. *Ein Herre mit zwei Gesind* (1905)	ASI Sk67
8. *Apostatenmarsch* (1905–1906)	ASI Sk144
9. *Abendstille* (1905–1906)	ASI Sk150
10. [for orchestra] (1905–1906)	ASI Sk151
11. *Besuch* (1906)	ASI Sk211
12. *Des Friedens Ende* (1906–1907)	ASI Sk225
13. [for string quintet] (1906–1907)	ASI Sk224
14. *Wenn schlanke Lilien* (1906–1907)	ASI Sk229
15. [Lied] (1907 I)	ASI Sk247
16. [for chamber ensemble] (1907–1908)	ASI Sk282
17. *Gewissheit* (1908)	ASI Sk295
18. Psalm 94 [1912]	Maegaard 160
19. Psalm 95 [1912]	Maegaard 160
20. [for orchestra] [1913]	ASI U271
21. [for chamber ensemble] (1922 II)	ASI Sketchbook 22–23, 1
22. [Adagio] (1922–1923)	ASI Sketchbook 22–23, 21
23. [Melodie] (1922–1923)	ASI Sketchbook 22–23, 25
24. [for string quartet] (1923)	ASI Sketchbook 22–23, 26
25. [for solo violin] (1925)	ASI Sk637

TABLE 6   Sketches (Undated)

1. [Lied; no text]	ASI Sk705–706
2. Psalm 40	ASI U429–430
3. Psalm 43	ASI U431
4. Psalm 103	ASI U432
5. [for violin/piano]	ASI U109
6. [Violin Concerto]	ASI U305–307
7. *Was klagst du*	ASI Sk320

However, it could not have been easy for a young composer of that era to give up the idea of writing a symphony—a young composer who had witnessed the conclusion of Bruckner's and Brahms's careers and experienced the premiere of one Mahler symphony after another. Despite initial reservations about Mahler, Schoenberg's attitude at some time between 1904 and 1908 took a turn. When the Eighth Symphony was given its premiere in Munich in September 1910, an event that marked the climax of Mahler's career as a composer, Schoenberg would have studied the work carefully as a matter of course, even though he did not attend the performance. It is evident from his obituary lecture on Mahler, first held in Prague in March 1912, that he knew the work well, at least from study.[6]

Schoenberg's next symphonic project (dated outline no. 8) may well have taken its impetus from Mahler's Eighth Symphony. Although it also includes many sketches and fragments, I have found it most appropriate to place it in the category of outlines. The concept goes back further than the date of the item would indicate, to a short fragment of an oratorio from December 1912, entitled *Seraphita* and based upon Honoré de Balzac's novel of that name (dated fragment no. 36). At about the same time Schoenberg wrote to the poet Richard Dehmel, whom he greatly admired, about his intention to write an oratorio; he describes the contents he envisions:

> how this modern man, having passed through materialism, socialism, and anarchy and, despite having been an atheist, still having in him some residue of ancient faith (in the form of superstition), wrestles with God . . . and finally succeeds in finding God and becoming religious. Learning to pray![7]

As Schoenberg tells Dehmel, he had initially intended writing the text himself, then considered adapting Strindberg's *Jakob ringt,* and finally decided to start with positive religious belief by adapting the final chapter of Balzac's

Séraphita. "But," he writes, "I could never shake off the thought of 'Modern Man's Prayer,' and I often thought: If only Dehmel . . . !"[8] In his reply Dehmel sent Schoenberg his *Oratorium natale,* which he had written the previous year but not yet published.

In his subsequent work on the text of this symphony Schoenberg included poems by Dehmel—some of them from *Oratorium natale*—and by Rabindranath Tagore, along with several texts from the Old as well as the New Testament. By January 1915 he had finished his own text, *Totentanz der Prinzipien,* which he designated as "3rd Movement," and three days later he started writing the text of *Die Jakobsleiter* under the heading "4th Movement." This seems to have been completed in May 1917. This ambitiously designed work, which thus goes at least as far back as 1912, ended up as the extensive fragment *Die Jakobsleiter* (dated fragment no. 40). Later, when mentioning the work, Schoenberg always referred it to 1914–1915, which is actually when most of the musical sketches for it were composed.

The original concept, which was to undergo so many changes, bears some analogy to Mahler's Eighth Symphony. However, whereas it had been Mahler's endeavor to sum up European man's feeling for religion and love, from the medieval "Veni creator spiritus" to Goethe's *Faust,* Schoenberg's concept evidently was to interpret what was left of religious feeling and love in European man at the beginning of the twentieth century, and to do so by means strikingly similar to those of Mahler's symphony. Schoenberg conceived his work on an even larger scale. Not only did he at first plan to have five huge movements, but he foresaw an orchestra of ten to twelve flutes, oboes, and bassoons, twelve to sixteen clarinets, twelve French horns and tubas, six to eight trumpets and trombones, two to three contrabass tubas, and a number of harps, celestas, glockenspiels, and xylophones, in addition to the traditional complement of percussion instruments, twenty stands of violins, ten to twelve stands of violas, cellos, and double basses, and on top of that a number of soloists and a large chorus.

Schoenberg's concept is significant in yet another respect, in that it marks a radical departure from the expressionistic outburst of 1909, represented by the Three Piano Pieces, op. 11, Five Pieces for Orchestra, op. 16, and *Erwartung,* op. 17. In fact, the uncompleted concept would have been a far more radical departure than that of the completed and published works: the Six Little Piano Pieces, op. 19, *Herzgewächse,* op. 20, and *Pierrot lunaire,* op. 21.

Between June and September 1917 Schoenberg composed almost the entire first part—603 bars—of *Die Jakobsleiter.* Then he was called up for military service, and although he was released after less than three months, it proved difficult for him to resume work. During the following years, until 1922, he managed to compose only a further one hundred bars, which extended to the end of part 1 and the beginning of an interlude. It is readily apparent that Schoenberg was unable to continue work on the composition at the same time that the "method of composing with twelve tones only related to one another" was being born in a series of new works. The desire to complete *Die Jakobsleiter* remained alive, however, and in 1944, at the time of his retirement from UCLA, Schoenberg resumed work on the score. In 1945, when he applied unsuccessfully for a grant from the Guggenheim Foundation, *Die Jakobsleiter* was mentioned among the projects he hoped to complete. Finally, less than one month before his death in July 1951, he asked his former pupil Karl Rankl to help him finish part 1.[9]

Schoenberg's last attempt to write a symphony occurred in January and February 1937. On seven sheets he conceived the outline of a dodeca-phonic symphony in four movements, which in a programmatic manner was intended to depict the contemporaneous situation of the Jewish people, their frustrations, and their hopes.[10] But this project, too, remained uncom-pleted. Thus three of Schoenberg's four symphonic projects were not car-ried out beyond the preliminary stages, whereas the one project that ended up as a huge fragment was more oratorio than symphony.

In the 1920s Schoenberg started another ambitious work that was also destined to remain a fragment, the opera *Moses und Aron*. The circum-stances surrounding this work are well documented and do not need to be repeated in detail here. The idea for the text sprang from Schoenberg's theater play *Der biblische Weg* of 1926–1927 and had initially been intended as an oratorio text. Schoenberg apparently made the decision to turn it into an opera at the time he began to compose the music in 1930. He completed the first two acts within two years. But neither the final version of the text nor the music of the third act ever materialized. In 1933 Schoen-berg told Walter Eidlitz that he had had difficulties with the text because of contradictions in the Bible, and that he had rewritten it at least four times.[11] He is known to have resumed work on it again in 1934 and 1935. Years later he gave permission for a performance of *Moses und Aron* with the 1934 version of the third act either as a spoken dialogue or left out altogether.[12] Some musical sketches do exist for this act, but nothing that could justify an attempt to reconstruct it. Thus *Moses und Aron* too has re-mained a large fragment.

A third work of a comparable scale deserves to be mentioned in this connection—namely, *Gurrelieder*. Schoenberg composed the music during 1900–1901, and had completed the orchestration up to the Peasant's Song at the beginning of part 3 by 1903. Then he laid the work aside. Fortunate circumstances caused him to arrange for a performance of part 1 in a ver-sion for pianos in a concert in Vienna in January 1910; also on that program were the first performance of the fifteen songs from *Das Buch der hängenden Gärten*, op. 15, and the Three Piano Pieces, op. 11. In the often cited pro-gram note that Schoenberg wrote for that recital it is stated that the two new and groundbreaking works are presented together with the older one so as to show "that not lack of inventiveness or of technical ability or of familiarity with the demands of traditional aesthetics" had driven him in that direction, but that he had followed an inner compulsion stronger than education.[13]

That performance gave rise to a desire in Schoenberg to hear the entire *Gurrelieder* in the orchestral version and with the big choruses of part 3. An added inducement was Franz Schreker's eagerness to perform it with his newly founded Vienna Philharmonic Chorus. As a result Schoenberg completed the score during 1910–1911, and Schreker conducted the first performance of the work in Vienna in 1913, which was a great success. That Schoenberg was able to take up and finish this large work after eight years of stylistic development seems to be due to the fact that in this case the music had actually been composed at an earlier stage.[14] It only remained for Schoenberg to complete the orchestration as of the end of the Peasant's Song. If the situation had been otherwise, *Gurrelieder* might well have shared the fate of *Die Jakobsleiter* and *Moses und Aron*.

There is only one additional fragment of a length exceeding 150 bars—namely, the Serenade in D major from 1896. Schoenberg completed the first movement, an Andante, but the two subsequent movements, a Scherzo and Finale, remained fragments of 63 and 198 bars, respectively. There is no reason to believe that he would have felt inclined to complete this work at any later stage.

The consideration of big fragments in Schoenberg's oeuvre would be incomplete without a word about the *Moderner Psalm* for narrator, mixed chorus, and orchestra, op. 50C. This was certainly also intended to be a work of considerable dimensions, as can be seen from the texts. Ten psalms seem to have been intended as a first group; beyond that there are five further psalms and a text fragment. Schoenberg began composing the music in October 1950 but had notated only eighty-six bars, together with a few sketches for the continuation, before his death on 13 July 1951. The last words Schoenberg ever set to music were "*Und trotzdem bete ich.*" (And nevertheless I pray).[15]

•   •   •   •   •

In the course of half a century Schoenberg's music passed through stylistic changes more far-reaching than had ever been seen in music history during such a short span of time; his musical language developed through many stages, and not always in a straightforward fashion. That state of constant change allowed very little time for the composition of large, time-consuming works. Almost as if he were aware of this, Schoenberg at an early stage developed the ability to compose very quickly. Thus the 426 bars of the monodrama *Erwartung* were composed in one burst of inspiration in the two weeks between 27 August and 12 September 1909. But whenever Schoenberg was interrupted in the middle of a big project, it was usually impossible for him to pick up the thread again. In 1917 work on *Die Jakobsleiter* was interrupted, first by military service and then by Schoenberg's preoccupation with developing the dodecaphonic technique. In 1932 work on *Moses und Aron* was interrupted, first by difficulties with the text and then by Schoenberg's flight from Germany in October 1933. In 1902 the orchestration of *Gurrelieder* had been similarly interrupted by Schoenberg's need to earn money by orchestrating operettas; he resumed work on *Gurrelieder* in 1903 but again gave it up, presumably because the possibility of having the colossal work performed in Vienna at that time seemed so slight. Fortunately Schoenberg was able to finish the score when the opportunity presented itself in 1910, but he himself admitted that the parts orchestrated in 1910 and 1911 sound different from the rest.

The same is true of another work that was saved from remaining a fragment. Schoenberg began his Second Chamber Symphony in 1906, right after completing the First Chamber Symphony, but soon thereafter gave it up. After resuming it in 1911 (upon completion of the *Gurrelieder* orchestration) and again in 1916, he did eventually complete the work in 1939, more than thirty years after its initial stages. No wonder that in this work, composed over a span of so many years, there are striking differences to be heard between the various parts.

Taking the pace of Schoenberg's stylistic development and the turbulence of his life into consideration, it is not surprising that throughout his creative life one or two of his most ambitious compositional projects were always pending, waiting to be completed. From 1900 on it was *Gurrelieder,* which took another twelve years to reach completion; from 1912 on it was the symphony that ended up as the *Jakobsleiter* fragment; and from 1930 on it was *Moses und Aron.* Given this situation, it is truly amazing—and testifies to his enormous vitality—that in September 1950, despite old age and failing health, Schoenberg had the courage to enter upon yet another big project, the *Moderne Psalmen.* There is no other great composer in whose oeuvre huge unfinished works play a role as decisive as they do in the oeuvre of Arnold Schoenberg.

NOTES

1. Schoenberg, *Fundamentals of Musical Composition,* ed. Gerald Strang and Leonard Stein (London: Faber and Faber, 1967), 8.

2. Quoted and translated from Rudolf Stephan, "Schönbergs Entwurf über 'Das Komponieren mit selbständigen Stimmen," *Archiv für Musikforschung* 29/4 (1972), 239–256. Unless otherwise indicated, all translations are by the author.

3. "Linear Counterpoint," in *Style and Idea*, 289–295, esp. 290.

4. Schoenberg to Reiner, 29 October 1944, translated in Rufer, *Works of Arnold Schoenberg*, 72.

5.

Fortsetzung folgt... Wenn ich nur wüsste, wie die Fortsetzung sein wird!—Zweimal habe ich mich darüber getäuscht. Jetzt wage ich nichts mehr zu hoffen, und zu befürchten. Folgt Fortsetzung?—Arn. Sch. Im Februar 1901.

6. The manuscript for Schoenberg's March 1912 talk on Mahler in Prague, which he repeated in Berlin and Vienna later that year, is dated 13 October 1912; it was later significantly revised and first published in *Style and Idea*, 449–471.

7. Schoenberg to Dehmel, 13 December 1912, *Schoenberg Letters*, 35–36, esp. 35; see also Joachim Birke, "Richard Dehmel und Arnold Schönberg, Ein Briefwechsel," *Die Musikforschung* 11/3 (1958), 279–285.

8. Schoenberg to Dehmel, 13 December 1912, *Schoenberg Letters*, 36.

9. After Schoenberg's death, Gertrud Schoenberg entrusted Winfried Zillig with the preparation of the score that was used for the first performance, which took place in Vienna in 1961.

10. The manuscript, formerly owned by Winfried Zillig, seems to have been lost, but two photocopies have been preserved; see Nikos Kokkinis, "Schönbergs Entwüfe zu einer jüdischen Programmsymphonie," *Mitteilungen der Internationalen Schönberg-Gesellschaft* 2 (October 1987), 5–6.

11. Schoenberg to Walter Eidlitz, 15 March 1933, *Schoenberg Letters*, no. 151, 172.

12. Schoenberg to Francesco Siciliani, the artistic director of Maggio Musicale Fiorentino, 27 November 1950, *Schoenberg Letters*, no. 255, 285. The performance never took place.

13. The program note, preserved in the ASI, is quoted in full in Maegaard, *Entwicklung des dodekaphonen Satzes*, 2:124.

14. For a chronology of the composition, see Schoenberg's letter to Alban Berg, dated 24 January 1913, which Berg quoted almost verbatim in both the full and abridged editions of his *Gurrelieder Führer* (Vienna: Universal Edition [1913 and 1914]), 18; for an English translation of the letter, see *Berg-Schoenberg Correspondence*, 147–148.

15. The sketches, particell, and texts were published in facsimile by Rudolf Kolisch in his edition of the score of *Moderne Psalmen* (Mainz: B. Schott's Söhne, 1956).

TEN

Schoenberg's Philosophy of Composition

Thoughts on the "Musical Idea and Its Presentation"

Patricia Carpenter and Severine Neff

Throughout his creative life Schoenberg wrote about various aspects of his philosophy of composition—that is, the system of motivating beliefs, concepts, and principles that constitutes his basic theory. Here we are concerned not with his technical theory but rather with the ground for technical matters. We shall discuss the development of Schoenberg's concept of the "musical idea" first by describing the chronology of manuscripts dealing with his theory and philosophy of composition, then by tracing the intellectual evolution of the concept of the "musical idea" in his theoretical writings. Finally we shall turn to Schoenberg's notion of the "musical idea" and its presentation by glossing the familiar passage on artistic creation in the 1941 twelve-tone lecture "Composition with Twelve Tones"[1] in light of the theoretical and philosophical concerns of earlier manuscripts.

I

Upon publication of the *Harmonielehre* in 1911 Arnold Schoenberg wrote to his publisher Emil Hertzka at Universal Edition:

> I would perhaps be ready to draw up a contract for my entire activities as a writer on music. I plan in the near future the following writings (in addition to the counterpoint [book][2]): an instrumentation text. There is nothing like this now, for all available books deal with the instruments themselves. I wish to teach the art of composing for orchestra!! This is a major distinction and something *absolutely new!!*
>
> Then a *Preliminary Study of Form: An Investigation into the Formal Causes of the Effects of Modern Compositions.* This writing will probably be limited to the study of Mahler's works. Then, later, also as a preliminary to the study of form, *Formal Analysis and Laws Resulting from It.* Finally, *Theory of Form.*

All of these books are texts or teaching aids. They form in their entirety an *Aesthetic of Music,* under which title I wish to write a . . . comprehensive work. For all of these works I already have ideas and also notes. I can finish all of them in the course of five years![3]

Not until six years later, however, in April 1917, did Schoenberg begin working simultaneously on the instrumentation and form books and on a counterpoint book distinct from *Das Komponieren mit selbständigen Stimmen,* to which he had referred in his letter to Hertzka.[4] At the same time, he also began work on a newly conceived book on musical coherence (rather than one on aesthetics).

By 1922 Schoenberg was planning both a *Lehre vom musikalischen Zusammenhang* (Theory of musical coherence) and a *Kompositionslehre* (Theory of composition).[5] However, two years later he wrote, "More recently I have made some discoveries which compelled me to revise the small work entitled *Lehre vom musikalischen Zusammenhang* into the more ambitious *Die Gesetze der musikalischen Komposition* [The laws of musical composition]."[6] The book on coherence and the book on compositional theory thus had become identified as a single project on composition.

The "discoveries" to which Schoenberg referred almost certainly concerned the twelve-tone method, which he began to use almost exclusively in 1923. A manuscript entitled "Der musikalische Gedanke" (The musical idea) also dates from 1923.[7] That same year he proposed a book to be entitled *Komposition mit zwölf Tönen* (Composition with twelve tones), but in 1924 he decided that an article with this title was sufficient.[8] This chronology suggests that his work on the twelve-tone method confirmed Schoenberg's belief that the nature of coherence in any piece of music (tonal, atonal, twelve-tone, and so forth) is the expression of a musical idea.

In one of the ensuing *Gedanke* manuscripts, "Der musikalische Gedanke, seine Darstellung und Durchführung" (The musical idea, its presentation and development), written between 1925 and 1929, Schoenberg again brought up the idea of a unified theory of composition:

At present the theories of harmony, counterpoint, and form mainly serve pedagogical purposes. With the possible exception of the theory of harmony, the individual disciplines completely lack even a truly theoretical basis emanating from other external criteria. On the whole, the consequence is that three different disciplines, that together should constitute the theory of composition, in reality remain separate because they lack a common point of view.[9]

By 1929 Schoenberg saw his concept of the musical idea as grounds for such a unified theory of composition: "Composition . . . is above all the art of inventing a musical idea and the fitting way to present it."[10] The concept of the musical idea thus superseded the earlier general theory of coherence as the core of Schoenberg's theory of composition.

Schoenberg's manuscripts on the "musical idea" were an ongoing attempt to formulate his unified theory of composition, a goal he never achieved to his satisfaction. There are twelve such incomplete manuscripts, written over a period of thirteen years, the first a brief paragraph from 1923, the last a 150-page text written between 1934 and 1936.[11]

1. "zu 'Darstellung des Gedankens' " (on "presentation of the idea"), dated 19 August 1923
2. "Der musikalische Gedanke, seine Darstellung und Durchführung" (The musical idea, its presentation and elaboration), dated 7 July 1925
3. "zu: Darstellung d. Gedankens" (on: presentation of the idea), dated 12 November 1925
4. "Der musikalische Gedanke und seine Darstellung" (The musical idea and its presentation), undated, with added notes dated 7 April 1929 and 1940
5. Untitled, undated[12]
6. "Zu: Darstellung des musikalischen Gedankens" (On: presentation of the musical idea), dated 16 August 1931
7. "Entwurf zum Vorwort/(Komp.lehre)" (Sketch for the preface/ [theory of composition]), dated 17 August 1931
8. "Zu: Darstellung des Gedankens" (On: presentation of the idea), dated 3 August 1932
9. "The Musical Idea," dated 4 June 1934
10. "Der musikalische Gedanke und die Logik, Technik, und Kunst seiner Darstellung" (The musical idea and the logic, technique, and art of its presentation), dated 5 June to 24 August 1934, and late September to 15 October 1936
11. "Der musikalische Gedanke; seine Darstellung und Durchfuehrung" (The musical idea: its presentation and elaboration), undated
12. Untitled, undated[13]

A phrase in the title of many of these manuscripts, "the musical idea and its presentation," expresses both the technical and philosophical sides of Schoenberg's theory of composition. In speaking of the musical idea and its presentation, the composer used a specific vocabulary. For "idea" he generally used *Gedanke,* a concrete thought, in contrast to *Begriff,* a concept. In its narrowest sense the idea is a musical relation, but in its broadest sense it is the totality of a piece, "the idea which its creator wanted to present."[14] Schoenberg used *Darstellung* (presentation) in a particular way—as he said, "to signify the presentation of an object to a spectator in such a way that he perceives its composite parts as if in functional motion."[15] The notion of a part "in functional motion" characterizes a nineteenth-century philosophy of the artwork as a living organism.

In the ensuing sections of this essay we will trace in Schoenberg's thought the theoretical and philosophical aspects of the "musical idea and its presentation."

II

Schoenberg opened *Gedanke* manuscript no. 6 (1931) with the statement "Composing is *thinking in tones and rhythms*. Every piece of music is the *presentation of a musical idea*." Schoenberg maintains that musical thinking is subject to the laws and conditions of all our other thinking. All thinking consists essentially in bringing things (concepts, and so forth) into relation. That being so, thinking searches out coherences; every idea is based on coherences. An idea is the production of a relation between things that would otherwise have no relation. Therefore an idea is always new.[16] In the opening of *Gedanke* no. 12 (undated) he distinguishes a "musical idea":

> A musical idea is sheerly musical. It is a relation between tones.

If one may designate as ideas the production of relations between things, concepts, and the like (thus also between ideas), then in the case of a musical idea such a relation can be established only between tones, and it can be only a musical relation.[17]

In the theoretical literature of the late eighteenth and early nineteenth centuries the musical idea (*Gedanke* or *Idee*) was commonly taken to be the theme or melody. Beginning with this traditional meaning, Schoenberg moved toward an understanding of the idea as standing for the wholeness of a work. He expressed this in the familiar passage in "New Music, Outmoded Music, Style and Idea":

> In its most common meaning, the term idea is used as a synonym for theme, melody, phrase or motive. I myself consider the totality of a piece as the *idea:* the idea which its creator wanted to present. But because of the lack of better terms I am forced to define the term idea in the following manner.[18]

Describing the manner in which a state of unrest or imbalance grows throughout most of a piece, he then goes on to state that "[t]he method by which balance is restored seems to me the real *idea* of the composition."[19] With this concept of the idea as the totality of a work he created a powerful conceptual tool, the development of which is demonstrated in the series of *Gedanke* manuscripts.

Already in the early *Gedanke* manuscripts Schoenberg confronted the problem of the integrity of the theme, and by 1925 he had begun to turn his attention from the theme as a whole to its smallest parts. Discussing the presentation of the idea independently of its substance, he distinguishes in the idea its components, *Gestalt* and *Grundgestalt*. On the one hand, the more primitive a musical idea and the piece based on it, the fewer and more closely related the Gestalten that may be enlisted; on the other hand, the more artful the idea, the richer the number of Gestalten and the more remote in form from the Grundgestalt.[20] He distinguishes even smaller components of an idea, its "characteristics"—that is, specific pitch and rhythmic relationships. Ultimately the characteristics of a motive—what he called its "features," its intervals and rhythms—could themselves be treated as motives.[21] By reducing the theme to these smallest components, Schoenberg destroyed its role as musical idea and transformed the material, freeing intervals and rhythms to be used for their own sake.

In an unpublished manuscript dated 5 October 1923 and entitled "Zur Terminologie der Formenlehre,"[22] Schoenberg raised the crucial matter of whole and part: Is the idea a part, the theme, or somehow the whole? He comments on the ambiguity of the term *musical idea*, observing that although it is preferable to *theme, motive*, or *phrase*, one must still distinguish the main or secondary ideas of an entire piece from individual smaller or smallest parts. This ambiguity is likewise taken up in *Gedanke* no. 12 (undated):

> The idea can be the subject of a longer or shorter work, it can exist for itself alone, but it can also be part of a larger whole. This larger whole will then itself usually break down into more or less numerous sections, steps, parts, and the like, which in part can again be ideas. Such ideas will in some way be connected with each other or juxtaposed, or will otherwise have a relation to each other which will probably be referable to the whole.[23]

Schoenberg resolved the relation of the idea to the whole by means of his remarkable vision of the dynamic of the musical work. He saw the potentiality for musical motion in the single tone, as he stated in the *Harmonielehre*.

> The primitive ear hears the tone as irreducible, but physics recognizes it to be complex. In the meantime, however, musicians discovered that it is capable of continuation, i.e., that movement is latent within it. That problems are concealed in it, problems that clash with one another, that the tone lives and seeks to propagate itself.[24]

In even the smallest component there is the potential for unrest and imbalance, as Schoenberg discussed in *Gedanke* no. 10 (1934–1936): "Through the connection of tones of different pitch, duration, and stress . . . an unrest comes into being: a state of rest is placed in question through a contrast. From this unrest a motion proceeds."[25] He conceived of the whole as a balance of forces between the unrest inherent in the material, the imbalance produced by such unrest, and the restoration of balance. The idea, then, is the contrast that challenges the state of rest—and the means by which that state is restored.

The source of Schoenberg's investigations of the musical idea was of course his experience as a composer. Ultimately he turned to his own experience to explain the relation of the idea to the wholeness of the work. A work is a totality because it is the realization of a single idea, the composer's vision—and that idea is always new.

III

Schoenberg's philosophy of composition is based on this principle of totality. He elaborated on it in a passage in the 1941 version of his lecture "Composition with Twelve Tones," which epitomizes his view of artistic creation. "To understand the very nature of creation," Schoenberg began, "one must acknowledge that there was no light before the Lord said: 'Let there be Light.' "

> We . . . should never forget what a creator is in reality.
> A creator has a vision of something which has not existed before this vision. And a creator has the power to bring his vision to life, the power to realize it.
> . . . . In Divine Creation there were no details to be carried out later; "There was Light" at once and in its ultimate perfection.
> Alas, human creators, if they be granted a vision, must travel the long path between vision and accomplishment; a hard road where, driven out of Paradise, even geniuses must reap their harvest in the sweat of their brows.
> Alas, it is one thing to envision in a creative instant of inspiration and it is another thing to materialize one's vision by painstakingly connecting details until they fuse into a kind of organism.
> Alas, suppose it becomes an organism, a homunculus or a robot, and possesses some of the spontaneity of a vision; it remains yet another thing to organize this form so that it becomes a comprehensible message "to whom it may concern."[26]

Having set up an antithesis between divine and mortal creation, between the composer's instantaneous vision and the arduous road from revelation to consummation, Schoenberg goes on to discuss several points in turn: inspiration, materialization, form, and idea.

A work, Schoenberg says, originates in an instant of inspiration. *Der Einfall,* or "inspiration," is a word he also uses for "idea," as in "*der blitzartige Einfall,*"[27] the idea that strikes like lightning. In 1931 he described the first thought that must dictate the structure and texture of the work as an "unnameable sense of a sounding and moving space, of a form with characteristic relationships."[28] The first thought is thus the source of the totality of a musical work.

But an instantaneous creative vision is one thing, its materialization quite another. The artwork materializes the vision in a particular way, as a kind of organism. Schoenberg's model for artistic creation is natural generation.

> [A]rt does not depend upon the single component part alone; therefore, music does not depend upon the theme. For the work of art, like every living thing, is conceived as a whole—just like a child, whose arm or leg is not conceived separately. The inspiration is not the theme, but the whole work.[29]

The distinction between organic form, achieved by a process analogous to natural growth, and mechanical form, imposed from without, was prevalent in the nineteenth century and was stated succinctly by August Wilhelm Schlegel in his influential "Lectures on Dramatic Art and Literature" of 1809–1811:

> Form is mechanical when it is imparted to any material through an external force, merely as an accidental addition, without reference to its character. . . . Organic form, on the contrary, is innate; it unfolds itself from within, and reaches its determination simultaneously with the fullest development of the seed. . . . In the fine arts, just as in the province of nature—the supreme artist—all genuine forms are organic.[30]

Schoenberg espoused the same distinction in his most extensive *Gedanke* manuscript, no. 10 (1934–1936). In the final essay of that manuscript, entitled "Prinzipien des Aufbaus" (Principles of construction), he elaborated on the principle that in art the construct is not a mechanical one, like a clock, but an image resembling an organism in its vital unity.[31]

An organism implies totality—indeed, a certain kind of totality. The properties of an organic whole cannot be derived from the sum of its parts; it cannot, to use Schoenberg's metaphor, be built up the way a bricklayer, for example, builds a wall.[32] The whole is prior to the parts; its unity is therefore diametrically opposed to the aggregate of bricks gathered to build a wall. Organic unity entails a certain relation of parts and whole, a relation that is not arbitrary, but as close and intimate as that among the organs of a living body. An artwork conceived organically is a totality because its author, by virtue of his creative imagination, has fused its elements into a single entity.

In "Prinzipien des Aufbaus" Schoenberg pursues this traditional concept of organicism. He proposes that to symbolize the construction of a musical work, one can think of a living body that is whole and centrally controlled, that puts forth a certain number of limbs by means of which it is capable of exercising its life function. In music, he says, only the whole itself is that central body.[33]

Schoenberg declares that the composer must organize the form of that body in such a way that it can be grasped by the listener. Now, *form* is an ambiguous word, but Schoenberg is quite specific when in *Fundamentals of Musical Composition* he defines "musical form" as the organization of the whole, in which the parts function like those of an organism.[34] Form is not a schema to be abstracted from or imposed upon the work, not something separable from the work—"a solid and inflexible body like a mold in which to cast material."[35] As he defined it in his 1925 essay "Tonality and Form," Schoenberg's notion of form begins with the musical "body":

> The form of a composition is achieved because (1) a body exists, and because (2) the members exercise different functions and are created for these functions.[36]

Form organizes, articulates the musical organism.

Articulation is the central concept in Schoenberg's theory of form. As he wrote in *Fundamentals of Musical Composition,* articulation disposes parts to produce a "surveyable whole," entailing delimitation and subdivision, as well as the distinction between main and subordinate matters, by giving to each its correct place, length, importance, form, and so forth.[37] He discussed this in even greater detail in the *Gedanke* manuscript no. 10, where he wrote that parts of a work are differentiated according to function:

> Above all (perhaps always) a piece of music is an *articulated* organism, whose organs, limbs and their definite functions exercise their own external effect as well as that of their mutual relationship.[38]

Schoenberg goes on to distinguish the parts of an inanimate object from limbs of a biological body and states that truly functioning limbs are found only in organisms and that, unlike parts—which are actually dead, alive from event to event only through an external power—limbs sustain their power as a result of their organic membership in a living organism.[39] Our way of receiving music, he says, is mostly as the comprehension of parts. And only a very precise knowledge of the whole and all its parts and their functions enables a few among us to comprehend a whole.[40]

Finally, with regard to the idea, Schoenberg insisted that the material, tonal body is worthless unless it transcends itself to become something immaterial, a comprehensible message, an idea. He believed that the inner force giving the tonal body its life is the musical idea this body represents. Form, he wrote elsewhere, is the embodiment of a content, the "outside" of the "inside."

All form-making, all *conscious* form-making, is connected with some kind of mathematics, or geometry, or with the golden section or suchlike. But only unconscious form-making, which sets up the equation "form = outward shape," really creates forms.[41]

Because the outer form corresponds to the inner nature of the idea, it makes the idea comprehensible. In the *Harmonielehre* he wrote:

In music we assume that the components of . . . an idea are expressed as melodic or (harmonic) progressions. That is correct, insofar as it concerns the visible or audible in music that can be perceived by the senses; it is correct only by analogy for that which makes up the actual content of a musical idea. . . . We may still assume that, as in any well-built organism[,] . . . the form and articulation manifested by the notes corresponds to the inner nature of the idea and its movement, as ridges and hollows of our bodies are determined by the position of internal organs.[42]

As Schoenberg wrote in the 1934 article "Problems of Harmony," "The effort of the composer is solely for the purpose of making the idea comprehensible to the listener. For the latter's sake the artist must divide the whole into its surveyable parts, and then add them together again into a complete whole."[43] In his 1941 twelve-tone lecture Schoenberg continued that discussion:

Form in the arts, and especially in music, aims primarily at comprehensibility. The relaxation which a satisfied listener experiences when he can follow an idea, its development, and the reasons for such development is closely related, psychologically speaking, to a feeling of beauty.[44]

The form of the work therefore articulates the idea as well as the organic body. To borrow notions from the traditional concept of beauty, form so clarifies the musical body, makes it so lucid, that the idea it embodies shines through. Toward the conclusion of his article Schoenberg declares: "Formerly, sound had been the radiation of an intrinsic quality of ideas, powerful enough to penetrate the hull of the form. Nothing could radiate which was not light itself; and here only ideas are light."[45]

· · · · ·

These, then, are the main points of Schoenberg's philosophy of composition, from a description of his concept of the musical idea as representing the total dynamic of the artwork to a discussion of its role in artistic creation. Schoenberg's creative process begins with the idea, the instantaneous inspiration of the whole, the first thought. It proceeds with its materialization or presentation in the musical organism, the work. And this in turn is so articulated, so formed, as to clarify the material, allowing the idea and its presentational body to be grasped as a unity. As Schoenberg says in his short essay "Konstruierte Musik" (Constructed music), written around 1930:

[I]n my case the productive process has its own way; what I sense is not a melody, a motive, a bar, but merely a whole work. Its sections: the movements; their sections: the themes; their sections: the motives and bars—all that is detail, arrived at as the work is progressively realized. The fact that the details are realized with the strictest, most conscientious care, that everything is logical, purposeful and organically deft, without the visionary images thereby losing fullness, number, clarity, beauty, originality or pregnancy—that is merely a question of intellectual energy. . . .

The inspiration, the vision, the whole, breaks down during its presentation into details whose constructed realization reunites them into the whole.[46]

NOTES

1. Schoenberg, "Composition with Twelve Tones (1)" (1941), in *Style and Idea*, 214–245. This essay is based on a lecture presented at the University of California at Los Angeles on 26 March 1941. Much of the material goes back to a lecture presented at Princeton University on 6 March 1934.

2. Schoenberg is referring to the text *Das Komponieren mit selbständigen Stimmen* (Composing with independent voices), which he had begun outlining in 1911. For a description of that manuscript, see Rufer, *Works of Arnold Schoenberg*, 135. For an edition of the text, see Rudolf Stephan, "Schönbergs Entwurf über 'Das Komponieren mit selbständigen Stimmen,' " *Archiv für Musikwissenschaft* 29/4 (1972), 239–246.

3.

Ich wäre eventuell bereit, einen Vertrag auf meine ganze musikschriftstellerische Tätigkeit zu machen. Ich plane folgende Schriften in der nächsten Zeit (ausser dem Kontrapunkt).

Eine Instrumentationslehre; die gibt es nämlich auch jetzt nicht; denn alle vorhandenen Bücher sind Instrumentenkunden. Ich aber will die Setzkunst für Orchester lehren!! Das is ein grosser Unterschied und etwas *absolut Neues!!*

Dann eine "Vorstudie zur Formenlehre": "Untersuchung über die formalen Ursachen für die Wirkung in modernen Kompositionen".

Diese Schrift wird sich wahrscheinlich nur mit *Mahlers* Werken befassen.

Dann später:

ebenfalls als Vorstudie zur Formenlehre: "Form-Analysen und Gesetze, die sich daraus ergeben." Schliesslich hierauf: "Formenlehre."

Alle diese Bücher sind Lehrbücher oder Lehrhilfsbücher. Das Ganze zusammen ergibt dann eine Aesthetik der Tonkunst, unter welchem Titel ich ein . . . zusammenfassendes Werk schreiben will.

Zu allen diesen Werken habe ich bereits Ideen und auch Notizen.

Im Lauf von fünf Jahren kann alles fertig sein!

Schoenberg to Hertzka, 23 July 1911; quoted and translated in Bryan R. Simms, review of *Harmonielehre*, by Arnold Schoenberg, trans. Roy E. Carter, *Music Theory Spectrum* 4 (1982), 155–162, esp. 156–157.

4. For a detailed discussion of these projects, see Arnold Schoenberg, *Coherence, Counterpoint, Instrumentation, Instruction in Form*, ed. Severine Neff, trans. Charlotte M. Cross and Severine Neff (Lincoln and London: University of Nebraska Press, 1994); translation of *Zusammenhang, Kontrapunkt, Instrumentation, Formenlehre*.

5. Schoenberg mentions both the book on coherence and that on composition in a letter to Vasili Kandinsky dated 20 July 1922; see *Schoenberg Letters*, no. 42, 70–71, esp. 71.

6. Arnold Schoenberg, "Zu meinem fünfzigsten Geburtstag: 1924" (first published in *Anbruch* 6/7–8 [August/September 1924], 269–270), in Reich, *Schoenberg: Schöpferische Konfessionen*, 98–101; translated as "On My Fiftieth Birthday: September 13, 1924," in *Style and Idea*, 23–24.

7. See manuscript Mus 56, ASI. This document is the first of the *Gedanke* manuscripts listed on page 148.

8. For a reference to a book of that title, see the letter from Schoenberg to Matthias Hauer, 1 December 1923, *Schoenberg Letters*, no. 78, 103–104, esp. 104. For a reference to an article (*einer Schrift*) to be entitled "Gesetze der Komposition mit zwölf Tönen" (Laws of composition with twelve tones), see Schoenberg, "Zu meinem fünfzigsten Geburtstag," 98–101, esp. 100; "On My Fiftieth Birthday," 23–24, esp. 24.

9.

> Harmonielehre, Kontrapunkt und Formenlehre sind gegenwärtig hauptsächlich zu pädagogischen Zwecken aufgebaut. Mit Ausnahme vielleicht der Harmonielehre fehlt den einzelnen sogar eine wahrhaft theoretische Anlage, die von anderen äusseren Merkmalen ausgeht, vollkommen, welcher Mangel im ganzen zur Folge hat, dass die drei verschiedenen Disziplinen, die zusammen die Kompositionslehre bilden sollten in Wirklichkeit auseinander fallen, da ihnen ein gemeinsamer Gesichtspunkt fehlt.
> "Der musikalische Gedanke, seine Darstellung und Durchführung," no. 11, 4.

For particulars on this and the other *Gedanke* manuscripts, see note 11.

10. Schoenberg, "Zur Frage des modernen Kompositionsunterrichtes," *Deutsche Tonkünstler-Zeitung* (5 November 1929); translated as "On the Question of Modern Composition Teaching" (1929), in *Style and Idea*, 373–376, esp. 374.

11. The manuscripts, located at the Arnold Schoenberg Institute, bear the following catalog numbers: *Gedanke* no. 1: T34.29; *Gedanke* no. 2: T37.4, T37.7–8; *Gedanke* no. 3: T35.2; *Gedanke* no. 4: T37.4, T37.7–8; *Gedanke* no. 5: T39.33; *Gedanke* no. 6: T35.40; *Gedanke* no. 7: T35.41; *Gedanke* no. 8: T35.48, T1.15; *Gedanke* no. 9: T20.13; *Gedanke* no. 10: T65.1–4; *Gedanke* no. 11: T37.4–6; *Gedanke* no. 12: T37.4–6. The excerpts quoted here have been translated by Charlotte M. Cross.

For a complete description of the *Gedanke* manuscripts, see Arnold Schoenberg, *The Musical Idea and the Logic, Technique, and Art of Its Presentation*, ed. and trans. Patricia Carpenter and Severine Neff (New York: Columbia University Press, 1995), app. 1.

12. In Schoenberg's bibliographic classification of his prose works, this manuscript is described as "Verm 341, Der Gedanke u. die Zange" (The idea and pliers).

13. Catalogued by Schoenberg as "no. 3, Ab Gedanke" in a list he compiled entitled "Unfinished Theoretical Manuscripts."

14. Arnold Schoenberg, "New Music, Outmoded Music, Style and Idea" (1946), in *Style and Idea,* 113–124, esp. 123.

15.

Darstellung heisst, ein Objekt auf solche[r?] Weise einem Beschauer vorführen, dass man Teile, die es zusammensetzen, gleichsam in funktioneller Bewegung wahrnimmt.

Schoenberg to Hertzka, 160.

16. Schoenberg summarized this aspect of the idea in the short English-language *Gedanke* manuscript no. 9, "The Musical Idea," written on 4 June 1934:

An idea is the establishment of relations between things or parts between which no relation existed before that establishment. An intelligent relation can only be found between things or parts which ressemble [*sic*] one another.

This manuscript continues with an elaboration of kinds of resemblance—direct, mediated, and indirect.

17.

Wenn man als Gedanken bezeichnen kann: die Herstellung von Beziehungen zwischen Dingen, Begriffen u. dgl. (also auch zwischen Gedanken), so ist beim musikalischen Gedanken eine solche Beziehung nur zwischen Tönen herstellbar und es kann nur eine musikalische Beziehung sein.

In content this seems to be a continuation of the thoughts discussed in the 1931 *Gedanke* no. 6.

18. Schoenberg, "New Music, Outmoded Music," 113–124, esp. 122–123.

19. Ibid., 123.

20. See Schoenberg, *Gedanke* no. 2 (1925), "Der musikalische Gedanke, seine Darstellung und Durchführung."

21. See Arnold Schoenberg, *Fundamentals of Musical Composition,* ed. Gerald Strang and Leonard Stein (London: Faber and Faber, 1967), 8.

22. Mus 66, T65.5, ASI.

23.

Der Gedanke kann Gegenstand einer längeren oder kürzeren Arbeit sein, kann allein für sich selbst bestehen, aber auch Teil eines Grösseren sein. Dieses Grössere wird dann selbst meistens in mehr oder weniger zahlreiche Abschnitte, Stufen, Teile, u. d. zerfallen, die zum Teil wieder Gedanken sind. Solche werden irgendwie miteinander verbunden oder nebeneinandergestellt sein, oder sonst ein wohl auf das Ganze beziehbares Verhältnis zueinander haben.

24. Schoenberg, *Harmonielehre* (1922), 378; *Theory of Harmony,* 313.

25.

Durch die Verbindung von Tönen verschiedener Höhe, Dauer und Betonung (Stärke???) entsteht eine *Unruhe:* eine Ruhe wird in Frage gestellt durch einen Kontrast. Von dieser Unruhe geht eine Bewegung aus.

Schoenberg, *Gedanke* no. 10 (1934–1936), "Der musikalische Gedanke und die Logik, Technik, und Kunst seiner Darstellung," 15.

26. Schoenberg, "Composition with Twelve Tones (1)," 214–215. For comments on the metaphysical nature of the idea as well as divine and mortal creation, see Karl Wörner, "Schönbergs Oratorium *Die Jakobsleiter:* Musik zwischen Theologie und Weltanschauung," *Schweizerische Musikzeitung* 105 (1965), 250–257, 333–340; and John R. Covach, "Schoenberg and the Occult: Some Reflections on the 'Musical Idea,' " *Theory and Practice* 17 (1992), 103–118.

27. See Schoenberg's manuscript "Inspiration," trans. Wayne Shoaf, *Serial: Newsletter of the Friends of the Arnold Schoenberg Institute* (Winter 1987), 3, 7.

28. In answer to the question, What are the most important phases in the composition of a song? see Julius Bahle's study on song composition (1931), reprinted in Reich, *Schoenberg: A Critical Biography,* 238. Schoenberg describes the musical idea as the "first thought" in an interview with José Rodriguez in Merle Armitage, ed., *Schoenberg* (New York: Schirmer, 1937); reprinted in H. H. Stuckenschmidt, *Arnold Schoenberg: His Life, World, and Work,* trans. H. Searle (New York: Schirmer, 1977), 419.

29. Schoenberg, "Gustav Mahler" (1912, 1948), in *Style and Idea,* 449–472, esp. 458.

30. A. W. Schlegel, "Vorlesungen über dramatische Kunst und Literatur" (1809–1911), in *Sämtliche Werke* (Leipzig: Weidmann, 1846), 6:157; translated in *A Course of Lectures on Dramatic Art and Literature,* trans. John Black (Philadelphia: Hogan and Thompson, 1833), 335.

31. See Schoenberg, *Gedanke* no. 10, 217–227.

32. Ibid., 108–109.

33. Ibid., 223.

34. See Schoenberg, *Fundamentals of Musical Composition,* 1.

35. See Schoenberg's unpublished fragment entitled "Form," ASI; cataloged as manuscript no. 180 in Rufer, *Works of Arnold Schoenberg,* 162. The manuscript is transcribed in its entirety in Severine Neff, ed., "Two Fragments: (1) Tonality, (2) Form by Arnold Schoenberg," *Theory and Practice* 17 (1992), 2–3.

36. Schoenberg, "Tonality and Form," *Christian Science Monitor* (19 December 1925); published as "Tonalität und Gliederung," in *Gesammelte Schriften,* 1:206–208, esp. 208; translated as "Tonality and Form," in *Style and Idea,* 255–257, esp. 257.

37. Schoenberg, *Fundamentals of Musical Composition,* 1.

38.

> Vor allem ist ein Musikstück (vielleicht immer) ein *gegliedertes Organismus,* dessen Organe, Glieder, und bestimmte Funktionen hinsichtlich ihrer äusseren Wirkung sowohl als hinsichtlich ihres gegenseitigen Verhaltens ausüben.
>
> Schoenberg, *Gedanke* no. 10, 220.

39. Ibid., 221.

40. Ibid., 226.

41. Schoenberg to Kandinsky, 24 January 1911, *Schoenberg/Kandinsky Letters,* 23–24, esp. 23.

42. Schoenberg, *Harmonielehre* (1922), 322–323; translation (here slightly adapted) in *Theory of Harmony,* 289.

43. Schoenberg, "Problems of Harmony" (1934; translated and adapted from the 1927 lecture "Probleme der Harmonie"), in *Style and Idea*, 268–287, esp. 285.

44. Schoenberg, "Composition with Twelve Tones (1)," 215.

45. Ibid., 240.

46. Schoenberg, "Konstruierte Musik" (1931–1934); translated as "Constructed Music," in *Style and Idea*, 106–108, esp. 107.

Connections

ELEVEN

Schoenberg and the Canon

An Evolving Heritage

Christopher Hailey

The current debate swirling around the literary canon is notable less for its novelty than for its self-consciousness. Every age wrangles over values and priorities, but seldom have the parameters of discourse been so studded with the brittle shards of contending ideologies. The forces of feminism and multiculturalism in the academy, the neuroses of political correctness in the society at large, the collapse of socialism, crises of late capitalism, and the postmodernist disintegration of metanarratives of progress and enlightenment are all signs of cultural adjustment to emerging global political and economic realities. In the United States shifting immigration and demographic patterns, economic dislocations, and the politics of affirmative action have heightened awareness of ethnic, racial, linguistic, gender, sexual, religious, and class differences and challenged long-standing assumptions about shared cultural values. As a repository of such values, literary canons, whether defined by reading lists, anthologies, or publishing projects such as the University of Chicago's Great Books series, are under scrutiny as to their makeup, their uses, the power structures they supposedly reflect, affirm, and perpetuate, and the diverse interests, backgrounds, and perceptions they demonstrably fail to represent.[1] Barbara Herrnstein Smith has pointed out that texts that endure are usually "those that appear to reflect and reinforce establishment ideologies,"[2] or, as Charles Altieri has paraphrased Smith's argument, those that speak to "nostalgia, conservative political pressures, stock rhetorical needs, and the inertia of established power."[3] In this spirit ideological challenges, from Marxism to feminism, have sought to demonstrate the relationship between canonicity and larger structures of oppression or coercion. This crisis has triggered responses ranging from the anxious hand-wringing of neoconservatives and political demagogues manning (literally) the ramparts of fortress culture against assault from the unwashed multitudes, to the objections of a committed rationalist such as Jürgen Habermas, who has identified a "legitimation crisis" that threatens to relativize values and criteria and derail the "incomplete project of Modernity."⁴ Although it is appealing to regard the canon as a self-adjusting image of societal consensus, there is an increasing understanding that any relevant—that is, practically applicable—canon will have to become a heteronomous construct subject to conscious modification and expansion.⁵

Such challenges to the legitimacy of the canon and the assumptions that undergird it must necessarily affect our understanding of Arnold Schoenberg, for whom a musical canon was axiomatic.⁶ Few composers have been so shaped by their identification with a canon—which for Schoenberg served as both his own artistic frame of reference and the source of those criteria by which he insisted that others judge the meaning and value of his works. His ideal was a music of organic process whose impetus and justification were the fulfillment of its own self-defined and historically grounded needs. Indeed, in making his modernist style the consequence of history, he aimed the canon in his direction. The result was an aesthetic of limited context, in which a premium was placed on the integrity of organic relatedness both within a work and between works in a historical continuum. In a real sense, then, Schoenberg's musical persona was a response to and a self-conscious fulfillment of a century of musical-canon formation that had resulted from a combination of aesthetic advocacy and the changing material conditions of musical practice.⁷ His experience is paradigmatic for understanding the relationship between twentieth-century canonic ideology and the rise and crisis of modernism.

•   •   •   •   •

It is readily apparent from the works that Schoenberg performed, taught, analyzed, and wrote about that his active canon—those works upon which he continually drew and from which he learned as a composer—was relatively limited, indeed much more limited, for instance, than the range of his literary interests and influences. In his 1931 essay "National Music," Schoenberg cited Bach and Mozart as his principal teachers, and Beethoven, Brahms, and Wagner as secondary influences. Arrayed around these core figures Schoenberg set Schubert, Mahler, Strauss, and Reger, to whom one might also add Haydn, Schumann, and Wolf. A handful of others, such as Liszt, Berlioz, C. P. E. Bach, and Handel, appear only on the periphery. In all it is a list that is almost wholly German and restricted to two hundred years of music history. This is of course not to suggest that Schoenberg was ignorant of other music, but it does delimit a relatively closed sphere of productive relevance.

It is nonetheless important to recognize Schoenberg's encounters and involvement with a broader spectrum of musical styles—one end of which is represented by his firsthand familiarity with Viennese operetta and his cabaret experiences in Berlin, the other by the programs of the Verein für musikalische Privataufführungen—which show a remarkable catholicity of interests if not tastes. After his move to Berlin in 1926 Schoenberg, now remarried to a woman many years his junior and engaged in a far more active social life, was exposed to a still wider range of musical impulses through concerts, theater, radio, and film. Moreover, his essays from the twenties and early thirties document his awareness of contemporary explorations of non-Western and early music.[8] In the United States, and more specifically in Los Angeles, Schoenberg was drawn into domains of popular culture he had until then witnessed only from afar. As a private tutor to studio musicians, a social guest sought after by celebrities such as Charlie Chaplin, George Gershwin, and Harpo Marx, and a member of an émigré community largely co-opted by the entertainment industry, Schoenberg found himself in an environment in which many of his established hierarchies were inverted.

These experiences brought him into contact with ever more diverse audiences, students, social circles, and cultural references, in a world ever more saturated with technology and disparate information sources, and these elements were not without influence upon his ideas of canonicity. Through his letters and essays one can follow the transformation of a relatively stable hierarchy of high and low art in Vienna into a tentative acknowledgment of wider pluralities in Berlin and into, in America, an attempt, however cursory, to posit a cultural continuum extending from Maeterlinck to Mickey Mouse, from Tolstoy to the Marx Brothers.[9]

These observations suggest that while over the course of his career Schoenberg's core musical canon remained relatively stable, the *instrumentality* of that canon changed. The influences were of course many, and included cultural, psychological, professional, political, geographic, and temporal factors, among others. But it is possible to isolate three distinct phases relating to Schoenberg's experiences in, respectively, Vienna, Berlin, and Los Angeles—three settings in which the concept "canon" shifted from a record of historical cultural identity to a tool of cultural politics to, finally, a project of cultural enlightenment.

•　•　•　•　•

Karl Kraus once observed, "The streets of Vienna are paved with culture; the streets of other cities with asphalt."[10] Schoenberg's Vienna was comparatively small physically, and highly centralized. The media of her cultural identity—art, literature, and above all theater and music—were cultivated with an intensity scarcely known elsewhere. For Viennese musicians the weight of history was particularly heavy, for they lived in the city where many of the central figures of the canonic repertory had made their home. This gave Vienna's musical life its vibrancy but also encouraged a degree of complacency that by the turn of the century threatened to ossify a rich legacy into sterile academism and unthinking tradition. If there was a musical "crisis of language" corresponding to Hofmannsthal's search for literary integrity and authenticity, then it was in large part brought on by the appalling experience of a rich syntactical inheritance being bled dry of meaning. Mahler recognized as much with regard to performance practice. His famous dictum *"Tradition ist Schlamperei"* was less an injunction against tradition than against *Schlamperei,* and he did much to rescue hallowed performance traditions by elevating them to a level of conscious articulation.

Similarly, a generation of composers and theorists—Schoenberg most radically among them—sought to rescue the techniques of the classical tradition from the stale formulae of the academy. The remarkable number of gifted teachers emerging from the generation of the 1870s and 1880s (including Schoenberg and his circle, as well as Hauer, Marx, Schenker, Schmidt, Schreker, Weigl, and Zemlinsky) shared a devotion to a legacy of craft and the conviction that the complete assimilation of that craft could serve as a basis for aesthetic judgment, the mastery of its grammar as the means to original, individual expression. These self-appointed inheritors of the legacy became its protectors as well. They were an extraordinary collection of composers, performers, and theorists whose commitment to the continuing value of a shared canon of classical works and techniques made Vienna a rich resonating chamber for its own cultural history. Their works represent a revitalized dialogue with that legacy and a process of self-discovery within that culture, creating the kind of dense tangle of associations within and between works of the larger canon that Kraus would have appreciated. For Schoenberg and others, the crisis of integrity and authenticity was resolved in favor of creative individuality achieved through the mastery of craft.[11] Not surprisingly, Schoenberg's canonical priorities reflect the cultural practices of turn-of-the-century Vienna.

Although Vienna was a point of geographic intersection, with a significant representation of Italian and French opera, and Slavic and Scandinavian music, Schoenberg's canon (at least through Brahms) is the sanctioned pantheon of the Vienna Conservatory and as such differs little from the preferences of his more conservative contemporaries.[12] The fact that Schoenberg and so many of his contemporaries were drawn to teaching, and taught primarily through examination and analysis of this limited canon, reinforced the canon's normative, disciplinary value as a criterion for critical judgment. More important, mastering the canon and its language as craft was an act of creative imagination, actively knitting past with present into a cohesive whole. It was both a linear legacy and a pedigree. In this sense the canon in Vienna was self-defining and self-legitimizing.

· · · · ·

The idea of the canon as a means of individual definition and expression within a historical continuum continued to resonate in Schoenberg's thinking at a time when he was becoming increasingly aware of the canon as an agent of self-definition within a political context. It is not surprising that during the First World War Schoenberg identified his canon with the larger cause of the German nation, but it was in fact a rhetorical stance he would maintain throughout his remaining years in Europe, though with shifting emphases. There is a world of difference between writing in 1919 of the need to "ensure the German nation's superiority in the field of music"[13] and the 1931 essay "National Music," in which Schoenberg defends his own music, "produced on German soil, without foreign influences," as "a living example of an art able most effectively to oppose Latin and Slav hopes of hegemony."[14] Between those two essays are the incidents in Mattsee, the assault upon Schoenberg's "bolshevist modernism" by cultural conservatives, and Schoenberg's own embattled position as a political appointee in a highly politicized German capital.[15] From an unabashed identification with a national cause to an appeal to hallowed tradition as a credential, Schoenberg had come to recognize the canon as an instrument of cultural politics.

Beyond that, now removed from the safe cocoon of Vienna, Schoenberg found his sacrosanct canon under attack from within, by a younger generation lured away from Mozart and Beethoven, Wagner and Brahms, by American jazz, Russian primitivism, French *ésprit,* Italian soul, experimental technology, and a feverish succession of fashions and fads from *Neue Sachlichkeit* to *Gebrauchsmusik, Spielmusik,* and neoclassicism. For a time, 1922 to 1930 by his own account, Schoenberg lost his influence over youth and, like other leading figures—Busoni and Schreker among them—was bewildered and dismayed by his students' craving for novelty.[16] In this context an appeal to the hallowed repertory was an appeal for stability—an appeal that befitted his position as a professor of the august Prussian Academy of the Arts. It was also an appeal with more than a hint of his own conservative agenda, which by 1930 had become a balancing act between artistic responsibility and the appearance of political opportunism.

· · · · ·

Schoenberg's emigration to the United States offered release from the anguished tangle that cultural identity in Germany had become, but at a price. In America, Europe's highly structured supports for cultural identity and authority were lacking. Schoenberg, now more object than subject, was a representative of an "old world" European culture. His writing is more patient, pragmatic, and cautiously articulated; his vision of the canon, more tolerant and inclusive, takes on a supranational cast that advertises itself as vaguely European, or simply "Western."[17] Both feted and marginalized, Schoenberg submitted to his own commodification as the "learned professor," though not without irony, as when he once tellingly likened his public persona to a statue on a pedestal.[18]

In the United States Schoenberg's students lacked the preparation and breadth of experience he could have expected in Europe. Their knowledge of music literature, he wrote in 1938, "offers the aspects of a Swiss cheese."[19] In the absence of a context, the canon could no longer serve as an anchor of identity as it had in Vienna, or as an article of political and aesthetic confession as in Berlin, but was instead marketed like a medicinal balm for which Schoenberg, the distinguished physician, offered testimonial. Schoenberg had become the kindly missionary patiently instructing the natives in higher truths.

But Schoenberg's canon was not simply competing against ignorance and an omnipresent popular culture; it was also challenged by a specifically American art music consciously seeking to free itself of its European—that is, German—heritage. Many of the colleagues and music students from whom Schoenberg most needed support were themselves torn between their search for indigenous roots and those alternative influences—most particularly from France, Stravinsky, and neoclassicism—that might assist them in that quest. The result was that Schoenberg's canon was further relativized by the presence of several contending canons.[20]

• • • • •

It is to his credit that Schoenberg recognized the necessity of this process, and recognized also the complexity of America's cultural growing pains.[21] He could even rationalize the marginalization of his music, for by this time he felt sufficiently secure of his *own* place in the canon to await the judgment of history.[22] At the same time he had become a modernist icon, more written about than performed, more cited than sighted. This is the point at which certain aspects of Schoenberg's attitude toward the canon become pertinent to his identity as a modernist.

During the late 1930s the art critic Clement Greenberg began to formulate a view of modernism as a process by which each medium discovered its own inherent forms and techniques. "It is by virtue of its medium," he wrote in 1940, "that each art is unique and strictly itself."[23] In eliminating effects borrowed from other media and other arts, Greenberg argued, "each art would be rendered 'pure,' and in its 'purity' find the guarantee of its standards of quality as well as of its independence."[24] This formalist preoccupation with medium-specific autonomy is explicitly present in literary and artistic modernism and is arguably a key element running through musical modernism from expressionism to *Neue Sachlichkeit* and neoclassicism.[25] It also came to be associated—at least as a subtext—with central tenets in Schoenberg's modernism. In such a quest the canon fulfilled a crucial role as means of assuring autonomy, for by crystallizing and applying to one's own work those "timeless" techniques that give the canon its coherence and integrity, one could assure both purity of lineage and resistance to temporal influences. What is more, I do not doubt that for a composer like Schoenberg, subject to a succession of cultural and geographic dislocations, the canon was a valuable guarantor of continuity and moral identity.

Concomitant with Schoenberg's quest for continuity and identity was the need to posit an ideal audience, an audience steeped in his canon and defined in *his* terms. In his compositions, performance coaching, analyses, and insistence upon structural listening Schoenberg created a canon viewed from a modernist's perspective, the artwork as a chiseled entity of self-referential perfection.[26] This, more than the leap—or slither—into atonality, more than the development of the twelve-tone system, has been, I would maintain, the most influential legacy of Schoenberg's teaching.[27] The result is not merely an idealized canon but also an idealized audience, an audience that took shape in Schoenberg's Verein für musikalische Privataufführungen, whose members were to be that model community, conversant with the canon and the lessons it taught. Performance was *realization* and listening a *contemplative immersion*. Strict injunctions against any public display of favor or disfavor, and the exclusion of critics, were intended to purge Verein performances of the theatrical impurities of normal concert life.[28] But the very nature of performance encourages interpretive interplay, challenges autonomy, and undermines intentionality and control; any performance, no matter how carefully prepared and faithfully executed, no matter how intelligently and respectfully heard, creates a dialogue in which all sides set terms. Such a dialogue, ever changing, is the currency of contemporary relevance.

· · · · ·

Schoenberg is in need of contemporary relevance, but it will not come on his terms. The price of taking Schoenberg into the musical canon, of accepting him as a modernist icon, has been to accept his definition of the canon and his place within it. That price is too high. His works, both as historical artifacts and as a part of living experience, can come alive to us only through unfettered dialogue, and a first step toward that dialogue is restoring Schoenberg to his time through a process of historical contextualization.[29]

The effect of Schoenberg's attempt—or our perception of his attempt—to associate his work with timeless canonic principles has been to rob it of its temporality.[30] This has not only tended to remove his music from what Steven Connor has called the "dust and heat of history" but also sped the process by which it has become an inert artifact of the past, more readily subject, as Connor observes, to being commodified and "museumized" by cultural institutions and the academy.[31] This ossification into monumentality has been accompanied by the flattened historical perspective of post-modernist theories, resulting in what Connor has called a "furious polyphony of decontextualized voices."[32] This is a trend to which Schoenberg's articulate self, for all its insistence upon historical origin, offers scant resistance. And yet it is precisely Schoenberg's articulate self, with his embrace of performance and pedagogy, that undermines his own quest for autonomy and open perspectives for revitalizing his creative legacy.

The interest in reader response and reception history that has helped revolutionize literary theory over the past quarter century is not a mere academic fad but a reflection of the way in which literature, art, and history itself have been called to account by the increasing self- and "other"-consciousness of our culture. Lay and professional audiences have begun to set terms of engagement that reflect an increasingly pluralistic cultural environment and a heightened awareness of the contingencies of individual perspectives. This array of contending perspectives has stimulated the search for critical categories that are more all-encompassing and that address perspectives such as those of gender, race, and class.

These same processes have been operative in transforming musical culture and have at long last begun to be reflected in musical criticism and scholarship.[33] Theoretical discourse, for instance, long dominated by a bias toward pitch and harmony (which assured a central position for works reflecting the development and dissolution of tonality and the structural and thematic means of tonal articulation), has recently begun to accommodate a range of music (including areas of new music as well as popular and non-Western styles) governed by other organizational principles such as timbre and rhythm. What is more, extramusical parameters such as the significance of popularity, gender identification, and psychological response have become sanctioned areas of inquiry. This has not only opened new repertories to critical scrutiny but also created an arena in which disparate works and repertories, from plainchant to punk rock, can be discussed within a single framework.

To abandon a narrowly defined set of critical criteria is to undermine the authority of any single canon as well as of individual works or bodies of

works that derived their authority from their consonance—or defiance—
of its principles. The authority of Schoenberg's works (and as a man and
artist, authority was one of the central categories of his life) derives from
both their consonance with and defiance of his chosen canon. The question
thus arises: How central is the maintenance of that authority for assigning
quality, value, or relevance to Schoenberg's work? That question can best
be answered by asking whether, within the shifting categories of contemporary evaluation, Schoenberg's works can continue to engage and reward
our interest.

At this point it is well to remember that Schoenberg's canon was in part
a construct of personal choices; his understanding of Mozart, Beethoven,
Wagner, and Brahms was selective and self-serving. Our own no less selective and self-serving ideas of canonicity (or even multi-canonicity) are a
reflection of the processes by which we adjust ourselves to transformations
in our own culture and find a means to assign value and meaning. The
eclectic quality of our culture has fostered interdisciplinary dialogue, cross-
cultural exchange, and a hermeneutics of heteronomy. Under such circumstances the autonomy of Schoenberg's music, its integrity on its own terms,
becomes but one evaluative factor among many. Of greater significance is
its contextual richness.

Schoenberg was passionately engaged with his times—in his activities,
in his writings, and most importantly in his works. It is evident that his artistic temperament was shaped by a range of influences in literature, theology, art, and philosophy, as well as by music far outside his admitted canon.
And one can follow his shifting preoccupations through the various stages
of his career and in a series of influential and provocative works, most of
which lay outside the traditional canonical formal categories.[34] Moreover,
an extraordinary number of Schoenberg's works are datable by the very
nature of their genre, form, content, musical language, and style. The gar-
gantuan dimensions of *Gurrelieder* could scarcely have been conceived in
1920 any more than the moral and theatrical austerity of *Moses und Aron*
belongs to a prewar mentality. *Pierrot lunaire*, *Von heute auf morgen*, the *Satires*
for chorus, the Serenade, op. 24, and the Piano Suite, op. 25, the Suite for
String Orchestra, *A Survivor from Warsaw*, and the *Ode to Napoleon* are just a
few of the works linked to specific contexts deriving from Schoenberg's
intense and ever broadening discourse with his time.[35] The intensity of this
discourse also accounts for the large number of fragments and torsos whose
concerns and musical means had outlived their moment of inspiration.[36]

There is a sense in which Schoenberg's oeuvre is refreshingly dated, and
no more so than in his insistent appeal to historical truths.[37] And yet it is
what Schoenberg *made* of that canonic inheritance within concrete cultural
and political conditions that lends him and his works new relevance. Con-
textualizing Schoenberg, reintegrating his work into the historical and tem-

poral flow of his time, has the double benefit of rescuing him from his defenders as well as creating a richer, more complex figure capable of resisting both facile commodification and reactionary deconstruction. Thus even if the authority of Schoenberg's canon can never be restored, even if the very idea of canonicity is undermined, one can create a context that allows Schoenberg and his works to resonate across a wider network of associations. It is part of what Steven Connor calls the "struggle between a modernist restricted field, with its stress on individuality, purity and essence, and the postmodernist expanded field, with its embrace of the contingent conditions."[38] The contingent conditions in Schoenberg's work are what create its most valuable and instructive tensions. We must be willing to separate Schoenberg's articulate vision of himself and his canon from his works and allow the historical connectedness of both to inform *our* vision of the whole. We must free his canon from being a preserve of timeless truth to becoming a theater of present possibilities. To delimit Schoenberg is not to abandon him but to welcome him into the productive discourse of our time.

NOTES

1. It is debatable whether a single overarching canon exists at all since its definition has proved so fluid and varied. Nonetheless, the idea of a canon has considerable conceptual force if only because it implies the existence of a coherent set of value assumptions.

2. Barbara Herrnstein Smith, *Contingencies of Value: Alternative Perspectives for Critical Theory* (Cambridge: Harvard University Press, 1988), 51.

3. Charles Altieri, *Canons and Consequences: Reflections on the Ethical Force of Imaginative Ideals* (Evanston, Ill.: Northwestern University Press, 1990), 52.

4. See Jürgen Habermas, *Legitimation Crisis*, trans. Thomas McCarthy (Boston: Beacon Press, 1975); and "Modernity—An Incomplete Project," in *The Anti-Aesthetic: Essays on Postmodern Culture,* ed. Hal Foster (Seattle: Bay Press, 1983), 3–15.

5. It goes without saying that the principal thrust of such arguments is directed toward the academy, where conscious decisions shape curricula and reading lists. In the real world political and market forces significantly complicate any planned articulation of a cultural program.

6. I am well aware that the idea of a "musical canon" is problematic, though I believe that musical canonicity is a concept that Schoenberg would have understood and endorsed in both its narrow disciplinary (pedagogical) and more broadly repertorial senses. It is readily apparent that Schoenberg embraced the idea of a body of works that was exclusive, exemplary, and normative.

Joseph Kerman was among the first to address the specific application of canonicity to music in "A Few Canonic Variations," *Critical Inquiry* 10/1 (September 1983), 107–125. He cautions in particular about the need for differentiating between a canon and a repertory. "A canon," he writes, "is an idea; a repertory is a program of action" (107), adding elsewhere, "repertories are determined by performers, canons, by critics" (114).

Other important contributions to the discussion of musical canonicity include the essays in Katherine Bergeron and Philip V. Bohlman, eds., *Disciplining Music: Musicology and Its Canons* (Chicago: University of Chicago Press, 1992); Marcia J. Citron, *Gender and the Musical Canon* (Cambridge: Cambridge University Press, 1993); Susan McClary, *Feminine Endings: Music, Gender, and Sexuality* (Minneapolis: University of Minnesota Press, 1991); and William Weber, "The Eighteenth-Century Origins of the Musical Canon," *Journal of the Royal Musical Association* 114/1 (1989), 6–17.

7. Kerman ("A Few Canonic Variations") traces the historical roots of the idea of a musical canon to those early early-nineteenth-century German critics and aestheticians such as E. T. A. Hoffmann who sought to "endow music with a history" (120). As such, the enterprise of musical-canon formation was both conscious and programmatic, nurtured by "a strong component of nationalism along with historicism, organicism . . . and what Carl Dahlhaus has aptly called 'the metaphysics of instrumental music' " (114). By the end of the century the repertory and its (predominantly German) canonic core extended back to the early eighteenth century (Bach and Handel) and up to and including Brahms. Of course, this development was closely related to the complex of economic, political, and social phenomena that created a network of institutions and practices that served both to stimulate and to stabilize cultural life. A stable repertory was both a precondition of and a corollary to the establishment of performing institutions such as orchestras and concert series, as well as a mediating linguistic apparatus for music critics, journalists, and historians. Weber ("The Eighteenth-Century Origins of the Musical Canon") offers valuable caveats to several of Kerman's principal points, arguing that musical-canon formation began in the eighteenth century and evolved unobtrusively from the practice of cultivating selected older works. However, the actual origins or dynamics of canon formation are of little relevance to a discussion of Schoenberg, for whom canonicity was an inherited concept, largely colored by the legacy of Romanticism.

8. See, for instance, Schoenberg's 1922 essay "About Ornaments, Primitive Rhythms, etc. and Bird Song"; "Folk-Music and Art-Music" of c. 1926; and "Old and New Counterpoint" of 1928—all published in *Style and Idea,* 298–311, 167–169, and 288–289, respectively.

9. See in particular Schoenberg's 1940 essay "Art and the Moving Pictures," in *Style and Idea,* 153–157. While urging the motion-picture industry to fulfill a higher cultural mission ("I had dreamed of a dramatization of Balzac's *Séraphita,* or Strindberg's *To Damascus,* or the second part of Goethe's *Faust,* or even Wagner's *Parsifal*"), Schoenberg nonetheless acknowledges that the institutions of popular culture had produced works that "had the same appeal to the more highly educated as to the average citizen," works that "satisfied the whole of a nation, or even of the entire word, like Mickey Mouse, or some of the films of Charlie Chaplin, Harold Lloyd, and the Marx brothers; like some operas of Rossini, operettas of Offenbach and Johann Strauss, and plays by popular poets like Raimund and Nestroy; or popular music of Strauss, Offenbach, Foster, Gershwin, and many jazz composers" (154).

10. Karl Kraus, *Sprüche und Widersprüche* (Frankfurt am Main: Suhrkamp Verlag, 1977), 157.

11. These ideas are developed more fully in my paper "Craft and *Kultur:* Karl Weigl, Vienna, and the Question of Mastery," delivered at the conference "Viennese Crosscurrents," University of Chicago, 1–2 December 1989.

12. The presence in Vienna of reactionaries like Schenker and progressives like Schoenberg should not obscure the fact that both "wings" were essentially conservative in nature. This is evident above all from the strongly articulated moral didacticism in their writings. The difference was one of emphasis. Whereas Schenker fought offensive and defensive battles against radical innovation with cultural political arguments, Schoenberg defended himself against reactionary critics and the inroads of mass culture by espousing an aristocracy of the spirit; Schoenberg cited the canon not to resist stylistic change but to enlist "eternal values" on its behalf.

13. See the 1919 proposal "Music" for the "Guide-Lines for a Ministry of Art," ed. Adolf Loos, in *Style and Idea,* 369–373, esp. 369.

14. Schoenberg, *Style and Idea,* 172–174, esp. 173.

15. Anti-Semitic agitation in the resort town of Mattsee, near Salzburg, forced Schoenberg and his family to break off their summer vacation there in July 1921. At the end of 1925 the Prussian Ministry of Culture appointed Schoenberg to succeed Ferruccio Busoni as the director of a master class at the Prussian Academy of the Arts.

16. I discuss these generational tensions in *Franz Schreker 1878–1934: A Cultural Biography* (Cambridge: Cambridge University Press, 1993), especially in the chapter "A Clash of Generations," 155–175.

17. This stance is complicated by Schoenberg's embrace of Judaism and the obviously awkward cross-loyalties with his German heritage. In a letter of 19 July 1938 to Jakob Klatzkin, Schoenberg wrote, "The non-Jews are 'conservative,' and the Jews have never shown any interest in my music. And now, into the bargain, in Palestine they are out to develop, artificially, an authentically Jewish kind of music, which rejects what I have achieved." *Schoenberg Letters,* no. 178, 205. Of particular note is the letter written to Frank Pelleg of 26 April 1951 concerning Schoenberg's election as honorary president of the Israel Academy of Music. He emphasizes the "technical, intellectual, and ethical demands of our art" as well as the "morality of art" and envisions an academy "fit to serve as a counterblast to this world that is in so many respects giving itself up to amoral, success-ridden materialism." He writes in conclusion, "For just as God chose Israel to be the people whose task it is to maintain the pure, true, Mosaic monotheism despite all persecution, despite all affliction, so too it is the task of Israeli musicians to set the world an example of the *old kind* that can make our souls function again as they must if mankind is to evolve any higher." *Schoenberg Letters,* no. 257, 287.

18. See Schoenberg's 1934 essay "Why No Great American Music," in *Style and Idea,* 178.

19. See "Teaching and Modern Trends in Music" (1938), in *Style and Idea,* 376.

20. Schoenberg seems to have made his peace with some, if not all, of his competitors for influence upon America's young composers. In a letter to G. F. Stegmann of 26 January 1949 he writes, "It would not be so bad to imitate Stravinsky,

or Bartók, or Hindemith, but worse is that they have been taught by a woman of Russian-French descent, who is a reactionary and has had much influence on many composers. One can only wish that this influence might be broken and the real talents of the Americans be allowed to develop freely." *Schoenberg Letters*, no. 233, 266. A little over three months later, however, Schoenberg wrote ruefully to Rudolf Kolisch on 12 April 1949, "The tendency is to suppress European influences and encourage nationalistic methods of composition constructed on the pattern adopted in Russia and other such places." *Schoenberg Letters*, no. 237, 270.

21. Particularly revealing in this regard is the 1934 essay "Why No Great American Music," in *Style and Idea*, 176–181. In an undated letter (c. 1944) to Lester Trimble, Schoenberg wrote, "I see you are aiming at a contemporary American style in some of these compositions. This is of course perfectly all right. It is your task, all of you young American talents, to create a style of your own, and it is every single man's duty to contribute as much as possible to this goal." Schoenberg goes on to caution: "On the other hand there are two points on account of which I would advocate that everybody should become perfectly acquainted with the achievements of the masters of the past, with the development of the musical language up to our times. Firstly: after some time most of these national characteristics fade and only the idea remains. Secondly: It would be too great a loss, if this technique, produced by centuries [were to] be abandoned and a new technique started at the point where the European started long, long ago."

22. As, for instance, when he writes in 1948 in "Turn of Time," "I know that history repeats itself, and I understand that works produced at a turn of time—that is, when a new period is in the process of development—have always been viciously attacked. I expect history to repeat itself this time also; real merits, if they are present, will not be ignored, will not be forgotten." Schoenberg, *Style and Idea*, 139–141, esp. 141.

23. Clement Greenberg, "Towards a Newer Laocoon," in *Perceptions and Judgments, 1939–1944*, vol. 1 of *Clement Greenberg: The Collected Essays and Criticism*, ed. John O'Brian (Chicago: University of Chicago Press, 1986), 23–38, esp. 32.

24. Clement Greenberg, "Modernist Painting" (1965), in *Modern Art and Modernism: A Critical Anthology*, ed. Francis Frascina and Charles Harrison (London: Harper and Row and Open University Press, 1982), 5–6.

Some feminist criticism posits a more sinister role for modernism. Paraphrasing such arguments, Marcia J. Citron describes how "modernism arose as a means of countering the feminization of literature and music. This placed men in the uneasy position of having to react to foremothers, thus presenting a fundamental problem for Oedipal resolution. One outcome of this male dilemma was the formation of an aesthetic intended to exclude women, namely modernism" (*Gender and the Musical Canon*, 50).

25. See Christopher Hailey, "Musical Expressionism: The Search for Autonomy," in *Expressionism Reassessed*, ed. Shulamith Behr, David Fanning, and Douglas Jarman (Manchester and New York: Manchester University Press, 1993), 103–111. Jost Hermand pursues a related argument to make the same point in "Musikalischer Expressionismus," in his essay collection *Beredte Töne: Musik im historischen Prozess* (Frankfurt am Main: Peter Lang, 1992), 97–117.

26. Schoenberg's conscious articulation of canonic principles served to deemphasize sociohistorical context and stress structural and stylistic constants. There is a striking corollary with this modernist appropriation of historical styles and contemporary efforts by Hugo Riemann and others to make style the basis of music-historical narrative. See Citron, *Gender and the Musical Canon*, 32.

27. A related phenomenon has been the proliferation of a school of formalist analysis that has increasingly concerned itself with performative operations divorced from any larger context, a self-validating and self-perpetuating circle of enterprise more concerned with method than meaning. In the decade since Joseph Kerman argued this point in *Contemplating Music* (Cambridge: Harvard University Press, 1985), musicology has undergone a striking transformation in which criticism and historicizing tendencies have acquired new relevance and authority. See Kerman's "American Musicology in the 1990s," *Journal of Musicology* 9/2 (1991), 131–144.

28. Citron points out the similarities between the closed circle of connoisseurs at the Verein evenings and the social settings for music before 1750 (*Gender and the Musical Canon*, 29). In this context there is an intriguing overlap between the ideas behind the Verein and the aesthetic theory of "absorbed presence" formulated by Michael Fried in his discussion of Diderot and eighteenth-century aesthetics of painting in *Absorption and Theatricality: Painting and Beholder in the Age of Diderot* (Chicago: University of Chicago Press, 1980). Diderot abhorred theatricality and proposed an ideal of unselfconscious participation in the work of art (which by its subject matter and style must invite such absorption). "The object of his distaste," Fried writes, "was not exaggeration or caricature or *politesse* as such but the awareness of an audience, of being beheld, that they implied. And it was above all else the apparent extinction of that awareness, by virtue of a figure's absolute engrossment or absorption in an action, activity, or state of mind, that he demanded of works of pictorial art" (99). To be sure, Schoenberg's ideal was not the naive absorption of Diderot, but rather an intellectual immersion that was conscious and alert. Nonetheless, there is something of the same paradox in the resulting relationship between the work of art and its beholder. "Diderot's conception of painting," Fried writes, "rested ultimately upon the supreme fiction that the beholder did not exist, that he was not really there, standing before the canvas" (103). But, as we all know, art and music presuppose their audience, so the work of art must at once attract the beholder and command his absorption, while negating his presence: "only by establishing the fiction of his absence or nonexistence could his actual placement before and enthrallment by the painting be secured" (103). Similarly, with the Verein ideal Schoenberg created a setting in which the work of art existed only for the listener, who was, however, invisible—at least according to the conventions of the concert experience.

Hans-Georg Gadamer is still closer to Schoenberg in his neo-Kantian apologia for modern art in "The Relevance of the Beautiful," in *The Relevance of the Beautiful and Other Essays*, ed. Robert Bernasconi (Cambridge: Cambridge University Press, 1986), 3–53. He argues that older representational and twentieth-century abstract styles share the demand that they be taken as an autonomous experience. "The identity of the work," he writes, "is not guaranteed by any classical or formalist criteria, but is secured by the way in which we take the construction of the work upon ourselves as a task" (28). In musical matters, incidentally, Gadamer makes clear that his aesthetic perspective derives from canonical priorities at whose pinnacle sits "absolute music, that great achievement of musical abstraction in Western culture which reached a peak of development in imperial Austria with the classical Viennese school" (38).

29. John Guillory has made a similar plea "to resist homogenizing canonical works" and suggests instead historicizing them and reinstating "historical context as a ground of interpretation." John Guillory, "Canon," in *Critical Terms for Literary Study*, ed. Frank Lentricchia and Thomas McLaughlin (Chicago: University of Chicago Press, 1990), 244.

30. Barbara Herrnstein Smith has made the point succinctly: "we make texts timeless by suppressing their temporality" (*Contingencies of Value,* 49–50). Harold Bloom bemoans the similar, if more profound, phenomenon in his discussion of the biblical text he attributes to the author he calls "J." "Few cultural paradoxes are so profound, or so unnerving, as the process of religious canonization by which an essentially literary work becomes a sacred text. When script becomes Scripture, reading is numbed by taboo and inhibition." *The Book of J,* ed. Harold Bloom, trans. David Rosenberg (New York: Grove Weidenfeld, 1990), 35.

31. Steven Connor, *Postmodernist Culture: An Introduction to Theories of the Contemporary* (Oxford: Basil Blackwell, 1989), 238.

32. Ibid., 176.

33. The stylistic and aesthetic multiplicity in the new music, programming practices, and recording projects of the last thirty to forty years significantly anticipated the critical and scholarly formulations of the 1970s and 1980s, including postmodernism, deconstructionism, poststructuralism, and feminism. And musical scholarship has been at least twenty years behind developments in the study of literature, art, and history.

34. This was no less true of the nineteenth century, in which most genres were outside the preserve of the classical teaching canon. Lieder and opera, for instance, laid little claim to canonic status and were only loosely bound by canonic rules. The century's major innovations in harmonic language and form took place, as it were, on the margins, often in "extramusical" terrain and in genres that were not sanctioned by or transmitted through the academy. These extraterritorial challenges undermined the preeminence of canonic genres, which were threatened from within by imitation and academicism. Schoenberg's emphasis upon process and procedure served to deemphasize the primacy of genre as an emblem of canonicity.

35. It is interesting to note how many of the later works are specifically tied to particular events or settings. The political/historical references of the *Survivor from Warsaw* and the *Ode to Napoleon* come readily to mind, but the Suite for String Orchestra, the *Kol Nidre,* and the Organ Variations had ready practical applications for a specifically American context.

36. The most famous example of these is *Die Jaokobsleiter* and the related projects that preceded it.

37. Schoenberg's historicism was strongly colored by the pervasive historicism of late-nineteenth-century Vienna, which is a major theme in Carl Schorske's *Fin-*

de-Siècle Vienna: Politics and Culture (New York: Alfred A. Knopf, 1980), especially the chapter titled "The Ringstrasse, Its Critics, and the Birth of Urban Modernism," 24–115. Other aspects of Schoenberg's worldview that are distinctly related to his time would include his attitude toward women (most particularly manifest in his stage works), religion, and philosophy, as well as his own political sensibilities. These elements were largely suppressed in the Schoenberg literature of the 1940s, 1950s, and 1960s, out of an impulse of self-censorship that Barbara Herrnstein Smith (*Contingencies of Value,* 49–50) observes is typical of the treatment of works of canonical status. "For one thing," she writes,

> when the value of a work is seen as unquestionable, those of its features that would, in a noncanonical work, be found alienating—for example, technically crude, philosophically naive, or narrowly topical—will be glozed over or backgrounded. In particular, features that conflict intolerably with the interests and ideologies of subsequent subjects . . . will be repressed or rationalized, and there will be a tendency among humanistic scholars and academic critics to "save the text" by transferring the locus of its interest to more formal and structural features and/or by allegorizing its potentially alienating ideology to some more general ("universal") level where it becomes more tolerable and also more readily interpretable in terms of contemporary ideologies.

38. Connor, *Postmodernist Culture,* 99.

TWELVE

Schoenberg's Concept of Art in Twentieth-Century Music History

Hermann Danuser

Translated by Gareth Cox

When considering Schoenberg's concept of art, his *Kunstbegriff,* it is necessary to supplement his terminological and authorial concept of art—insofar as this essential aspect of the concept can be deduced from his writings and statements—with that other aspect that is revealed by his actual musical oeuvre. It is in this dual sense, in which the explicit poetics (the way Schoenberg the artist perceived himself, his *Selbstverständnis*) are considered together with the implicit poetics of what can be deduced from his music, that I intend to examine Schoenberg's Kunstbegriff. In doing so the contradictions that are rooted in the specific nature of Schoenberg's artistic development will be deliberately disregarded to allow us a clearer view of the unchanging principles behind his idea, or conception, of art. After a very brief, general outline of his Kunstbegriff I intend to consider the extent to which its specific characteristics contrast with those in the music history of the nineteenth century and with the contemporary context of the first half of the twentieth;[1] in conclusion I will outline some aspects of the historical influence of Schoenberg's Kunstbegriff in the latter half of the twentieth century.

I

Although "New Music," as both an idea and a catchword, is now outdated, the term had a formative influence on Schoenberg's understanding of art. He was outspoken in setting emphatic requirements: "Art means: *New Art*"; and earlier he declared: "Music insofar as it has to do with *art,* must always be new! Because *only* something *new,* something *previously unexpressed* is worth saying in art."[2] This demand for newness in art has of course nothing to do with innovation at any price. For Schoenberg, novelty in itself was neither an asset nor a liability; rather, he was concerned with the reasons for art being new. What he prescribed so emphatically for composers—the idea of New Music—he rejected with vehemence the moment he saw it reduced to a catchword by critics and historians. There is hardly a composer in the history of the twentieth century who combined, indeed merged, tradition and innovation more radically than Schoenberg. It was with good reason that in his dedicatory 1934 article "Der dialektische Komponist" Theodor W. Adorno quoted Stefan George's dictum "*Höchste Strenge ist zugleich höchste Freiheit*" (the greatest stringency is at the same time the greatest freedom),[3] for this most productive paradox pervades Schoenberg's music. The dialectic that characterizes Schoenberg's Kunstbegriff was recognized and captured early on in such article and book titles as Hanns Eisler's "Arnold Schönberg, der musikalische Reaktionär"[4] and Willi Reich's *Arnold Schönberg oder Der konservative Revolutionär.*[5] The fact that Schoenberg was so persistently conscious of tradition prevented him from taking a "modern" position akin to that artistic modernism that since Baudelaire has associated itself with randomness, with the everyday and commonplace, but also with "*épater le bourgeois.*"[6]

The poles of tradition and innovation are not the only ones that define the dialectics of Schoenberg's Kunstbegriff. Another formulation—to draw on Schoenberg's own words about compositional process—is defined by the concepts "heart" and "brain" in music; this configuration implies that even the categories of rationality and intuition (or inspiration) in Schoenberg's musical poetics are governed by a singular dialectic. This dialectic is particularly applicable where reception history has created an impression of one-sidedness—namely, in the period of free atonal expressionism (suspiciously irrational) in which Schoenberg's sense of form, governed solely by the rational basis of traditional musical expression and its syntactic mechanisms, was summed up in his declaration "*Ich entscheide beim Komponieren einzig und allein durch das Gefühl, durch das Formgefühl*" (in composing I make decisions only according to feeling, according to the feeling for form).[7] Conversely, though, the dialectic is also reflected in the twelve-tone period (suspiciously rational) in which Schoenberg, while admittedly employing a technique of greater rationality as regards the selection of pitch classes, composed as before so far as the art of developing variation was concerned—composed "as before," with the old rationality of spontaneous fantasy, without any hint of constructivism for its own sake.

But what of Schoenberg's dialectical/dynamic Kunstbegriff in his own compositional development from work to work? If we presuppose a very individual synthesis in Schoenberg of the tradition of German art music from Bach to Wagner/Brahms and Mahler/Strauss, on the basis of which he was able to create his new art, then the question follows whether we can assume if not a teleological then at least a problem-historical compositional progress. Certainly the main lines of development can be recognized, even sometimes a progression from work to work, but it would be an oversimplification to say that the succession of works in Schoenberg's oeuvre follows a model where, in seamless continuity, a musical problem is established in one work and solved in the succeeding one. Such a view would pervert the concept of a history of musical problems, a history that certainly cannot disregard the paradigm Schoenberg. Rather we should, in this respect, take as our point of departure the idea of a dialectical form of art production, one that favors the unorthodox and in which the rationally deducible is found alongside the unexpected, and recourse to compositional and genre tradition alongside bold inroads into new musical and music-historical territory.

II

In what way, then, does Schoenberg's dynamic concept of tradition differ from corresponding nineteenth-century concepts—in particular, from those of Beethoven, Brahms, and Wagner, from whose works he drew central creative stimuli? Schoenberg evaded the well-established dichotomy of the second half of the nineteenth century—between instrumental music in Brahms's line of development and music theater in Wagner's—and, by boldly breaking through the entrenched mechanism of the "art text" (*Kunsttext*) at the end of the century, transcended the dichotomy. He composed both and thereby manifested in his range of genres the same force of synthesis that can be seen in his compositional technique, where he adapted Brahmsian as well as Wagnerian means.

What appears new is that he relinquished any compositional-historical continuity of genre in his work. Although Wagner had drastically modified the category of genre, he did nonetheless remain true to music theater, and—despite what he said to the contrary—it in no way rendered the other areas of creativity superfluous. The only—partial—exceptions to this rule of transcending genres in Schoenberg's oeuvre that might be considered are the string quartets and, with respect to his early works, the lied. But the fact that the first quartet has a single-movement form and the second an integrated voice part shows just how loose the traditional concept of genre had become. In fact, both dodecaphonic quartets are closer to the traditional genre—also a sign of dialectical composition—just as general classical features reasserted themselves in the early dodecaphonic period.[8]

New traits also emerge in Schoenberg's Kunstbegriff with respect to its pragmatic realization. Ever since Mozart, and particularly Beethoven, had paved the way for the idea of original composition as an indication of artistic autonomy—analogous to the bourgeois emancipation of the subject—a more or less "aesthetic detachment" (in the words of Hans Robert

Jauss) between a new work and what was expected of it by the audience became part of successful composing.[9] Whereas Brahms worked within the traditional genres and relied upon their institutional contexts, Wagner created an appropriate institution for himself in Bayreuth, whereby this unique project also found its fulfillment in a single genre. With Schoenberg, however, the paradox was that while in terms of aesthetic reception he relied mainly on his oeuvre's connectedness to tradition (he was tireless in associating his works with the tradition of great German music),[10] the reality of the aesthetic reception was characterized by a nearly insurmountable rupture with the public, who were, apart from the early works, aware only of the innovative and not the traditional features in his music. Schoenberg's Kunstbegriff, then, compared with that of the nineteenth century, is revealed as one that, though conceived traditionally by the composer, functioned in the pragmatic sphere in a more innovative fashion with concomitant institutional consequences (evident particularly in Schoenberg's Viennese Verein für musikalische Privataufführungen). However, Schoenberg's works are so diverse and follow such individual designs that here, too, one can hardly speak of uniform consequences.

Is the entwinement of aesthetics and ethics in Schoenberg new, or was it already anticipated in Beethoven or Brahms? It was precisely in this respect that Gustav Mahler proved so important a model for Schoenberg, perhaps even more important than in any direct compositional sense. Implied entwinement of aesthetics and ethics culminated in Schoenberg in a rigorous artistic morality that is unparalleled. It is because of this concept— artistic morality—that Schoenberg gained such pathbreaking importance, not only as a composer but also as a teacher and a thinker. Concrete instruction and imparting rules of composition were far less important than the realization that only an extraordinary compositional problem was worthy of a truly artistic effort. Therefore it was more important to him to solve incorruptibly the unorthodox problem and thus exert lasting influence through the example of his moral artistic position than to offer illusory means for solutions that in reality failed. Perhaps it is for this reason that Schoenberg is the only truly great composer of recent music history who taught with passion and corresponding success and exerted such formative influence;[11] the Festschriften and compositions dedicated to him by his pupils testify to this.

III

In the context of twentieth-century music history, depending on the operative phase, it has been alternately either the innovative or the conservative features of the Schoenbergian Kunstbegriff that were manifest. All in all it is unprecedented with what consistency and innovative richness Schoenberg salvaged the concept (as derived from Schopenhauer's metaphysics) of an absolute musical art well into the twentieth century, all the more remarkable for the period after World War I, when new paradigms were established and the prewar era was considered a bygone world.

It would be well to outline here, very briefly, the various stages of Schoenberg's development. In his youth, and indeed during his whole life, Schoenberg was for the most part an autodidact. In his 1949 English-language essay "My Evolution" he names three people who played an important role in his artistic development: Oscar Adler, David Bach, and Alexander Zemlinsky.[12] There is unquestionably a connection between Schoenberg's unacademic side, his awareness that only original solutions endure, and this nonscholastic education. It helped him attain greater independence in his musical thinking and allowed him to develop his Kunstbegriff in so original a way.

As of 1899, the date of the string sextet *Verklärte Nacht,* op. 4, and in what is generally referred to as the first and second main periods—those of the tonal early works and subsequent free expressionistic atonality—work succeeded work in an intense, vigorous development of his musical thinking. In the context of musical modernism (in the sense in which that turn-of-the-century period is best understood),[13] there were overlapping, epoch-specific traits—for instance, the trend toward programmatic subjects, toward the transcendence of genre, toward the monumental song—but already here Schoenberg's Kunstbegriff developed more radically and more dynamically than that of any of his European colleagues. The dynamics of the development charted by this series of works, written one after another in an incredibly short period of time, were historically unprecedented. Schoenberg recalled this burst of creative energy when he admitted at the 1910 Vienna premiere of the *George-Lieder,* op. 15, that in this work he had succeeded for the first time in realizing a new ideal of expression that he had had in mind for years. The heading "Schoenberg and Progress" for the chapter on Schoenberg in Adorno's *Philosophy of New Music* was absolutely justified. Strauss, Mahler, Reger, Debussy—all the leading contemporary composers—being children of their own time, were in one way or another committed to the idea of progress, but none realized it as radically in his work as did Schoenberg when around 1910 he ventured into totally new territory with his expressionistic art.

In the twenties Schoenberg embarked on a new stage of his work, and of music history, with his method of composition with twelve tones related only to one another. At this time his Kunstbegriff, without any involvement on his part, became subject to the dichotomous misunderstanding that it was on the one hand "brain music," the dead monster of a musical engineer who tries to compensate for his lack of artistic inspiration with mathematical calculations, and on the other "heart music," the Romantic echoes of an outmoded composer whose legacy no longer represented a truly contemporary musical art. The first of these two polemical arguments against Schoenberg—which taken together serve to illuminate the composer's complexity—stemmed from the position of a preserved post-Romantic traditionalism (for example, that of Pfitzner); the second, from an alienating neoclassicism (for example, that of Stravinsky). Nonetheless, despite such attacks it was precisely at this time that Schoenberg's Kunstbegriff asserted itself in its complete individuality. Yet its author saw himself as an unappreciated artist. Having at the end of 1925 attained the pinnacle of public recognition with his position as the director of a master class in composition at the Prussian Academy of Arts in Berlin, he was forced to acknowledge that a younger generation of composers, seeing the times in a new way and with their concept of *"mittlere Musik,"*[14] had already passed him over and that it was they who were at the focal point of the music world's attention, an interest that could not be ascribed to mere fashion.

It is not easy to assess the extent to which Schoenberg's Kunstbegriff changed during the last two decades of his life in the United States, after his exile from National Socialist Germany. On the one hand "committed works" take on greater significance as a result of Schoenberg's declaration that he would make the political struggle for Judaism his main mission. On the other hand his Kunstbegriff changed hardly at all, since his commitment was a fermentation more of autonomous than of functional art, and his occasional works, unlike those of composers of *"mittlere Musik,"* remained, as in the nineteenth century, separate from his proclaimed Kunstbegriff. In no sense did Schoenberg conform to popular contemporary taste in the thirties and forties;[15] his artistic personality was too fixed to have allowed the pressure of external circumstances substantially to change his Kunstbegriff. During those two decades he gives the impression of an antediluvian boulder resistant to any softening toward a musical populism with an eye on the tastes of the broader public. Schoenberg knew that that isolated him, but because of his unshakable belief in himself and his idea of art he also foresaw that the future would belong to him.

IV

Naturally the question of Schoenberg's Kunstbegriff in twentieth-century music history addresses not only its specific qualities in comparison with other Kunstbegriffe but also its historical influence. Schoenberg's singularity and the predominance of his personal and artistic physiognomy became apparent in the fact that in Europe in the second half of the century, at the expense of the scholastic tradition, he was considered less important than his principal pupils, Webern and Berg. Reception is also always deformation. Those two main factors "heart" and "brain"—that is, intuition and rationality—which were dialectically intertwined in Schoenberg (and in both his pupils), in the course of reception history became sundered and fixed in separate strands of reception. On the one hand there developed that branch of Schoenberg reception that followed from the (suspected) constructivism of his twelve-tone technique and from which, with the expansion of his idea of the row in all dimensions (or parameters) of the texture, an integrated serial music emerged; because of the connection with Anton Webern this can be seen only as indirect reception. The Schoenberg patricide (committed by Boulez) from a historical distance—the dictum "*Schoenberg est mort*" is an artistic program, not a statement of fact—and the crowning of his pupil Webern in his place were presented in such a way that indirectly Schoenberg remained historically influential, though in a doubly deformed way as a result of aesthetic expression diminished by the reception of serialism (and the "brain" dimension made absolute, as it were). On the other hand the composers who, having grown up still within the populist aesthetic, feared the "constructivist ideology" and strove to reconcile the serial technique with tonality and expression attached themselves not to late Schoenberg but to Alban Berg, whose constructive profundity was not widely recognized; here too, where the "heart" was the focal point of attention, Schoenberg proved after 1950 to be, for the time being, of only indirect relevance. Likewise Adorno's emphasis on the "freely" atonal, expressionistic—as opposed to the dodecaphonic—Schoenberg (developed in his 1961 essay "Vers une musique informelle,"[16] which succeeded his criticism of serial technique in the *Philosophy of New Music*) was not to have reception-historical effect until later.

Schoenberg's dialectical Kunstbegriff, which the exponents of a serially organized music had criticized insofar as its constructive and expressive dimensions were considered inadequate and a relic of the aesthetic expression of an antiquated, bygone era, gained new relevance after the breakdown of the idea of the avant-garde in the 1970s. Here Schoenberg's own skepticism about "modernism" (not to mention the avant-garde), whose "fashionable" character he rejected and surmounted through rigorous connectedness with tradition, proved to be well-founded. So, at least in Germany, an authentic Schoenberg succeeded in gaining new credence after Adorno's Schoenberg—that is, the Schoenberg defined in *Philosophy of New Music*—had been buried. It was suddenly recognized that Schoenberg's artistic morality accords the individual a significance over and above philosophical-historical frameworks and beyond an avant-garde *Kanon des Verbotenen* (canon of the forbidden); his artistic morality corresponded exactly with the intentions of a younger generation who were growing weary of the obligation imposed on them by avant-garde progress. And so Schoenberg, and especially the expressionistic Schoenberg who so unreservedly followed his singular need to express himself, became a model for Wolfgang Rihm and his contemporaries. It was not that these younger composers wanted only to tend the "heart"; rather, they did not, and indeed do not, want the dictates of the "heart" to be any longer regimented by a procedural "brain" mechanism.

If Schoenberg's concept of art is measured against his perception and understanding of himself, it must be declared a "failure." The German music tradition that Schoenberg aspired to perpetuate for a further hundred years no longer exists; national ties, in the nineteenth-century sense in which Schoenberg still perceived them, have become irrelevant. But beyond his authorial intention we can discern the continuing relevance of certain elements of Schoenberg's Kunstbegriff that manifest themselves in a number of different ways. Indeed, the very fact that in our times we cannot share his absolute view of art in the sense of Schopenhauer and Nietzsche means that his Kunstbegriff, having acquired that special dignity of something from the past, has now also attained a sentimentally refracted contemporary relevance.

NOTES

1. In this context, see the proceedings of the Second Conference of the Internationale Schönberg-Gesellschaft, *Die Wiener Schule in der Musikgeschichte des 20. Jahrhunderts,* ed. Rudolf Stephan and Sigrid Wiesmann (Vienna: Verlag Elisabeth Lafite, 1986).

2. From the original 1933 article "Neue und veraltete Musik, oder Stil und Gedanke," in Schoenberg, *Gesammelte Schriften,* 466–477, esp. 466. Revised and translated as "New Music, Outmoded Music, Style and Idea," in *Style and Idea,* 113–124, esp. 114.

3. Theodor W. Adorno, "Der dialektische Komponist," *Arnold Schönberg zum 60. Geburtstag 13. September 1934* (Vienna: Universal Edition, [1934]), 18–23, esp. 20. Unless otherwise indicated, all translations are by Gareth Cox.

4. Hanns Eisler, "Arnold Schönberg, der musikalische Reaktionär," special Schoenberg issue of *Anbruch* 6/7–8 (August/September 1924), 312–313. The article closes with the words: *"Er ist der wahre Konservative: er schuf sich sogar eine Revolution, um Reaktionär sein zu können."* (He is the true conservative: He even created a revolution so that he could be reactionary.)

5. Published in English as Reich, *Schoenberg: A Critical Biography.*

6. See Schoenberg's humorous rejection of the characterization *"mutige[r] Vertreter der Wiener musikalischen Moderne"* (courageous representative of the Viennese modern school of music) in his letter to Emil Hertzka of 31 October 1911 (*Schoenberg Letters,* no. 8, 31–32, esp. 31). See also Schoenberg's declaration *"ich bin kein Moderner"* (I'm not a modern) in his letter to Oskar Kokoschka of 3 July 1946 (*Schoenberg Letters,* no. 211, 242–243, esp. 243); and his derisive treatment of the *"épater le bourgeois"* stance in his 1949 essay "My Evolution": "Fifty years later, the finest ears of the best musicians have difficulty in hearing those characteristic fea-

tures that the eyes of the average musicologist see so easily" (Schoenberg, *Style and Idea*, 70–92, esp. 88.).

7. Schoenberg, *Harmonielehre* (1922), 502; *Theory of Harmony*, 417.

8. See Rudolf Stephan, "Schoenberg und der musikalische Klassizismus," in *Bericht über den Internationalen Musikwissenschaftlichen Kongress, Berlin 1974*, ed. Hellmut Kühn and Peter Nitsche (Kassel: Bärenreiter, 1980), 3–11.

9. See Hans Robert Jauss, *Toward an Aesthetic of Reception* (Minneapolis: University of Minnesota Press, 1982).

10. See Constantin Floros, "Die Wiener Schule und das Problem der 'deutschen Musik,' " in *Die Wiener Schule und das Hakenkreuz: Das Schicksal der Moderne im gesellschaftspolitischen Kontext des 20. Jahrhunderts*, Studien zur Wertungsforschung, vol. 22, ed. Otto Kolleritsch (Vienna and Graz: Universal Edition, 1990), 35–50; see also Hermann Danuser, "Arnold Schönberg und die Idee einer deutschen Musik," lecture delivered at the symposium "Was ist deutsch in der Musik?" Dresdner Zentrum für zeitgenössische Musik, October 1991 (forthcoming).

11. See also Rudolf Stephan, ed., *Die Wiener Schule*, Wege der Forschung, vol. 643 (Darmstadt: Wissenschaftliche Buchgesellschaft, 1989), in particular the editor's introduction, 1–19.

12. Schoenberg, "My Evolution," in *Style and Idea*, 70–92, esp. 79–80.

13. See Carl Dahlhaus, *Die Musik des 19. Jahrhunderts*, vol. 6 of *Neues Handbuch der Musikwissenschaft*, ed. Carl Dahlhaus (Wiesbaden: Akademische Verlagsgesellschaft Athenaion, 1980), 279 ff; English translation, *Nineteenth-Century Music*, trans. J. Bradford Robinson (Berkeley and Los Angeles: University of California Press, 1989), 330 ff.

14. See Hermann Danuser, "Die 'mittlere Musik' der zwanziger Jahre," in *La musique et le rite sacré et profane: Kongressbericht Strassburg 1982*, ed. Marc Honegger and Paul Prevost (Strasbourg: Association des Publications près les Universités de Strasbourg, 1986), 2:703–721.

15. See Hermann Danuser, "Was ist Populismus in der Musik?" lecture delivered at the March 1991 symposium "Ethnomusikologie und historische Musikwissenschaft," ed. Christoph-Hellmut Mahling (forthcoming); published in Italian translation as "Che cos'è il populismo in musica?" *Musica/Realtà* 12/36 (December 1991), 117–133, esp. 117 ff.

16. Theodor W. Adorno, "Vers une musique informelle," in *Darmstädter Beiträge zur neuen Musik* (Mainz: B. Schott's Söhne, 1962), 4:73–102; English translation in *Quasi una fantasia: Essays on Modern Music*, trans. Rodney Livingstone (London and New York: Verso, 1992), 269–322.

THIRTEEN

Schoenberg and Present-Day Theory and Practice

Jonathan Dunsby

In 1971 Allen Forte wrote the following:

> The scope and variety of contemporary musico-theoretical investigations, especially in the U.S. beginning in the 1950s, is remarkable. . . . There seems to be ample evidence that musical theory in the twentieth century is once again what it has occasionally been in the past: a vital intellectual component of music.[1]

These words were partly a tribute to Arnold Schoenberg, who is mentioned in Forte's article "Theory" (from which this quote is taken) essentially for the notions of extended tonality that evolved between the 1911 and 1922 editions of the *Harmonielehre*.

One must doubt whether Forte had much inkling even as late as 1971 — bearing in mind the composers who were then in vogue — that the end of our century would see a surge of artistic evolution that now has its very firmly established name borrowed from wider trends in Western society that became (fatally for "modernism") conspicuous in the 1980s — namely, "postmodernism." There does not appear to be significant commentary from the late 1960s that predicts the household names of the next wave of composition, though the likes of John Adams, Arvo Pärt, and Toru Takemitsu were alive and musically kicking at the time.[2] Now, so soon afterward, even that ongoing — and, as it were, institutional — European masterpiece *Répons*, by Pierre Boulez, has a new, sensuous, repetitive, multivalent quality to stamp it as a work of the 1990s and beyond. In Boulez the new way — in Schoenberg's wake but not in his manner — seems to have shed its skin in yielding to an even newer way. So it is hardly to Allen Forte's discredit that he could not foresee the concomitant swing toward the present-day antiformalist character of much that is on offer in the name of new music theory.

Of course, one may make too much of this new Zeitgeist as an orderly, interlinked phenomenon of the creative and the contemplative. The very plurality of postmodernism suggests that Zeitgeist is itself a formalist, if last-century Hegelian, notion that perhaps should be allowed to die quietly beside other old modernisms adopted in the twentieth century. Nowadays fashionable creativity and fashionable commentary do not necessarily go hand in hand, but this does not necessarily imply any conflict. After all, such distinguished West Coast antiformalist writers as Kerman and Taruskin do pay more attention publicly to old music than to new, as we find of those more recent darlings of the music-academic press, Abbate and Kramer, and the ascendant Korsyn. In this curious scenario antiformalism and anticontemporaneity seem to go in tandem. Such writers as Joseph Straus talk about remaking the past.[3] One gets the feeling that that is where they would really like to live.

It is tempting to declare that modern music theory, of the kind Schoenberg would recognize, not only saw its beginnings in the thinking he himself conducted in Vienna and Berlin many decades ago but is now drawing to its close in America and, given our transcultural age, elsewhere too. We can now begin to discern the true curve of the arch that is twentieth-century music theory—or, as some nostalgic historians of music might say, we can now begin to see the light at the end of the tunnel. As a result it is possible to get a sense of how deep and enduring was the view of music that Schoenberg, above all, put on the agenda. That "above all," of course, needs some gloss, and it seems to me that there are both an easy way and a hard way to provide it.

The easy way is to examine the development of theorizing about dodecaphonic and what have come to be called "serial" forms of composition in general. Despite the excellent contribution made by other theorists in the early years of musical modernism, it was Schoenberg who provided the golden key. Forte has put this succinctly. "Schoenberg's brief consideration of new atonal harmonies," he wrote, "inspired others to examine systematically the resources of the twelve-tone method. . . . This in turn led to projections of other systems and resources."[4] From this line of development were to emerge the great trends of postwar American activity, in the work of what is usually termed the "Princeton axis," and in the dissemination and elaboration of pitch-class set theory. This well-known and oft-told story is a transatlantic matter. It may well be that *Die Reihe,* for instance, which grew out of the postwar Darmstadt ethos, put down a more focused historical marker than, say, the early *Perspectives of New Music;* certainly one must acknowledge the continuing, lively, creative theoretical developments of the European scene.

It has been a natural tendency for the prospective and proactive aspects of Schoenberg the composer-theorist to be praised at the expense of their genealogy. What unlocked the "oft-told" story to which I just referred was Schoenberg's insistence that, putting it somewhat whimsically, consonance is a lower form of dissonance. There is such a hackneyed familiarity in the air whenever we are asked to contemplate emancipated dissonance that the historical leverage of the idea is forgotten. When Heinrich Schenker illustrates the lack of tonal prolongation in a Stravinsky excerpt, all we are being offered is an image of the end of music history, or of a future that never did arrive. When Schoenberg illustrates how Mozart's dissonance can be understood only in terms of the total chromatic, we are being offered a link from the past to a future that did arrive and that did in this century yield many marvels of the human spirit. And thus we reach the center of my own view on these matters. There has been only one comprehensive theorist of our age—so far—who has regenerated the spirit of his European past into a progressive, contemporary resource. Not every composer of genius could have achieved this, or wanted to; on the other hand, only a real composer interested in theory could have achieved it.

This brings me to what I called the "hard way" of providing a gloss to the claims I have made for Schoenberg. For how is it that in many respects Schoenberg the theorist has been marginalized?

It often appears to be a matter of wheels within wheels, as is exemplified almost canonically in a little clash between Walter Frisch and Kofi Agawu, two of the most energetic and imaginative musical commentators in what might still be called the younger generation. Many readers will have sympathized with Frisch's difficulties in addressing his subject in *Brahms and the Principle of Developing Variation*.[5] It was not just a matter of high expectations, given that this was the book Schoenbergians had been longing for since 1932 and even before. Everyone assumed, too, that Frisch would be in the position of the quixotic homicide officer who has just the two clues: "A" (who is missing and presumed dead), developing variation; and "B" (who looks a bit guilty), Schoenberg. Agawu replies, though, that what Frisch has missed, and by implication what the Schoenbergians in this area have missed in general, is the very point on offer in the first place:

> It is often said that Schoenberg formulated the notion of developing variation too vaguely and that he failed to provide demonstrations *in extenso* of how it works. . . . I would contest the extent to which Schoenberg's analyses are ambiguous; in fact . . . we need not look beyond his essay "Brahms the Progressive" in order to form a fairly clear idea of what developing variation means. The emphasis in Frisch's own analytical plot on an absence of "sustained illumination" in Schoenberg's own analysis only propagates a myth.[6]

On the contrary, Agawu is arguing, Schoenberg's analytical work is relatively brief not because it lacks some ideal musico-critical lyricism but just because it is, at its best, systematic.[7] I do not have the temerity to adjudicate between these two positions.[8] All the same it is intriguing, at the risk of being unfair to two subtle writers, to summarize them: on the one hand Schoenberg is frustrating but ultimately good because he does not formalize; on the other Schoenberg is constructive and good precisely because he does formalize or at least leads the way to it.

Is it too much to infer from all debates of this type that one of the reasons Schoenberg has been marginalized in music theory is because theorists have been unequal to the task of taking up his ideas during the era of formalism? Have the ideas been almost too advanced for music theory as a discipline? Considering current theory and practice in respect to "developing variation," it is pertinent to see how cleanly and helpfully Ethan Haimo has at last been able to stitch the concept into his new account of the evolution of Schoenberg's twelve-tone method, some sixty to seventy years after the event.[9] Along with some of the best recent work in music theory, this indicates at least some continuing contemporaneity in Schoenberg's legacy, as we become able to see the things that were not to be seen before. Arnold Whittall formulated the matter in 1980:

> From a perspective where the consequences of Schoenberg can be contemplated, the study of Schoenberg himself is becoming increasingly concerned with analysis and less with criticism. Only now, therefore, are the essential technical issues beginning to be adequately explored and expounded.[10]

Here Whittall is contemplating the critical treatment of Schoenberg's own music, but again commentary folds into itself, and his comment applies perfectly well to the position of Schoenberg's theories. Once we have taken on board the idea of historical perspective, there remains the challenge of assimilating Schoenberg's thinking as a guide to analysis, explored thoroughly.

Although I have in fact already introduced him by name and in principle, in practice this is the point to come clean about Schenker. One cannot speak of Schoenberg as the "above all" in music theory without returning to Vienna and that other ascendant—but not, I believe, transcendent—theorist. It has been implied here that Schoenberg has been marginalized by large cultural forces, matters of time, place, intention—simply the contingencies of history that we historians struggle to comprehend. Yet the obsession of a large class of music theorists, myself included, with Schenkerian theory and practice is something identifiable and indeed obvious. The serpent is to some extent biting its tail. I have already indicated that notions of approaches to musical structure in terms of pitch-class set (and, one must certainly add, genera) would be unthinkable without Schoenberg's work as a composer-theorist, and there is a pungent scent of postmodernism in all the current research that combines pitch-class-set and neo-Schenkerian posttonal voice-leading theories, as there is in the idea of the trichordal pitch genus. However, in the study of First Viennese music, Schenker's insights have proved so attractive—mainly, I would say, to those who are not primarily concerned with musical composition—that they have distracted the attention of a large community of potential students of Schoenberg's theories. Schoenbergians may take some grim satisfaction in knowing that this has happened to Schenker too, who has been marginalized in the German-speaking world by yet other cultural forces.

If there is any justice and balance in twentieth-century life, some confirmation of this might be found in the theoretical marginalization of Schoenberg the composer, who insisted that it does not matter how a piece of music is made. If it does not matter, why did Schoenberg spend so much time trying to discover how pieces of music by other composers were made, and explaining this to his many students? The answer, for sure, is that Schoenberg could theorize only as a composer and yet could not theorize about his current practice: theory had to be a notch behind what he was actually creating, as has often been stated.[11] The years of rapid atonal evolution, approximately 1907 to 1912, could easily spawn Schoenberg's theoretical magnum opus, the 1911 *Harmonielehre*. After that it was very much slower work compositionally. I feel that to his dying day Schoenberg was preoccupied with a compositional breakthrough he had made in his forties, about which he had little to say because it required more than a lifetime's quiet reflection. Here I would wish to supplement Reinhold Brinkmann's portrayal of the politico-religious projects dating from Schoenberg's middle age. It was overall surely a *philosophic*-politico-religious project; to society and to the spirit we have to add the intellect, even if Schoenberg's intellect was less overtly at work in the second part of his life.

Although Schoenberg has been marginalized as a theorist, insofar as institutionalized theorizing is concerned, in books, journals, and debates, his pedagogical importance is well-nigh universally recognized, at the highest level through study of the *Harmonielehre,* and in common practice through the American textbooks. This is not the occasion to discuss those volumes, but they are the obvious signs of a core of thinking through which Schoenberg intended to pass on more than simple descriptions. Description is the best result of most theory, in the hands of those who really want to discover how a composer managed to work. The contemplative armchair theorist is in awe of creativity and cultivates an intellectual, quasi-scientific detachment. Even the brilliant Schenker, a very failed composer but by all accounts a superb performer, has the demeanor of the detective—of the fascinated operative whose whole claim on our attention nevertheless depends on acts committed by others. In the past, minds such as those of Johann Fux, Heinrich Koch, and Paul Hindemith have also been oriented in this way, while attempting to pass on a degree of compositional know-how. Such theorists in this intermediate group are less in awe of compositional practice and do not have an idealistic—one might almost say European—view of what it means to be a composer.

Among first-order theorists, Rameau provides the atavism, an unusual Franco-Austrian embrace. His task may have been a little easier than Schoenberg's because he was part of the march of Enlightenment thinking—not, as inevitably the case more recently, one of many lone voices speaking different tongues. Rameau, who managed to forge a new musical language while theorizing about it enduringly, is the paradigm of the composer-theorist in the modern sense: he left indelible creative and intellectual acts to future generations. It is not I who posit this well-established paradigm, and it is for the reader to decide whether the coincidence of art and reflection at a transcendent level is a good and useful thing. If it is, we must accord to Schoenberg an importance in twentieth-century culture that goes beyond what one must thus dare to call a mere appreciation of his compositions.

Heinrich Schenker, who has been an inescapable subtopic of this essay, provides us with a profound method for studying and discussing the many jewels of First Viennese music, and much more besides, from Scarlatti to Chopin. This method is of universal interest. Yet in the end Schoenberg has done something potentially more important: he has offered us the means of understanding a continuity between First and Second Viennese musics and, in a way, whatever else is to follow. This is probably what the composer, rather than the pure theorist, most needs, and is certainly what many composers of the mid to late twentieth century have demonstrably exploited creatively. For decades arcane commentary has been recycling a fixation with what is called Schoenberg's "historical self-justification." In perspective it is time to start discussing his theoretical comprehensiveness, to investigate this as a live issue. It has recently been reasserted in the telling words of Ian Bent: "[W]ith Schoenberg's powerfully suggestive concepts . . . the organic model, aesthetic, and technical array of tools that can be seen to have arisen in the late eighteenth and early nineteenth centuries were transmitted to the twentieth century."[12] And I note with interest how in his very recent major article "Debussy's Significant Connections" Craig Ayrey brings Schoenberg squarely into a current music-theory heartland, noting that "the organicist metaphor in Schoenberg asserts a preference for metonymy,"[13] confirming the impetus in the "old" thinking for the thinking of the poststructuralist future.

Returning to my opening theme, I stress the crucial element of postmodern pluralistic approaches as far as they concern not only music theory, but music history in its broadest sense. As various cultural historians are now expounding, we find in these new movements not some kind of deathly return to old values but a modernism that has taken a new turn, away from formalisms that require us to learn and to imitate, and toward a pluralist approach that constrains us to ask questions and accept no easy answers. In arguing the case for musical prose, for developing variation, for the musical idea and the logic, technique, and art of its presentation, for the emancipated dissonance, indeed for the plenty of good music still to be written in C major—in all of this Schoenberg has been the greatest irritant to the orthodoxies, not just of theorists, but of musicology in general and the music making it merely reflects. We may question his formalist credentials but not his modernist ones, and this is what renders him such a central architect of present-day theory and practice. Any composer or musicologist, whether twenty or eighty years old, will see this. One has only to read *Style and Idea.*

NOTES

1. Allen Forte, "Theory," in *Dictionary of Twentieth-Century Music,* ed. John Vinton (London: Thames and Hudson, 1974), 759. Forte's article originally appeared in the 1971 U.S. edition of this publication.

2. Historians were of course already tracking the rapid changes in contemporary life. For example, Eric Salzman, in the second edition of *Twentieth-Century Music: An Introduction* (Englewood Cliffs, N.J.: Prentice-Hall, 1974), concludes that "the age of modern music is drawing to a close. The music of the avant-garde, growing out of modern music, is in fact a transition to something new. The old categories are purely historical and no longer really relevant" (200).

3. Joseph N. Straus, *Remaking the Past: Musical Modernism and the Influence of the Tonal Tradition* (Cambridge: Harvard University Press, 1990).

4. Forte, "Theory," 756.

5. Walter Frisch, *Brahms and the Principle of Developing Variation* (Berkeley and Los Angeles: University of California Press, 1984).

6. Kofi Agawu, review of *Brahms and the Principle of Developing Variation,* by Walter Frisch, *Music Analysis* 7/1 (March 1988), 99–100.

7. Agawu's second example provides a "fundamentalist's application of the principles implicit in Schoenberg's analysis" to a Brahms song, revealing a "contiguous intervallic process almost exhaustively described thereby" (Agawu, review of Frisch, 104). It is a most elegant example of formalist countercriticism.

8. Protocol demands mention, however, of chapter 5 of my *Structural Ambiguity in Brahms* (Ann Arbor, Mich.: UMI Research Press, 1981), which put me, rather long ago, in the Agawu camp.

9. Ethan Haimo, *Schoenberg's Serial Odyssey* (Oxford: Clarendon Press, 1990).

10. Arnold Whittall, "Schoenberg and the English," *Journal of the Arnold Schoenberg Institute* 4/1 (June 1980), 32.

11. Silvina Milstein, the author of *Arnold Schoenberg: Notes, Sets, Forms* (Cambridge: Cambridge University Press, 1992), has put it to me first that Schoenberg meant that the permutational pitch structure does not reveal the real secrets of musical construction, and second that one must never underestimate the extent to which Schoenberg's thinking was driven by his current compositional evolution.

These are both points well worth recording, but I feel they have to do with nuance, and I stick to my argument. I would like here to record my thanks to Dr. Milstein for her advice on various points of this article.

12. Ian Bent, *Music Analysis in the Nineteenth Century* (Cambridge: Cambridge University Press, 1994), 1:17.

13. Craig Ayrey, "Debussy's Significant Connections," in *Theory, Analysis and Meaning in Music*, ed. Anthony Pople (Cambridge: Cambridge University Press, 1994), 145.

FOURTEEN

Schoenberg the Contemporary

A View from Behind

Reinhold Brinkmann

Let me begin outside the picture, as it were.[1] The last book of the late Bruno Bettelheim, the famous psychiatrist, bears the title *Freud's Vienna*.[2] From the title essay of this book, I cite the following passages:

> It is not by chance that psychoanalysis was born in Vienna and came of age there. In Freud's time, the cultural atmosphere in Vienna encouraged a fascination with both mental illness and sexual problems in a way unique in the Western world—a fascination that extended throughout society. . . . The origins of this unique cultural preoccupation can be traced to the history of the city itself, but most especially to the concerns and attitudes foremost in the minds of Vienna's cultural elites just before and during the period in which Freud formed his revolutionary theories about our emotional life. . . .
>
> With the appearance of *The Interpretation of Dreams* in 1900, psychoanalysis became established. This greatest of Freud's works is one of introspection; in it all interest is devoted to the innermost self of man, to the neglect of the external world, which pales in comparison to the fascination of this inner world. That this turn-of-the-century Viennese *chef d'oeuvre* was indeed the result of desperation at being unable to change the course of the external world and represented an effort to make up this deficiency by a single-minded interest in the dark underworld, is attested to by the motto which Freud put at the beginning: Virgil's line *"Flectere si nequeo superos, Acheronta movebo"* ("If I cannot move heaven, I will stir up the underworld"). This motto was a most succinct suggestion that turning inward toward the hidden aspects of the self was due to a despair that it was no longer within one's ability to alter the external world or stop its dissolution; that therefore the best one could do was to deny importance to the world at large by concentrating all interest on the dark aspects of the psyche.

Bettelheim's text may be reread as a statement on Schoenberg's new music with but a few changes of words in these passages—substituting "Schoen-

berg" for "Freud," "atonality" for "psychoanalysis," "*Erwartung*," for example, for "*The Interpretation of Dreams*"; and introducing historically significant
musical categories (such as "the emancipation of dissonance" or "the dissolution of the tonal system") instead of psychoanalytical terms. The underlying sociocultural analysis and the central idea of introspection as the
primary figure of thought characterize the origin and the structure both
of Freud's psychoanalytical theory and of Schoenberg's atonal compositions. Thus, with an identical social and historical accentuation, "Freud's
Vienna" could also be named "Schoenberg's Vienna," just as philosophers
rightly call it "Wittgenstein's Vienna" and art historians could claim it to be
"Schiele's Vienna."

Schoenberg's foundation of the Viennese atonality as a new paradigm
for a contemporary music, besides being embedded in a music-historical
process, was indeed the reflection of a very specific and problematic historical, social, cultural, and psychical situation in Vienna around 1900.
Schoenberg's music is at once a direct expression and reflecting mirror of
this situation and, for some exceptional moments, its anticipation: it is at
once a subject of this state of mind and its complex symbolic representation. And its most general principle seems to be the gesture that Bruno
Bettelheim named "introspection"—the concentration on the "inner
world," its exploration, reflection, and manifestation. Ernst Bloch would
later characterize this principle as "*der interne Weg*" (the internal way) — "*der
interne Weg, auch Selbstbegegnung genannt, die Bereitung des inneren Worts, ohne
die aller Blick nach aussen nichtig bleibt, und kein Magnet, keine Kraft, das innere
Wort auch draussen anzuziehen, ihm zum Durchbruch aus dem Irrtum der Welt zu
verhelfen.*"[3] Elsewhere I have related this thought to the gesture with which
Schoenberg in an oft-quoted aphorism of 1910 characterizes the creative
act.[4] In this *Fragment*, to use a Romantic term, art is defined—and I paraphrase Schoenberg—as the "cry of despair uttered by those who experience
at first hand the fate of mankind." Artists are seen as sensitive individuals
"who hurl themselves in among the moving wheels, to understand how it
all works." They open their eyes—they "open them wide"—"to tackle what
must be tackled" so as to grasp the world and its mechanisms. But, most
important, they "often close their eyes, in order to perceive things incom-
municable by the senses, to envision within themselves the process that only
seems to be in the world outside. The world revolves *within*—inside them:
what *bursts out* is merely the echo—the work of art."[5]

I am interested in what I have called the specific gesture, or figure of
thought, contained in these three statements (by Bettelheim, Bloch, and,
in particular, Schoenberg) and their three layers. The first layer betrays
desperation about the "external world," an attempt to intervene, and the
experience of one's inability to change its dissolution; in a second layer
we find a turning inward, an introspection, and the stipulation that there

is an inner world that is intact—unhurt and intact in spite of everything, and therefore superior; and, finally, we have a third layer: the artistic out-burst, the figure of the *Durchbruch* (breakthrough)—the work of art as the utopian message, confronting the "world" with truth—that is, spiritual truth. It seems to me not only that this figure of thought is Schoenberg's most fundamental aesthetic creed—a creed deeply rooted in European middle-class culture and nineteenth-century history—but that this intellec-tual gesture can serve as a metaphorical characterization of his life and work.

In parentheses, and briefly: The term Durchbruch is familiar as a repre-sentational category in musical criticism, in particular since Adorno's Mahler monograph; the term mediates art form with what Adorno called the *Weltlauf,* the course of the world.[6] But it certainly goes back to nine-teenth-century compositional strategies and was probably introduced into the critical vocabulary for music by Paul Bekker in *his* book on Mahler, dating from 1920.[7] And it should be noted that both Ernst Bloch and Schoenberg himself use this energetic term to characterize the creative situation—Bloch in the sentence quoted above—the Durchbruch of the "inner word" to the world "outside"—and Schoenberg in his well-known statement of 1910 that with the *George-Lieder* he was "conscious of having broken through every restriction of a bygone aesthetic."[8]

Schoenberg's quest for contemporaneity in his art can be concentrated first in the question of *how* to realize artistically the paradigmatic Durch-bruch; this question governs his search for a pertinent musical language. His quest for contemporaneity can be concentrated second in the ques-tion of *what*—of, in other words, the goal of this strategy; this governs his search for meaning. To illustrate this vague general statement I will use three images from different periods of Schoenberg's life: a pictorial image for "Schoenberg's Vienna" (notice the *genitivus possessivus!*), a linguistic im-age for "Schoenberg in Berlin," and a musical image for "Schoenberg in America." In my understanding of this life's work and its historical place, the first period sets the *fundamentum.* I will therefore devote considerably more time and space to Schoenberg's "project Vienna" than to "Berlin" or "America."

SCHOENBERG'S VIENNA

Shortly after World War I Darius Milhaud visited Schoenberg in his Möd-ling home. Decades later he still vividly recalled a visual impression:

> We had coffee in a dining room, the walls of which were hung about with Schoenberg's paintings. Faces and eyes, eyes, eyes everywhere![9]

This experience can be corroborated by a number of images: an amateur photo of a wall from the 1974 Schoenberg exhibition in the Vienna *Secession* displaying Schoenberg paintings; a photo of Schoenberg sitting in his Brentwood home in front of a wall hung with self-portraits;[10] one of the self-portraits from 1910; and the *Red Gaze,* also from 1910[11]. All of these paintings display Schoenberg's central pictorial idea: the human being's existence concentrated in open eyes—eyes of a specific intensity, direct, active, burning, confronting, questioning.[12]

Iconologically these faces resemble and at the same time differ from Edvard Munch's famous *Scream,* with its expression—in lines and eyes—of defensiveness and angst.[13] A particularly telling difference is that Schoenberg's portraits depict isolated individuals, concentrating them in their open eyes, whereas Munch's screaming face and body are shown within a realistic context of landscape and other background figures.

For me Schoenberg's "eyes" are pictorial realizations of the first layer of his artistic creed of 1910, eyes "wide open" as the "cry of despair" of the isolated individual, the artist attempting to grasp "world" and its mechanics, eyes wide open so as to "understand how it all works." These are eyes that are letting "world" enter—eyes, too, that leave the artist almost defenseless.

And I recall Schoenberg's remark, late in life, to Halsey Stevens: " . . . what painting meant to me. In fact, it was the same to me as making music." A painter friend of mine insists that these eyes are in fact "sounding," that they have an almost musical quality. The painted "cry of despair" can be aurally perceived. Indeed, there seems to be a strong connection between eye and ear in Schoenberg's perception of his world; seeing "world" and hearing "world" are linked, almost identical.[14] Schoenberg once remarked that a professional painter would always be able to express the entire person through the eyes, whereas Schoenberg himself, as an amateur painter, felt that his capacity in this field was limited, the "eyes" being primarily confined to representing only one side—that is, emotions, the expressive inwardness of their subject. That may well be true. But the active, confronting directness of these eyes indicates to me, in addition, a reflecting, critical quality, reflection as the basis for a critical distance, an assessment of both world and self.

The second level of Schoenberg's aphorism—close the eyes and listen to the world within—calls to mind Hegel's definition of the lyric:

> In lyric . . . it is feeling and reflection which draw . . . the objectively existent world into themselves and live it through their own inner element, and only then, after the world has become something inward, is it grasped and expressed in words. In contrast to the spread of epic, lyric has contracted concentration [*Zusammengezogenheit*] for its principle.[15]

Schoenberg's 1910 aphorism is like an expressionistic specification of this general perspective on the lyric; even the vocabulary is strikingly similar. Lyrical introspection is Schoenberg's Viennese answer to the artist's inability any longer to embrace and grasp the "world."

This introspection could be demonstrated in compositional terms. Strategies as applied to Schoenberg would include the antimonumental, antisymphonic poetics of the "critical years" around 1910; his speaking out against the representation of the "world" in Mahler's symphonies, his pointed withdrawal from the large genres and large, complicated formal constructions of the Viennese and German tradition; his rejection of the symphony, symphonic poem, and oratorio (this impulse would return later, but both the oratorio *Die Jakobsleiter* and the opera *Moses und Aron* would remain fragments). Rather would there be a predominance of lyrical genres such as lied and character piece. The subject of Viennese atonality around 1910 is a lyrical one. There are a chamber symphony for solo instruments (op. 9), a string quartet (op. 10), lieder (opp. 14 and 15), lyrical piano pieces (opp. 11 and 19), character pieces for orchestra (op. 16), and the monodrama *Erwartung.*[16]

Hegel's *Zusammengezogenheit* (contracted concentration) as a compositional category quite obviously coincides with Schoenberg's, Webern's, and even Berg's seemingly short pieces from around 1910, those intense moments of inwardness that are in fact contracted, compressed long ones. *Erwartung* is the paradigmatic work, and Marie's death in *Wozzeck* is its concentrated reflection. I could demonstrate similar strategies in compositional and dramaturgical details. Take, as one example only, the light-and-storm scene at the center of *Die glückliche Hand.* Schoenberg's stage directions instruct the Man to act "as if" the crescendo of light and storm originates in himself; in other words, the events of the outer world are mere projections of an inner world.

It is illuminating to note, in this context, that Schoenberg's lieder belong to a very specific period in his compositional output—namely, the period from his early works to the freely atonal ones: that is, the time leading up to World War I. From the 1920s onward Schoenberg abandoned the genre of the intimate musical lyric, and his later oeuvre, his vocal music in particular, is located beyond the realm of the lyric as a paradigm of contemporary thought.

Among Schoenberg's numerous self-portraits from around 1910 one painting is of specific interest for our discussion of inwardness as the second layer. It is the well-known *Self-Portrait from Behind,* painted in 1911.[17] The composer is walking, obviously on a sidewalk, arms crossed behind the body, holding a walking stick and a cap (it does not, unfortunately, seem to be a sketchbook); the shadow shows that the sun is behind him. The gesture of the moving body suggests that the walker is concentrating, meditating,

Fig. 12. Schoenberg, sketch for *Self-Portrait from Behind*. Reproduced courtesy of Lawrence Schoenberg.

thinking. One particular aspect of the genesis of this painting interests me at this point. There is a pencil sketch, a drawing, that precedes the oil painting (see figure 12).[18] Here the artist is walking in the inner city, approaching an intersection with people and traffic. We see tall houses, two street-cars, a *Fiaker,* and two women and another man, either going in the opposite direction or crossing. Though the artist is already isolated in the sketch, an important decision is made in the step from sketch to final painting to exclude reality, the "world outside"—or, viewed positively, to concentrate on the isolated individual and, with that, and within the context of the Viennese "psyche," on the problem, the crisis, of the Self. Thus the genesis of the self-portrait follows Bloch's "inner way."

The third layer of Schoenberg's artistic creed is concerned with the breakthrough of the work of art from its inner existence to the world outside. This step entails the question of representation or communication. Schoenberg's problem seems to lie in the finding, or defining, of the message or goal of his art; in a letter to Rudolf Kolisch he refers to "what it *is*" overriding the "how" of artistic communication.[19] During these Vienna years, the need to go ahead, to walk, and the direction of the path seem clear; what is not clear, at this point, are the ends (the quasi-Nietzschean "the new man" in Schoenberg's *Harmonielehre* defines them in an abstract manner). In the words of the Archangel Gabriel in *Die Jakobsleiter,* "Whether right or left, forward of backward, uphill or down, one must go without asking what lies behind or ahead."[20]

There are well-known compositional strategies to realize the Durchbruch and to communicate the message "from within," particularly those strategies related to the nineteenth-century symphonic plot archetype. These include not only formal processes but structural dispositions as well. Schoenberg made use of such strategies throughout his career. Characteristic of his Viennese free atonal period, however, is the uncertainty about the "what" of the artwork, the final destiny of the artist's engagement.

The early *Gurrelieder* defines the grandiose climax of the work's massive choral ending as "Panic" nature; it is, to use Rudolf Stephan's term, "*Weltanschauungsmusik*" in the post-*Gründerzeit* spirit, deeply influenced by prevailing ideas from Schopenhauer and Nietzsche.[21] Mahler's Third Symphony seems to indicate a similar, though more sophisticated, philosophical stance. Schoenberg's Second String Quartet, with its purely aesthetic goal of a new musical language ("*Ich löse mich in tönen*"—I dissolve myself in sounds), characterized with Stefan George as "*luft von anderem planeten*" (air from another planet), combines its aestheticism with the proclamation of the artist as a prophetic voice at the climax of the last movement: "*Ich bin ein dröhnen nur der heiligen stimme*" (I am only a rumble of the holy voice). The monodrama *Erwartung* then ends with a utopian gesture toward an unknown and uncertain future. The Woman's last words are "*Ich suchte. . . . ,*" which close without identifying, or allowing us to identify, *what* she is searching for. And the orchestral wedge with which the two lines disappear in the highest as well as deepest registers—breaking off, not ending— leaves the final musical motion wide open; the "what" remains unspecified indeed. Ernst Bloch would call this gesture "*Sich ins Blaue hinein bauen*" (to build oneself into the unknown future); it appears here, at the open end of *Erwartung,* as a similar searching for "the true, the real, where the merely actual disappears"[22] without the certainty of the "incipit vita nova." What remains at this point is the artist's reflection of his own situation: his being an object only of the world's dissolution (for which a particular sensitivity must have existed in the capital of the fading Hapsburg empire), limited to an expressive, perhaps prophetic, statement but unable to offer a goal, let alone any advice for actually changing the course of the external world. The open eyes—the orchestral wedge—"*ich suchte. . .* "—in search of meaning.

Here Schoenberg's *Self-Portrait from Behind* can again come into play. I should like to make a few iconographical remarks—quite incomplete, given the complex history of this image. I will not even touch on the gothic figures from behind, or the baroque *repousseurs,* or Tischbein's *Goethe at the Window in Rome*—to name just a few more distant examples. But the nineteenth-century history of the *Rückenfigur* can be illuminating for my purpose. And certainly Caspar David Friedrich must be mentioned. I offer three examples: Friedrich's *Traveler Looking over the Sea of Fog,* painted in 1818; *Woman in Front of the Setting Sun,* also from 1818; and the later *Evening Landscape with Two Men,* from the early 1830s.[23]

Depicted are isolated back-view figures resting before a silent landscape, preferably in the twilight. They are alone, solitary, sometimes in pairs, confronting nature, sometimes as though sanctified by the spectacle of nature. It is an important formal quality of the Rückenfigur in general that the back view has the tendency to draw the beholder into the canvas, tempting the beholder to assume the protagonist's place. The traditional scholarly interpretation of Friedrich's paintings, renewed by Jens Christian Jensen, stresses the unifying quality of the silent conversation with nature and includes the beholder in this assessment:

> These figures do not so much stand in front of the picture, they are part of the picture. Man and nature meet: the divine universe unfolds in the tableau of nature, it manifests itself in transcendental infinity. . . . The individual's solitude is replaced by the fusion of contemplation, visibility and thought, the arrival of the godly in the infinite and the entrance of man into this unearthly realm. One might generally say that Friedrich's back-view figures fulfilled a demand which he himself called perhaps the greatest demand on the artist: "Thus it is the artist's great, and possibly greatest, merit to stimulate the viewer spiritually and arouse thoughts, feelings, and sensations."[24]

This reflects the Romantic quest for the unity of man and creation, the traditional interpretation of Friedrich's Rückenfiguren already expressed by his contemporaries, Carl Gustav Carus in particular; further, this interpretation extends its claim of a unifying experience of "man and nature" to include the beholder too (the perspective on the viewer is already present in Friedrich's own statement as quoted above by Jensen). It views the beholder as being drawn, through the Rückenfigur, into the picture and thus becoming part of the divine tableau of nature. A new and contrasting, destabilizing, and more skeptical approach to Friedrich's landscape paintings, most recently developed by Joseph Leo Koerner, takes its criteria from another contemporaneous source, Heinrich von Kleist's essay on Friedrich, published jointly with the dialogical review of a Friedrich painting by Achim von Arnim and Clemens von Brentano. Koerner stresses the ambiguity of an experience of the paintings that tries to mediate the solitary back-view figure with the landscape it is facing. For Koerner this experience results not in unity but in separation. Or rather, in an explication of Romantic irony, the experience of both, figure and beholder, remains ambiguous, remains the motion of entering the picture and bringing figure and nature closer together, at the same time as it explicitly distances figure and beholder from nature because the separation between them seems unrevokable. "The Rückenfigur," says Koerner, "indeed draws the beholder into the canvas, making the landscape seem closer and more immediate, yet his otherness to landscape makes nature something experienced only from afar, from the standpoint of the Burger who has lost a natural bond to the land and seeks it now with his gaze. His gaze, which defines his surroundings not as his home but as something 'beautiful,' distances him from the landscape."[25] Schoenberg's *Self-Portrait from Behind* too depicts an individual distanced from, or distancing himself from, his surroundings.

I move on to two other examples from the rich arsenal of nineteenth-century Rückenfiguren, examples much closer to Schoenberg's time— namely, Edvard Munch's *The Lonely Woman,* a woodcut from 1896, and *The Lonely Ones,* a mezzotint engraving from 1899.[26] Again, like Friedrich, the I and nature. But now the emphasis is clearly not on spiritual unity. Expressed in these works are isolation, loneliness, and alienation. If there is a pair, as in *The Lonely Ones,* the two are separated (despite the fact that in this painting the man seems ready to take a step toward the woman); this is most poignantly seen in the oil-painting version of *The Lonely Ones* from 1908, which is on loan in Harvard's Busch-Reisinger Museum.

Schoenberg's *Self-Portrait from Behind,* with its concentration on the self, the isolated subject, is in this pictorial tradition. Here, too, the structural, compositional strategy of the figure from behind seems to draw the beholder into the canvas, into moving along with the protagonist. But this protagonist is not confronting nature; rather, he is part of a modern city—a street scene, so to speak. And the man is not standing still, not resting in contemplation, but walking forward, even uphill, while thinking. This motion within the picture away from the beholder counteracts the possibility of an identification in a way different from Friedrich's Rückenfigur. The

beholder, even if seemingly drawn into the canvas, will never reach the protagonist, who will always be ahead; the beholder will be able to do no more
than follow. In Schoenberg's self-portrait as the "upright walker" (I allude
to Bloch's later metaphor of the *"aufrechter Gang"* and its ethical connota-
tions),[27] placed within the tradition of the nineteenth-century Rückenfigur,
we have the artist presenting himself as a divinely inspired, moral leader;
he proposes that he is leading to the new, to the realm of the future, or—in
Schoenberg's words from his 1911 *Harmonielehre,* with its strong Nietzschean
resonances—anticipating in art the "new man," announcing a renewed human world through the "new sound."[28]

   There is also another source for Schoenberg's identification of the isolated Rückenfigur with the modern artist. It is a popular one, and it gives his
back-view figure a specifically musical and, as such, a specifically Viennese
component. I refer to drawings depicting Ludwig van Beethoven walking
through the streets of Vienna. Among them there is one from behind, an
isolated figure whirling his walking stick; there is another one from the side,
Beethoven wearing a hat, his arms crossed behind him (as are those of
Schoenberg's pedestrian), with buildings in the background and a couple
watching from the distance; and there is a third one, also with a hat, but
again isolated and from behind. These drawings refer to Beethoven's well-
known habit of composing, thinking in music, while walking in and around
Vienna, lost in thoughts and in his sonorous inner world.[29]

   The image of the walking composer originated in the early nineteenth
century; it became prominent within the emerging public middle-class culture of the big cities, and is first tied to Beethoven as its paradigmatic figure.
It developed from there and became very popular toward the turn of the
century, iconologically as part of the prevailing Beethoven reception, particularly in Vienna. Depicting a composer as a lonely pedestrian on the
streets of the city placed him in the great Beethoven tradition; its was an act
of legitimation—in our case, of self-legitimizing. Like the pictures of conducting musicians, the image also played its role in caricature and satire.
There are pictures of Bruckner walking through Vienna with his umbrella
(with little Hanslick, Kalbeck, and Heuberger following him), as there are
of Bruckner conducting. We have Brahms, with his cigar and his heavy
tread, on his way to the "Roter Igel" restaurant.[30] And we continue into the
age of photography with the late Brahms "from behind" (again with arms
crossed behind him—a photo that was clearly staged and thus refers to
Beethoven), and with *Direktor* Gustav Mahler walking around his Viennese
Hofoper.[31]

   There is yet another source for the tradition of the reflective walker. I
would very much like to think that Schoenberg knew this drawing. Unfortunately I cannot prove it. Wilhelm Busch, the north-German caricaturist,
drew the old Schopenhauer "from behind," also with his arms crossed be-

hind the body, a stick in one hand, a hat in the other, with an almost bald head, and in addition with his beloved poodle.[32] Despite its ironic distancing (already as a picture within a picture, as if it were a sheet of paper, torn out of a notebook), this drawing adds the philosophical thinker to our series of reflecting Rückenfiguren. Moreover, it adds the one philosopher who, both because he identified musical art with the universal principle "will" and because Wagner championed his ideas, meant so much to Schoenberg and his fellow composers at the turn of the century.[33]

In his painting Schoenberg sees himself in the Viennese tradition after Beethoven,[34] as the reflective artist leading his generation, at a critical moment within the historical process and through the paradigmatic art form music, into the future. The question, however, remains: Where is he leading to; what is the content of his message to be followed? The self-portrait poses the same questions as the compositional strategies of the Durchbruch. And again the questions remain open at this point.

It is obvious that almost all the "plots" of Schoenberg's free atonal works deal with the dark side of life and the psyche, with distress, disorder, even madness and destruction, and at best with no more than a longing for a positive solution:

—the Second String Quartet, op. 10, with its "nimm mir die Liebe—gib mir dein Glück" (take love from me and give me your bliss);

—the George Songs, op. 15, with the crisis of the "I" in no. 14, and the isolation and loneliness at the end;

—*Erwartung*, op. 17, with the experience of death, disorder, and madness, and the unanswered "Ich suchte . . . ";

—*Die glückliche Hand*, op. 18, with its last words of pain and longing: "Und suchst dennoch. Und quälst dich, und bist ruhelos" (And nevertheless you search. And torture yourself, and are restless);

—*Pierrot lunaire*, op. 21, with the self-sacrifice and self-destruction of the artist in no. 11, the exact center of the twenty-one melodramas.

Thus at the end there is, as a final word for this stage, Pierrot the fool, the *Hanswurst,* or better, the ironic mask of the artist, who, knowing the truth, can survive only as a fool. Schoenberg's dedication letter of the *Pierrot* score to Zemlinsky, dated Christmas 1916, explicitly makes this identification:

> It's banal to say that we're all such moonstruck fellows; yes, the poet thinks that we insist on trying to scrub the stubborn moonbeams from our clothes, as we pray to our crosses. We should be happy that we have wounds; because from them we gain something that helps us, and that is not to set much store by material things. Out of the contempt for our wounds comes the contempt for our enemies, comes our strength to sacrifice our lives for a moonbeam. We become suddenly solemn when we think about the Pierrot poem. But, for heaven's sake, isn't there more than the price of grain?[35]

This immediately calls to mind Robert Schumann's illuminating remark on Berlioz and "the spirit of the day, which tolerates a burlesque *Dies Irae.* . . . For a few moments in an eternity, Poetry has put on the mask of irony to cover her grief-worn face. Perhaps the friendly hand of a genius may also one day remove it."[36] Schumann's commentary, from around the beginning of the "historical century," rightly understands the artists's alienation as a historical phenomenon, as caused by history. But history did not bear out the mild optimism Schumann expresses at the end of the passage. On the contrary, what Schumann indicated was in fact the beginning of "modernism," the movement of an age for which alienation, suffering, and sacrifice were fundamental artistic experiences. Looking at the twentieth century and at Schoenberg's life, it seems that there were an eternity of grief and at best a few moments of *Glück*. Schoenberg's lifelong striving for the "new" in art and society can be seen as an attempt to overcome this situation, to enable the artist to "remove" the mask of irony, to anticipate eternal *Glück* in a world of peace and outer as well as inner freedom.

With this diagnosis as a background, a third look at Schoenberg's *Self-Portrait from Behind* may offer another perspective on the painting. (A premise for this would be to accept the actual realization of the various pictorial elements at face value as aesthetic qualities and to put in abeyance, for a moment at least, any doubts about Schoenberg's craftsmanship as a painter.) Wolfgang Rihm, in a conversation I had with him, insisted on the skeptical, "broken" quality of Schoenberg's portrait. Indeed, the walking composer does not, on the surface, show an optimistic, self-confident attitude, is not moving forward with his head held high as did Beethoven or even Brahms. Instead, he is walking with a stoop, the shoulders as if weighed down by a heavy burden. In addition, the coloring of the entire painting is subdued, a mixture of gray and pale blue. Acknowledging this self-presentation as a bundle of compositional strategies, I see these "shadings" as indications of the "nevertheless," "in spite of everything" in Schoenberg's creed, discussed earlier. Metaphorically, even if confronted by a wall of difficulties, the walker is moving on; even if the outward appearance seems to indicate a skeptical mood, he continues inwardly upright. Ernst Bloch's "*aufrechter Gang*" does not refer to a physical stance, but is an inner category, a moral imperative.

Thus "Schoenberg's Vienna" provides the basic structure for his life and work; "Vienna" poses the central questions. The 1920s would develop Schoenberg's "Vienna project" as an answer to this basic configuration.

SCHOENBERG IN BERLIN

Here I will be brief and extremely general. My starting point for an assessment of Schoenberg's work in the twenties, and of the twenties in general, is Schoenberg's 1922–1923 correspondence with Vasili Kandinsky. In his letter of 20 July 1922 he writes:

> I expect you know we've had our trials here too: famine! It really was pretty awful! But perhaps—for we Viennese seem to be a patient lot—perhaps the worst was after all the overturning of everything one has believed in. That was probably the most grievous thing of all.
>
> When one's been used, where one's own work was concerned, to clearing away all obstacles often by means of one immense intellectual effort [*Gewaltakt*] and in those 8 years found oneself constantly faced with new obstacles against which all thinking, all power of invention, all energy, all "idea" [*Idee*], proved helpless, for a man for whom everything has been "idea," this means nothing less than the total collapse of things.[37]

And it is at this point that Schoenberg introduces religion. The "overturning of everything one has believed in" refers not only to Schoenberg's pre–World War I artistic or aesthetic principles but to conditions of his human existence in general. The twenties, the decade after the collapse, were to be, or were intended to be, or had to be, a period of stabilization. (In addressing attempts at stabilization, I will not talk about concrete political and social aspects, though the term *stabilization*, probably first used by Adorno for music of the twenties, aims at bridging artistic and social matters.)

As for the artistic perspective, from our present view Schoenberg's formulation of rules governing composition—that is, the foundation of his twelve-tone method—is in its general historical signification an act of stabilization not unlike Stravinsky's neoclassicism or the younger Hindemith's neobaroque. But there was more than an artistic method at stake. In the wording of Schoenberg's letter to Kandinsky, the pure belief in "idea" had been falsified by history and therefore a much deeper and more concrete fundament had to be laid out. Schoenberg was aiming at a law, a unifying law for both life and art—that is, for his actual and real, as well as for his spiritual and artistic, existence.

I see his work of the 1920s following a double strategy. There is on the one hand the foundation and expanding application of his new method of composing. Retrospectively we witness a carefully designed approach, incrementally extending to include all genres, from the soloistic and monochromatic piano to different kinds of chamber ensembles to the large orchestra and the stage. There are, first, the piano works, opp. 23 and 25; there is, then, music for chamber ensemble: the Serenade, op. 24, Wind Quintet, op. 26, Suite (with piano), op. 29, String Quartet, op. 30; parallel, there are chamber ensembles plus voices, opp. 27 and 28; then comes the orchestral score, op. 31; and, finally, there is the stage work *Von heute auf morgen*, op. 32. (One remembers the sequence of genres around 1910: lied, piano piece, orchestra piece, stage work; and one recalls the famous examples in music history: Beethoven's "new way" with piano and violin sonatas, piano variations, the *Eroica* symphony, then *Fidelio;* Schumann with the years of piano works, then the realm of song, the orchestral dimension, chamber music, oratorio, and opera; and Brahms with his careful approach to the grand symphony over more than two decades.) And there is, at the same time and running in parallel, Schoenberg's preparing for another dimension—namely, the realm of the artist as *Homo religioso-politicus,* the political prophet. This thread is represented by the text of *Der biblische Weg,* by some of the vocal pieces from opp. 28 and 35, and by the *Hauptwerk*—that is, *Moses und Aron.*

The cause for this double strategy and for the concretization of Schoenberg's artistic creed is to be found in the political conditions in 1920s Europe, especially in Germany and Austria; for Schoenberg in particular it is the growing threat of anti-Semitism. I see this development as follows. At the same time that Schoenberg was intensely working on the conceptual and practical stabilization of his art (following the collapse of the "project Vienna"), an eroding destabilization of his personal existence took place. The 1921 Mattsee experience[38] and the offensive anti-Semitism he encountered in Berlin after being appointed *Preussischer Kompositionslehrer* questioned not only his artistic integrity but the very basis of his human existence; this sharpened his political mind as well as his awareness of being a Jew. The 1923 letters to Kandinsky reveal that Schoenberg had a clear vision of what Hitler and the Nazi movement were striving for: the exiling or even extermination of the Jews. I shall quote one paragraph only from his 4 May 1923 letter to Kandinsky:

> But what is anti-Semitism to lead to if not to acts of violence? Is it so difficult to imagine that? You are perhaps satisfied with depriving Jews of their civil rights. Then certainly Einstein, Mahler, I, and many others, will have been got rid of. But one thing is certain: They will not be able to exterminate those much tougher elements thanks to whose endurance Jewry has maintained itself unaided against the whole of mankind for 20 centuries. For these are evidently so constituted that they can accomplish the task that their god has imposed on them: to survive in exile, uncorrupted and unbroken, until the hour of salvation comes![39]

This is a diagnosis and, in the second part of the passage, a program: to survive and to prepare for salvation. And this program was to be transformed into an artistic project. In the plot of *Moses und Aron*—that is, the Exodus—Schoenberg's project was to receive its first artistic realization. The metaphor for his program is to be found in an unpublished letter to Alma Mahler. Written on 19 January 1929, Schoenberg's letter refers to the scandal surrounding the 1928 premiere of the Variations for Orchestra, op.

31, with Furtwängler and the Berlin Philharmonic. The central passage, in translation, reads as follows:

> Since the scandal at Furtwängler's I have lost all joy and interest in living in Berlin. Berlin has had almost no other advantage for me, than that there are a good many people one does not need to see; at the same time it is possible to perform *Wozzeck* undisturbed. The latter privilege could not be transferred to me [the following image is untranslatable, so I continue in the original German] *denn mit mir ist es ein Hakenkreuz: ich bin ein schuftiger, unverständlicher Jude.*[40]

The traumatic experience of a violent anti-Semitism is turned into a horrifying image, a metaphor of biting irony. Schoenberg's command of language forces together the popular everyday simplification of the Christian cross metaphor (colloquial sayings such as *"Es ist schon ein Kreuz mit dir"* or *"Jeder hat halt sein Kreuz zu tragen"*)[41] with the Nazi *Hakenkreuz*, or swastika. This is similar on the surface to, but quite different in essence from, Brecht's song text about the swastika, with its cabaretlike tone: *"das Kreuz hat einen Haken"* (the cross has a catch to it). And Schoenberg's subsequent explanation of the metaphor is very carefully composed, combining a moral judgment (*"schuftig"*—that is, "rascally" or "mean") with an aesthetic one (*"unverständlich"*—that is, "incomprehensible," which certainly refers to the critical reception of his music).

Schoenberg's acts are metaphorical in a demonic way. A Jew, being persecuted by the Nazis, tacks their emblem, the swastika, on himself: *"mit mir ist es ein Hakenkreuz."* But this ability of the victim to name, to denounce the torturer is intended to ban the threat, and bans it. The act of intellectual defense is a sign of spiritual victory. It is in this sense that I see Schoenberg's *Hakenkreuz* metaphor as the new decisive signature for his future life and work. It is reflected in his various serious attempts to devote his life and artistic activities to politics, to the foundation of a Jewish party, a Jewish state. And it is reflected in his *Spätwerk*, the late works. The case of Jewry becomes a central focus; artist and Jew are seen as identical. And the artwork must express this identification.

This is a dramatic change for the composer. The 1916 *Pierrot* letter to Zemlinsky, with its devotion of the artist's life to the moonbeam (as the image for artistic creation and spirituality), the proudness in being wounded—this *Pierrot* interpretation was still primarily concerned with artistic rejection and alienation. But now, in the 1920s, a new situation has arisen, one fundamentally much more dangerous: to be denied as a German, as a *Homo politicus*, as a human being. This is indeed an attack on his entire existence and becomes a question of life and death. And for Schoenberg, the political conservative and German musical nationalist, it is of the utmost importance that his membership in the great German cultural tradition is threatened. The 1926 first version of the preface to the Satires, op. 28, is entitled "No longer a German" and addresses precisely this denial. Now it seems no longer possible to think in terms of a purely aesthetic creed. Out of this situation grows the new focus of Schoenberg's artistic production. It can be observed in his compositions with text, his choice of plots and topics, and his turning to his Jewish faith and to politics. All this governs his late work.[42]

Schoenberg's late work utters the voice of *Verbannung* (exile) and of victory. Acts 1 and 2 of *Moses und Aron*, the only ones composed, end with Moses' spoken words: "*O Wort, du Wort, das mir fehlt*" (Oh word, that word that fails me). But these words are spoken to the most expansive, most expressive melody Schoenberg ever wrote, played in unison in the first and second violins. The melody is anticipatory, projecting something that still cannot be pronounced in words.

SCHOENBERG IN AMERICA

As with "Berlin," I will be very brief. As is well known, Schoenberg's American output differs from that of the two European periods in various respects. One tendency defining the American works could be labeled classicism; the turn to traditional genres of the concert repertory, such as piano concerto or violin concerto, belongs here. And there are the works displaying a strong retrospective attitude: the Variations on a Recitative for Organ, op. 40, with their tonal orientation; or the Second Chamber Symphony, op. 38, begun in Vienna and only now completed. Here, too, belong the Brahms instrumentation and the German folk songs for a cappella choir, op. 49. Closely related to this group are the compositions with pedagogical intent: the Variations, op. 43, and the Suite in Old Style for String Orchestra. Besides those there are commissions such as the Prelude, op. 44 (originally for a projected Genesis film); even the Fourth String Quartet, op. 37, resulted from a commission. As a highly personal, intimate piece of chamber music, the String Trio, op. 45, stands isolated in this period; only the Fantasy for Violin with piano accompaniment, op. 47, comes close to the sphere and the language of the Trio. Central for the American period, however, are the religious and political compositions, which give the *Spätwerk* its unique physiognomy: *Kol Nidre*, op. 39, *Ode to Napoleon Buonaparte*, op. 41, *A Survivor from Warsaw*, op. 46, the works for choir, op. 50 (A, B, and C), and the continuing attempts to complete *Moses und Aron*. For my understanding of Schoenberg's life and work, it is in these works of a religious-political engagement that his path reaches its goal and fulfillment. It is no accident that *Moderne Psalmen* is his last word.

To characterize this *Spätwerk* it must suffice to concentrate on one work only. I take *A Survivor from Warsaw* as an example. In this, Schoenberg's most explicitly political work, the composer uses his own prose text and concludes with the Jewish prayer "Schema Israel." As stated in the text itself, the seven-minute work is a memory of the one "moment," brief but loaded with history. It is constructed as the report of one surviving witness—that is, a story told in the first person—as a sequence of a preceding reflection and a following narration, the story's perspective alternating between direct reportage and more distant reporting. The work is, from the very beginning, directed toward the "grandiose moment" where the melody of the old prayer, the "forgotten creed," emerges out of the holocaust and transcends this situation of bestiality and desperation into a moment of political eschatology. The work ends with the hymnlike prayer, sung in unison, and does not return to the narration. This again is the Durchbruch. The grandiose moment of A Survivor is in line with the formal strategies mentioned earlier, connected to Gurrelieder, to op. 10, and to Erwartung. The Durchbruch here is in the same tradition indeed—but with a new and precise goal and statement. As with the Hakenkreuz metaphor, Schoenberg takes the position of the victim who will be victor.

Late style has been characterized by Goethe as "stufenweises Zurücktreten aus der Erscheinung" (stepwise retreat from the phenomenon) and "sich selbst historisch werden" (seeing oneself historically). Schoenberg's late style is not a "Zurücktreten." Schoenberg did not "paint the velvet in a symbolic manner only," as the old Goethe believed both he and Titian were doing ("Tizian, der den Samt nur symbolisch malte.") Schoenberg's late style is a "Hineintreten" and an "Eintreten" in the twofold sense of the latter: "entering" or "facing," and "representing" or "standing for." But the older Schoenberg looks back at his own compositional career, sees himself historically, and "uses" formal strategies, textures, and stylistic elements of his expressionistic and his earlier twelve-tone periods for specific representational purposes.[43] The first part of A Survivor, with its broken textures, "fields" of colors, and motivic fragments, its dispersed "shocks" and illustrative gestures, is very close to the textural principles of Erwartung. The second part, beginning with the triumphant entry of the prayer melody, displays stable textures, a cantus firmus, and a coherent melody with accompanying figures. Christian M. Schmidt here sees a historical perspective on Schoenberg's own development, a critical commentary by Schoenberg about his free-atonal period versus his twelve-tone composition. I believe that in addition there is a broader perspective.

First, this design represents Schoenberg's "quest for language," his concern and insistence that music be language—understandable, conceivable, communicable, able to express, to transport ideas. To me the prayer, the music of liberation and of salvation, is this language. It conveys a message; even if the words were not added, tone, texture, plot, formal position, and entry would deliver this message of liberation.

Second, there are several levels of presentation in the text itself, and there are three verbal languages being spoken: English (by the narrator), German (by the sergeant), and Hebrew (by the Jews, singing the Prayer). Even more pointedly, the Sergeant speaks in a Berlin dialect. This refers back directly to Schoenberg's experiences during the twenties and to the *Hakenkreuz* metaphor. And in the formal gesture of *A Survivor* with the prayer hymn at the end, the program from the 1923 letter to Kandinsky now seems fulfilled: "to survive in exile, uncorrupted and unbroken, until the hour of salvation comes!"

Schoenberg's late works, the *Ode to Napoleon* and *A Survivor from Warsaw* in particular, are the fulfillment of his "Vienna project"; here his early artistic creed finds its appropriate plot and realization. From this perspective the prayer at the end of *A Survivor*, music as "language" again, is the corrective to Moses' "word that fails me," since it is the fulfillment of the great anticipating melody that counteracts these words.

· · · · ·

With this, in a sort of coda, I can return to the staring eyes and the walking artist. In his late *Geschichtsphilosophische Thesen* (Theses on the philosophy of history), completed in 1940, Walter Benjamin gives an interpretation of a 1920 painting by Paul Klee. Thesis IX reads as follows:

> A Klee painting named *Angelus Novus* shows an angel looking as though he is about to move away from something he is fixedly contemplating. His eyes are staring, his mouth is open, his wings are spread. This is how one pictures the angel of history. His face is turned toward the past. Where we perceive a chain of events, he sees only one single catastrophe which keeps piling wreckage upon wreckage and hurls it in front of his feet. The angel would like to stay, awaken the dead, and make whole what has been smashed. But a storm is blowing from Paradise; it has got caught in his wings with such violence that the angel can no longer close them. This storm irresistibly propels him into the future to which his back is turned, while the pile of debris before him grows skyward. This storm is what we call progress.[44]

Here again are the staring eyes, again wide open, as we remember, and they certainly are "experiencing the fate of mankind." But, to be more precise, they are, in Benjamin's view, looking back, and they are looking at the debris of the world, viewing a catastrophic development of which they themselves are a part.

Benjamin's text gives a contaminated view of historical materialism and Jewish messianism.[45] Within this conflation the collective and abstract power of the violent storm—that is, the view of "history" as an irreversible process—is Marxian. There is no subjective factor; the subject seems to remain powerless, reduced to an impulse of thought. But the notion of the

Paradise is Judaic: the storm, though blowing "irresistibly," comes from Paradise. One might want to assume that naming "Paradise" in this context already sends a signal of hope. (And Gershom Scholem in his commentary on thesis IX does exactly that, with a quasi-cyclical understanding of Benjamin's imagery.)[46] But I do not see that a messianic appearance is mentioned in, or could be concluded from, Benjamin's text. The storm blows *from* Paradise toward the future; it blows, and continues to blow, over the remaining debris of the world, which has already reached Heaven and continues to grow; the angel has his back turned to the future, and the future is, at best, unknown and cannot be anticipated. There may be an emotional-intellectual impulse toward the future hidden behind the text, but the text itself does not allow for such an assumption. Though the storm blows, moves forward, the angel remains in a quasi-fixed position. This indicates to me that Benjamin's thesis IX indeed represents the *"Dialektik im Stillstand"* (dialectic at a standstill),[47] a carefully designed position between the poles of political pessimism and spiritual optimism. The *"Dialektik von Zukunft und Vergangenheit, von Messianismus und Eingedenken"* (dialectics of future and past, of messianism and remembrance) that Peter Szondi refers to in his congenial essay on Benjamin[48] is brought to a halt, as if frozen in stone. Benjamin's thought "looks" back to see the future, because only in the past, in its origin, is the utopian idea of the future preserved, preserved as an undistorted promise. For the present this image is perverted, obliterated, ruined.[49] However, "[t]he angel would like to . . . make whole what has been smashed. But . . . " (Benjamin). A critical assessment comparing Benjamin's late text with his earlier essays would certainly acknowledge a touch of melancholy in this view, a melancholy[50] born of skepticism, if not pessimism, created at the strange crossroads of hope and despair.

In sharp contrast, Schoenberg's message in *A Survivor* is decidedly messianic. It carries the positive image of the artist as leader into the future through all political and spiritual breakdowns and, as such, articulates an old-fashioned, individualistic, nineteenth-century optimism. Schoenberg's image remains the artist as the leader into the future, the walking composer, to be seen by his contemporaries only from behind. But now, toward the end of his life, the direction and goal of the walk are finally defined. The artist, now bound to his roots, is the political prophet. Thus Schoenberg maintains his Viennese artistic creed of the Durchbruch to the better world, now as the anticipation of paradise, confined to his Jewish constituency. The Viennese creed for an aesthetic culture is redefined as the quest for a political culture based on religious grounds. As such Schoenberg's late work and word are not Leverkühn's *Dr. Fausti Weheklag* and the *"Zurücknahme,"* they are not the revocation of the Ninth Symphony. The Durchbruch in *A Survivor*, the "grandiose moment," is political eschatology—almost another, a modern "Ode to Joy," born out of the deepest desperation and terror of the twentieth century. The truly conservative Viennese individualist has become a commentator on matters of world politics. Composing and proposing this, the artist is back walking on the street, no longer lonely and isolated, but singing and strolling with his contemporaries. Will he be heard, and can he be understood?

NOTES

1. Unfortunately, I could not use the title "Schoenberg from Behind," because Heinz-Klaus Metzger had the idea first; see his "Arnold Schönberg von hinten," in *Musik-Konzepte: Sonderband Arnold Schönberg*, ed. Heinz Klaus Metzger and Rainer Riehm (Munich: text + kritik, 1980), 29–34. The reader is reminded that this text was conceived for aural presentation; only footnotes have been added. I am grateful to Juliane Brand and Michael Ochs for their help in correcting my English.

2. Bruno Bettelheim, *Freud's Vienna and Other Essays* (New York: Alfred A. Knopf, 1990), 3–17, esp. 3 and 14–15.

3. I confess my inability to translate this paragraph satisfactorily: "the internal way, also called meeting one's self, the making of the inner word, without which every glance outside remains void, and no magnet, no power to attract the inner word from outside, to help it break through from the error of the world." Ernst Bloch, *Geist der Utopie* (second version 1923; Frankfurt am Main: Suhrkamp Verlag, 1964), 13. Translations, unless otherwise noted, are by the author.

4. See Brinkmann, "Schönberg und das expressionistische Ausdruckskonzept," in *Bericht über den 1. Kongress der Internationalen Schönberg-Gesellschaft*, ed. Rudolf Stephan (Vienna: Verlag Elisabeth Lafite, 1978), 13–19.

5. Arnold Schoenberg, "Aphorism" (emphasis added by the author). The original German text appeared first in *Die Musik* 9/21 (1909/1910), 159–163, esp. 159; also published in Reich, *Schönberg: Schöpferische Konfessionen*, 12. See also the translations in Malcolm McDonald, *Schoenberg* (London: J. M. Dent, 1976), 58.

6. See Theodor W. Adorno, *Mahler: Eine musikalische Physiognomik* (Frankfurt am Main: Suhrkamp Verlag, 1960), 12–14. See also Adorno, "Arnold Schönberg," 147–172, esp. 153: "What he [Schoenberg] designated as the 'subcutaneous' . . . breaks through the surface, becomes visible and manifests itself independently of all stereotyped forms. The inward dimension moves outward."

7. See Paul Bekker, *Gustav Mahlers Sinfonien* (Berlin: Schuster & Loeffler, 1921), esp. 62. A terminological study would certainly go back to the nineteenth century, to prenaturalist literary critics such as Georg Brandes (1842–1927), for example, who elaborated on the notion of "the modern breakthrough."

8. "*alle Schranken einer vergangenen Ästhetik durchbrochen zu haben.*" From Schoenberg's program notes to the first performance of the *George-Lieder*, 14 January 1910, in Vienna; published in Reich, *Schönberg: Schöpferische Konfessionen*, 28; English translation in Reich, *Schoenberg: A Critical Biography*, 49.

9. Darius Milhaud, "To Arnold Schoenberg on His Seventieth Birthday," *Musical Quarterly* 30/4 (1944), 379–384, esp. 381.

10. For a reproduction of that photograph, see Walter Rubsamen, "Schoenberg in America," *Musical Quarterly* 37/4 (1951), 469–489, esp. 481.

11. For reproductions of the self-portrait (catalog no. 4) and *Red Gaze* (catalog no. 246), see Ellen Kravitz and Lawrence Schoenberg, "Catalog of Arnold Schoenberg's Paintings, Drawings and Sketches," *Journal of the Arnold Schoenberg Institute* 2/3 (June 1978), 185–231, esp. 190 and 230; see also Thomas Zaunschirm, ed., *Arnold Schönberg: Das bildnerische Werk* (Klagenfurt: Ritter Verlag, 1991).

12. The relationship of Schoenberg's "eyes" to similar expressive gazes in portraits and particularly self-portraits by Richard Gerstl, whose work predates Schoenberg's paintings, is striking. According to his student and friend Victor Hammer, Gerstl "placed great importance on the 'expression' of the eyes"; see Hammer, "Memories of Richard Gerstl," in the exhibition catalog *Richard Gerstl. Oskar Kokoschka*, ed. Jane Kallir (New York: Galerie St. Etienne, 1992), 28.

13. For reproductions of Munch's *Scream*, see Nicolay Stang, *Edvard Munch* (Dresden: VEB Verlag der Kunst, 1977), 61 (woodcut) and color plate no. 1 (painting).

14. Metaphorically speaking, Schoenberg's death mask, taken by Anna Mahler, seems to display this very powerfully, especially in the photo published on page 468 in Rubsamen, "Schoenberg in America."

15. Translation adapted from Georg Wilhelm Friedrich Hegel, *Aesthetics: Lectures in Fine Art*, trans. T. M. Knox (Oxford: Clarendon Press, 1975), 2:1,133. For the discussion that follows, see also Brinkmann, "The Lyric as Paradigm: Poetry and the Foundation of Arnold Schönberg's New Music," in *German Literature and Music 1890–1989: An Aesthetic Fusion*, ed. Claus Reschke and Howard Pollack (Munich: Fink, 1992), 95–129.

16. For a more detailed discussion of these strategies, see Brinkmann, "The Lyric as Paradigm."

17. For a reproduction of *Self-Portrait from Behind*, see Kravitz and Schoenberg, "Arnold Schoenberg's Paintings," no. 7, 191.

18. For a reproduction of the pencil sketch, see Kravitz and Schoenberg, "Arnold Schoenberg's Paintings," no. 6, 190.

19. Schoenberg to Kolisch, 27 July 1932, *Schoenberg Letters*, no. 143, 164–165, esp. 165.

20. "*Ob rechts, ob links, vorwärts oder rückwärts, bergauf oder bergab—man hat weiterzugehen, ohne zu fragen, was vor oder hinter einem liegt.*"

21. Rudolf Stephan, "Aussermusikalischer Inhalt; Musikalischer Gehalt: Gedanken zur Musik der Jahrhundertwende," in *Vom musikalischen Denken: Gesammelte Vorträge*, ed. Rainer Damm and Andreas Traub (Mainz: B. Schott's Söhne, 1985), 309–320, esp. 316.

22. "*das Wahre, Wirkliche, wo das bloss Tatsächliche verschwindet.*" Bloch, *Geist der Utopie*, 3. This passage is already included in the first version (1918) of *Geist der Utopie*.

23. See the color plates in Helmut Börsch-Supan, *Caspar David Friedrich* (New York: George Braziller, 1974), 3:109; and the catalog *The Romantic Vision of Caspar David Friedrich: Paintings and Drawings from the U.S.S.R.*, ed. Sabine Rewald (New York: Metropolitan Museum of Art, 1990), 75. Jens Christian Jensen summarizes the common interpretation of Friedrich's works in his *Caspar David Friedrich: Life and Work* (Woodbury, New York, and London: Barron's, 1981).

24. Jensen, *Caspar David Friedrich*, 175–176.

25. Joseph Leo Koerner, *Caspar David Friedrich and the Subject of Landscape* (New Haven and London: Yale University Press, 1990), 220.

26. For reproductions of *The Lonely Woman* and *The Lonely Ones,* see the color plates in Ulrich Weisner's catalog *Edvard Munch. Liebe. Angst. Tod. Zeichnungen und Graphiken aus dem Munch-Museum Oslo* (Bielefeld: Kunsthalle, 1980), 143, 144.

27. See, for example, Ernst Bloch, *Tübinger Einleitung in die Philosophie* 2 (Frankfurt am Main: Suhrkamp Verlag, 1964), 178.

28. *"Der neue Klang ist ein unwillkürlich gefundenes Symbol, das den neuen Menschen ankündigt, der sich da ausspricht."* Schoenberg, *Harmonielehre* (1911), 447.

29. The three drawings, selected from a great number of similar ones, are reprinted in H. C. Robbins Landon, *Beethoven: Sein Leben und seine Welt in zeitgenössischen Bildern und Texten* (Vienna and Zurich: Universal Edition, 1970), 144–147. The first is a watercolor drawing by Joseph Weidner, dating from the 1820s; the second is a drawing by Johann Peter Theodor Lysing, first published in 1833 in the journal *Cäcilia;* the third is a sketch by Joseph Daniel Böhm for a picture to be engraved on a small silver plate. Böhm had met Beethoven in 1819 or 1820.

30. These pictures were cultivated in fin de siècle Vienna by Otto Böhler (1847–1911); his silhouettes, often with an ironic twist, were very popular, and Schoenberg must have known them from Viennese newspapers. For a reproduction of the Brahms picture, see Christiane Jacobsen, *Johannes Brahms: Leben und Werk* (Wiesbaden: Breitkopf & Härtel, 1983), 157.

31. For a reproduction of the Brahms photograph, from the Fellinger collection, see Marie Fellinger, *Brahms-Bilder,* enlarged 2d ed. (Leipzig: Breitkopf & Härtel, 1912), 7. For the Mahler photographs, see Kurt Blaukopf, *Mahler: A Documentary Study* (New York and Toronto: Oxford University Press, 1976), nos. 222 and 223; for a photograph of Mahler walking in the countryside, see no. 306.

32. See the picture in Robert Dangers, *Wilhelm Busch—der Künstler* (Berlin: Rembrandt Verlag, 1937), 33; and the back cover of Walter Abendroth, *Arthur Schopenhauer in Selbstzeugnissen und Bilddokumenten* (Reinbek: Rowohlt Taschenbuch Verlag, 1967). Busch's satirical work includes a variety of figures from behind. Iconologically most of them do not belong to the "Romantic" line from Friedrich to Munch and Schoenberg. Busch's figures seem to distance themselves from the viewer; they either slink away as scapegoats or victims, or pointedly turn their backs and leave the viewer behind. Identification with these figure seems neither intended nor possible.

33. Schoenberg had volumes of Schopenhauer's works in his library, and his two editions of *Parerga und Paralipomena* are heavily annotated.

34. In editing this text for publication I came across Alessandra Comini's richly illustrated book *The Changing Image of Beethoven: A Study in Mythmaking* (New York: Rizzoli, 1987). Obviously, she was the first to connect Schoenberg's painting to the Beethoven and Schopenhauer drawings. However, her commentary—"Arnold Schoenberg would pay jocose homage to Beethoven" (43)—is inadequate.

35. Translated by Anne Shreffler. For the German text, see Brinkmann, "Was uns die Quellen erzählen," in *Das musikalische Kunstwerk: Festschrift Carl Dahlhaus zum 60. Geburtstag,* ed. Hermann Danuser et al. (Laaber: Laaber-Verlag, 1988), 679–693, esp. 691–692.

36. From the last paragraphs of Schumann's famous review of the *Symphonie fantastique*. Translation from Hector Berlioz, *Fantastic Symphony*, ed. Edward Cone, Norton Critical Scores (New York: W. W. Norton, 1971), 220–248, esp. 248.

37. Schoenberg to Kandinsky, adapted from the translation in *Schoenberg Letters*, no. 42, 70–71.

38. Schoenberg and his family, on vacation in Mattsee, Austria, were forced to leave because they were Jews.

39. Schoenberg to Kandinsky, *Schoenberg Letters*, no. 64, 89–93, esp. 92–93.

40.

> Seit dem Skandal bei Furtwängler habe ich alle Lust verloren, dort [in Berlin] zu leben. Fast hat Berlin für mich keinen andern Wert gehabt, als dass man dort sehr viele Leute nicht sehen muss und aber eben Wozzeck ungestört aufführen kann. Der letztere Vorzug hat sich auf mich selbst nicht übertragen lassen, denn mit mir ist es ein Hakenkreuz: ich bin ein schuftiger, unverständlicher Jude.
>
> Mahler-Werfel Collection, Van Pelt Library, University of Pennsylvania.

41. "It is a cross with you" (in other words, "You sure are a burden") and "Everyone must bear his cross."

42. I must acknowledge two important studies here, which contributed background to this discussion—namely, the late Michael Mäckelmann's dissertation *Arnold Schönberg und das Judentum* (Hamburg: Verlag Karl Dieter Wagner, 1984) and Alexander L. Ringer's *Arnold Schoenberg: The Composer as Jew* (Oxford: Clarendon Press, 1990).

43. See Christian M. Schmidt, "Schönbergs Kantate 'Ein Überlebender aus Warschau' op. 46," *Archiv für Musikwissenschaft* 33/4 (1976), 174–188, 261–277.

44. English translation in Walter Benjamin, *Illuminations*, ed. Hannah Arendt, trans. Harry Zohn (New York: Schocken Books, 1969), 257–258. It is irrelevant for my purpose whether Benjamin's view does justice to Klee's intentions, as it is irrelevant whether Benjamin's allegorical interpretation of the drawing itself is adequate. A reproduction of the Klee picture is published in *Zur Aktualität Walter Benjamins*, ed. Siegfried Unseld (Frankfurt am Main: Suhrkamp Verlag, 1972), 85. The drawing was owned by Benjamin and is now in the Israel Museum, Jerusalem. It was included in the 1991 Berlin exhibit *Jüdische Lebenswelten* as no. 20:6/61.

45. Benjamin's allegorical understanding of the Klee painting could be viewed as an actualization of Friedrich Schlegel's "Philosophical Fragment" no. 667: "*Der Historiker ist ein rückwärts gekehrter Prophet*" (The historian is a prophet turned backward); see Friedrich Schlegel, *Kritische Schriften und Fragmente* (Studienausgabe), ed. E. Behler and H. Eichner (Paderborn: Ferdinand Schöning, 1988), 5:28.

46.

> He [the Angel] announces the future, from where he came, but his face is turned to the past. . . . [P]aradise is both the origin and the primeval past for man and, at the same time, a utopian image of the future of salvation—in actually a more cyclical than dialectical understanding of history.
>
> Gershom Scholem, "Walter Benjamin und sein Engel,"
> in *Zur Aktualität*, 87–138, esp. 131.

The "actually" (*eigentlich*) reveals Scholem's problem.

47. See Walter Benjamin's *paralipomena* to his "Geschichtsphilosophische The-sen," in *Gesammelte Schriften* I/3, ed. Rolf Tiedemann and Hermann Schweppen-häuser (Frankfurt am Main: Suhrkamp Verlag, 1974), 1,236 and 1,249–1,250. See also Rolf Tiedemann, "Historischer Materialismus oder politischer Messianismus?" in *Materialien zu Benjamins Thesen "Über den Begriff der Geschichte,"* ed. Peter Bulthaup (Frankfurt am Main: Suhrkamp Verlag, 1975), 77–121. If one ignores Tiedemann's assuming the role of warden of the grail, this essay gives the most competent inter-pretation of the theses. The summary (110), in particular, provides a balanced ac-count of their assumed position between historical materialism and messianic the-ology. A slightly different and generally speaking more 'optimistic' interpretation, emphasizing "the redemptive urge behind Benjamin's view of the past" (David Stern), is given by Richard Wolin. See his study *Walter Benjamin: An Aesthetic of Re-demption,* 2d ed. (Berkeley and Los Angeles: University of California Press, 1994); and David Stern's review essay "The Man with Qualities," *New Republic,* 10 April 1995, 31–38.

48. Peter Szondi, "Hoffnung im Vergangenen: Über Walter Benjamin," in *Satz und Gegensatz* (Frankfurt am Main: Insel, 1964), 79–92, esp. 92. English translation in Szondi, *On Textual Understanding and Other Essays,* trans. Harvey Mendelsohn (Minneapolis: University of Minnesota Press, 1986), 155–156.

49. To quote Szondi again ("Hoffnung im Vergangenen," 91; *On Textual Under-standing,* 155): "A knowledge of ruin obstructed Benjamin's view into the future and allowed him to see future events only in those instances where they had already moved into the past. This ruin is not only Benjamin's, it is the ruin of his age."

50. On the notion of melancholy in Benjamin's thought, see Susan Sontag, *Un-der the Sign of Saturn* (New York: Noonday Press, 1980), 103–134.

CONTRIBUTORS

Joseph Auner is Assistant Professor of Music at the State University of New York at Stony Brook. He is the editor of the forthcoming *A Schoenberg Reader* and serves as the general editor for a new series on twentieth-century music for Garland Publishing.

Leon Botstein is President of Bard College, the music director of the American Symphony Orchestra, and the editor of the *Musical Quarterly*. His writings include a forthcoming revised translation of his *Judentum und Modernität: Essays zur Rolle der Juden in der deutschen und österreichischen Kultur, 1848–1938*.

Reinhold Brinkmann is the James Edward Ditson Professor of Music at Harvard University. His most recent publications include *Late Idyll*, a study of Brahms's Second Symphony, and an edition of Schoenberg works for piano solo. He has edited *Pierrot lunaire, Herzgewächse*, and *Ode to Napoleon* for the Schoenberg Gesamtausgabe.

Patricia Carpenter, Professor Emerita at Barnard College, Columbia University, studied with Arnold Schoenberg at the University of California at Los Angeles, and privately between 1942 and 1949. She is the coeditor, with Severine Neff, of *Arnold Schoenberg's Musical Idea and the Logic, Technique, and Art of Its Presentation*.

Hermann Danuser is Professor for Music History at the Humboldt University, research coordinator at the Paul Sacher Stiftung, and a coeditor of the periodical *Musiktheorie*. His writings include *Musikalische Prosa, Die Musik des 20. Jahrhunderts, Gustav Mahler: "Das Lied von der Erde,"* and *Igor Strawinsky: Trois pièces pour quatuor à cordes*.

Jonathan Dunsby is Professor of Music and Head of Department at the University of Reading. He is the founding editor of Music Analysis and a coauthor of *Music Analysis in Theory and Practice.* He has written on Brahms, Schoenberg, and Debussy, and his most recent book is *Performing Music: Shared Concerns.*

Walter Frisch is Professor of Music at Columbia University. He has served as the editor of *19th Century Music,* and his writings include *Brahms and the Principle of Developing Variation, The Early Works of Arnold Schoenberg, 1893–1908,* and a book on the Brahms symphonies. He is currently working on a book entitled *Music and German Modernism, 1885–1915.*

Christopher Hailey is Director of the Franz Schreker Foundation, Inc. His writings include *Franz Schreker: A Cultural Biography.* He served as the editor of *Der Briefwechsel zwischen Paul Bekker und Franz Schreker,* was a coeditor of *The Berg-Schoenberg Correspondence,* and prepared an edition of early songs by Alban Berg for the Berg Gesamtausgabe.

Ethan Haimo, composer and theorist, is Professor of Music at the University of Notre Dame. He is the author of *Schoenberg's Serial Odyssey* and *Haydn's Symphonic Forms,* as well as of many articles and reviews. His compositions have been widely performed and have been recorded recently by Centaur Records.

Alan Lessem (1940–1991) was a founding member of York University's Department of Music. He also taught at the Rubin Academy of Music in Jerusalem and the Telma Yellin School in Tel Aviv. His writings include *Music and Text in the Works of Arnold Schoenberg,* and from 1989 through 1991 he was the editor of the *Canadian University Music Review.*

Jan Maegaard is a composer and Professor of Musicology at the University of Copenhagen. He has published widely on twentieth-century music and the Schoenberg school. His writings include *Studien zur Entwicklung des dodekaphonen Satzes bei Arnold Schönberg.*

Severine Neff is Professor of Music at the University of North Carolina at Chapel Hill. She is the editor of *Coherence, Counterpoint, Instrumentation, Instruction in Form,* a collection of Schoenberg's theoretical manuscripts, and the coeditor, with Patricia Carpenter, of *Arnold Schoenberg's Musical Idea and the Logic, Technique, and Art of Its Presentation.*

Alexander L. Ringer, Professor Emeritus at the University of Illionois, is the author of *Arnold Schoenberg: The Composer as Jew* and *Musik als Geschichte.* He is a coeditor of the *Beethoven Interpretationen,* and he recently began overseeing the preparations for a new multivolume edition of Schoenberg's collected writings.

Bryan R. Simms is Professor of Music at the University of Southern California. He has served as the editor of the *Journal of Music Theory* and *Music Theory Spectrum* and is the author of *Music of the Twentieth Century: Style and Structure, The Art of Music: An Introduction,* and a biobibliography of Alban Berg.

Peg Weiss is Research Professor in the Department of Fine Arts at Syracuse University. She has lectured and written widely on Russian art and is the author of *Kandinsky in Munich—The Formative Jugendstil Years* and, most recently, *Kandinsky and Old Russia: The Artist as Ethnographer and Shaman.*

INDEX OF NAMES AND WORKS

A reference followed directly by a note number or numbers refers to the notes at the end of each chapter. Note numbers in parentheses serve to locate text citations or quotations in the main text that are not identified by title. Page references in italics denote illustrations or musical examples.

Compositor:	J. Jarrett Engineering, Inc.
Music setter:	George Thomson
Text and Display:	Baskerville
Printer:	Thomson-Shore, Inc.
Binder:	Thomson-Shore, Inc.